NOT THE GERMANS ALONE

NOT THE GERMANS ALONE

A Son's Search for the Truth of Vichy

ISAAC LEVENDEL

With a Foreword by Robert O. Paxton

Northwestern University Press
Evanston, Illinois

Northwestern University Press
Evanston, Illinois 60208-4210

Printed in the United States of America

ISBN 0-8101-1663-4

Library of Congress Cataloging-in-Publication Data

Lewendel, Isaac, 1936–
        Not the Germans alone : a son's search for the truth of
Vichy / Isaac Levendel ; with a foreword by Robert O. Paxton.
        p. cm.
        Includes bibliographical references.
        ISBN 0-8101-1663-4 (alk. paper)
        1. Lewendel, Isaac, 1936– . 2. Jewish children in the
Holocaust—France—Avignon—Biography. 3. Jews—France—
Avignon—Biography. 4. Holocaust, Jewish (1939–1945)—France—
Avignon—Personal narratives. 5. Lewendel, Sarah, 1904–1944.
6. World War, 1939–1945—France—Avignon—Collaborationists.
7. France—History—German occupation, 1940–1945. 8. Holocaust
survivors—Biography. 9. Avignon (France)—Biography. I. Title.
DS135.F9L487 1999
940.53'0944922092—dc21
[B]   99-19628
                                            CIP

Contents

Acknowledgments

My thanks to all who made this work possible. They are, of course, the numerous French archive curators who patiently guided me through a maze of information, helping me find my way without getting lost. Their impeccable erudition was coupled with sensitivity to the depth of my undertaking.

They are, too, my friends of always, who accompanied me from the beginning, and also the new friends I met along the way. All granted me their unlimited support. Professionals or witnesses of history, or simply outraged by the depth of the abyss, they broadened, by their advice, the scope of my undertaking far beyond my original intentions.

And foremost, I am indebted to my wife and my children for sticking with me on this unexpected journey.

Foreword

Isaac Levendel's mother was arrested near Avignon on June 6, 1944, deported to Auschwitz, and gassed to death. In this book, Levendel takes us along two quests: first, a search within himself for his "personal truth," as he struggles to come to terms with his experience as a boy of seven whose mother is taken away. This meant overcoming the silence and denial within which he wrapped himself for over forty years. His second quest was a search in the departmental archives of the Vaucluse for the persons responsible for his mother's death. This meant overcoming the restrictions imposed by the French state on access to police, prefectoral, and judicial records, as well as the preference of most of the people around him to forget the past.

Both quests are successful, at least on the surface. After many years of shutting out his unbearable memories, Levendel learns to confront them, accept the finality of his mother's death, and cope with his sense of guilt for not having accompanied her on the journey that led to her death. Levendel also succeeds, by dogged persistence and with some help from influential acquaintances, in finding out exactly who brought about his mother's deportation.

For years he had accepted the neighbors' explanation: "The Germans did it." It turned out, however, that the persons responsible for identifying and arresting Mme. Levendel were all French. The man who registered her on the prefecture's list of Jews, saw to its regular updating, and played a large role in a first arrest of foreign Jews for deportation in August 1942 was an eminent high civil servant in the Vaucluse, honored after the war as a victim of the Germans. His successors, respected civil servants, updated the lists and transmitted them, with some foot-dragging, to the local staff of the Vichy Commissariat aux Questions Juives, who passed them to the Gestapo. The men who, using that list, came to take Mme. Levendel away were members of a Marseille underworld gang who delivered Jews to the Gestapo in exchange for a fee and the liberty to pillage their belongings afterward.

These quests not only brought Isaac Levendel a sense of liberation; they also brought him a lot of pain—a pain he makes us share. This book is not always comfortable to read. Once we have begun it, however, it grips us with its intensity and authenticity. The author says what he thinks. He is angry.

Levendel has harsh things to say about practically everyone: not only the Nazis and their French collaborators, but, at times, his French neighbors, with their dislike of the "difference"—of people who are not like themselves; the American bombers' indiscriminate slaughter of civilians on the ground; the French Liberation Committee's summary justice after the war; self-satisfied veterans of the French Resistance; Catholics conditioned to envision Jews as "killers of Christ"; professional historians with their bloodless objectivity; archivists bent on keeping researchers away from their sensitive documents; civil servants who think only of their careers; and, last but certainly not least, his fellow Jews, with their propensity for lamentation and self-pity, their efforts to "pass," and their bland food.

Levendel's harsh judgment becomes bearable in the end, however, because he is also hard on himself. He admits he was a bit of a spoiled brat, and he continues to be willful and stubborn as an adult. Otherwise, he never would have persisted in these quests despite advice from friends and officials to let the past alone.

There are some heroes in this book, too. They are the Just Ones who helped the distressed child. The Steltzers, foreign Jews who also needed to hide, took the time to make sure the boy also had shelter. The Brès, a poor and uneducated but generous peasant family, took him in without hesitation and without the slightest calculation, in spite of the risks of trouble from the Gestapo or their French helpers. But the Just Ones were only a minority, and they could not change the course of events. The hospitality the Brès offered the Jewish child only magnified the neighbors' low opinion of them as irresponsible and improvident. They fit the theory that those who take risks to help members of a persecuted minority tend to be outsiders, people of independent values who are indifferent to respectable opinion.[1] Levendel declines to let us take the easy way out and consider the Brès representative of the French people as a whole.

After the Liberation, another French family, the Sourets, gave the young Isaac a warmer home than his bereaved father could. When his father returned after the war from internment in Switzerland, Isaac felt only stiff awkwardness with him. The wounded Levendel family was not able to knit itself back together. It was as a boarder with the affectionate Sourets, whose reluctance to wash, love of good food, resistance to rules, and spontaneous good humor remind the reader of Marcel Pagnol, that the nine-year-old began to construct a normal childhood. Like many rescued children, however, he was torn between his happiness with the Sourets and the Jewish identity of which his schoolmates never failed to remind him.

Levendel claims he has sought only his "personal truth." He situates himself on a middle ground between the professional historians, whose bloodless abstractions are devoid of memory, and the excesses of self-serving recollection, without self-awareness and perspective, in which some victims indulge nowadays. But his book contributes in a number of ways to the more general truths sought by historians.

Because Levendel was tenacious and lucky in gaining access to his archives, he can give us a vivid picture at the village level of how the Vichy machinery for identifying, making the census, and excluding Jews was subsequently taken up and used by the Gestapo and its French helpers for their much more radical goal of extermination. That machinery worked, even without ideological commitment on the part of the local *fonctionnaires,* and even after some of them had come to have doubts about Vichy. This reminds us that the cooling of French public opinion toward Vichy, stressed by recent historians,[2] was not sufficient to prevent that regime from functioning. The vast majority of French people were neither strongly in favor of nor strongly opposed to Vichy's anti-Jewish policies.[3] On which side of the account book, however, shall we enter the prevailing indifference? On the one hand, the neighbors did not denounce the Brès to the police; on the other, indifference allowed the deportation machinery to function until August 1944.

Levendel's discovery that his mother was identified, tracked, and stamped not by ideological collaborators but by respectable civil servants following orders makes us look hard at "collaboration d'état." It reminds us how many ordinary French public officials followed a complex itinerary during the Vichy period, from routine obedience to reserve and, in some cases, finally, to resistance. The very ambiguity of those common itineraries makes it difficult for those who lived through the Occupation, and for us, to establish any single serene memory of that period. But does the ultimate transformation of some "collaborateurs d'état" into latter-day Gaullists make them more admirable than the ideological collaborators, or only more adroit? Or were they, too, victims of their leaders' blunders? In his closing lines, Levendel forces us to ask ourselves, too, whether we would sacrifice our careers in such a situation.

The haphazard manner in which some Jews were taken away and others were not is strikingly apparent in Isaac Levendel's story. Chance and individual circumstances play considerable roles. That means that the perennial question of how it was that two-thirds of the Jews in France survived the Nazi occupation can receive no simple answer. And while that answer surely includes actions by good people in France, among them some *fonctionnaires*, it can only in very rare instances include official acts by the Vichy government and administration. One of those rare instances was Vichy's refusal to extend to the Unoccupied Zone the German ordinance of June 1942 requiring Jews to wear a yellow star. Although this refusal was more a reassertion of Vichy sovereignty than a moderation of Vichy anti-Semitism, it offered the Jews in the Unoccupied Zone a significant advantage. Levendel gives it due recognition. But the absence of external marks made the prefectures' lists even more fateful for the Jews inscribed on them, along with the word "Jew" stamped relentlessly by Vichy officials on all identity papers and ration cards.

Levendel sees evidence that Vichy *fonctionnaires* were trying toward the end to save French citizens of Jewish origin (and France's own sovereign status) by placating the Nazi agencies with the foreign Jews. That kind of discrimination was also practiced by Admiral Miklós Horthy's Hungary, Bulgaria, and other quasi-independent regimes under the sway of Nazi Germany. But it is not a bargain in which defenders of Vichy can take much pride. Nor was it a bargain that succeeded. Isaac Levendel was not on the list with his mother, but had he gone back to Le Pontet with her on June 4, he would have been taken away, despite the French citizenship he had acquired at birth. The completeness of Vichy's homegrown anti-Jewish program before 1942, which subjected long-established Jews to most of the same restrictions as recent immigrants, hobbled Vichy's efforts after 1942 to protect the French citizens among them from Eichmann's men.

Levendel gives us a sensitive look at the awkward matter of

living in France after 1945 with memories of the Occupation and deportations. He meets former school classmates on the street who once scrawled anti-Semitic graffiti on his door, and who now expect to be treated cordially, as if nothing had happened.

Should Levendel have left the past alone, as many people urged him to do? Does he have the right to look in the archives for those whom he holds responsible for his mother's death, and to make their names public? Readers will have to decide for themselves how to establish an appropriate balance between two conflicting goods: their right to privacy against Levendel's right to know what happened to his mother. Does an official's undoubted right to privacy in his personal life extend to actions accomplished in the exercise of official functions? In any event, it would be difficult to deny Isaac Levendel the possibility of understanding his own life, and his duty to tell the next generation about this century's violence in all its gritty, quotidian details.

Levendel is an accomplished computer technologist and manager who writes without the benefit of literary artifice or training in historical methods. His book has more basic values. He is blunt and honest with us, and aware of his own subjectivity. That unsentimental tough-mindedness makes this one of the most convincing and moving of this kind of memoir of the Final Solution in France.

Robert O. Paxton
Columbia University, New York

He Who . . .

He Who Loses One Single Life, It Is Counted Against
Him As If He Lost The World In Its Entirety, And He
Who Saves One Single Life, It Is Counted For Him As If
He Saved The World In Its Entirety.

     —The Babylonian Talmud, fifth century

These lines are dedicated to the people who made a difference in my life.

My thoughts particularly go to the daughter of Hersh Goldstein and Ruchli Lewendel of Poland, my mother Sarah Goldstein, whose ashes were scattered somewhere in Central Europe sometime at the beginning of July 1944. There she rejoined her brothers, sisters, and parents, and the other victims of Nazi barbarism and Christian anti-Semitism. Before parting, she showered me with unforgettable love and care for almost eight years. Her gift was enough for a lifetime. She resisted evil with her bare hands, but she was no match for it. This book is more a hymn to her life than a memorial for her death.

Before taking care of themselves, our friends Monsieur

Steltzer and his family acted as go-betweens to find me a refuge. They themselves were Jews hunted by the Nazis, but they took the time for my safety because they could not bear the thought of the alternative awaiting me; I had been sentenced to death by the laws of Vichy three years earlier, at the age of five.

Until they helped me, Monsieur Brès and his family had, as Christians, no reason to fear the Nazis. When I was left alone, they responded to Monsieur Steltzer's call. They extended for me a protective net and took me in as one of their own. In doing so, they suddenly had everything to lose in the face of Nazi hostility.

Monsieur Brès and Monsieur Steltzer formed a benevolent alliance to allow me to live. Without their help, I would have been delivered to the Nazis.

After the war, Madame Souret and her family revived me with simple warmth and understanding. They opened up their door and their hearts to me, and began my healing.

Finally, this book is also dedicated to a particular group among my peers, the youngest child survivors. My juniors by a few years, they lost everything and became orphans forever, because, unlike me, they were too young to have memories. Will they ever find their peace?

NOT THE GERMANS ALONE

1 | *The Cherry Season*

Absence is the worst of ills.

—Jean de La Fontaine, "The Two Doves"

It is June of 1990, and my wife, Elsa, and I are driving along a winding rural road toward Venasques, a small village on a spur of Mont Ventoux, the mountain towering above the town of Carpentras in French Provence. The valley below turns bluish toward the far edge. Here and there, rocks and aromatic scrub have yielded to meager patches of cherry trees. In the furnace of summer, scents of wild lavender and thyme blend with the relentless chirp of the cicadas. As a child, I knew by heart La Fontaine's fable of the cicada and the ant. It started with something like:

> *Cicada, having sung her song*
> *All summer long,*
> *Found herself without a crumb*
> *When winter winds did come.*[1]

Although it has been forty-six years since my last visit, I still remember this narrow road winding up and down on the edge of the hills, as, laboring along the protective row of cypresses, an old bus was taking my mother and me to Venasques on June 4, 1944. My mother had finally surrendered to the pressing advice of the Steltzers, our friends and fellow Jews, and had decided to seek refuge from the German Gestapo and the French Militia. I have forgotten the bus driver and the other passengers, but I remember my sense of relief. After two years of fear, my mother was taking me to a safe place.

German military trucks and foot patrols had filled the streets back in our village of Le Pontet, but the road to Venasques was quiet and seemed almost asleep. There were no black limousines like the ones that brought the Gestapo men who regularly visited Monsieur Gros, our neighbor. I was no longer afraid of the Germans and their French helpers. We had finally left our hostile neighborhood behind, and here, in the mountains, there would be no more bombings by the Allied planes.

I remember well that hot day in 1944. Our destination was a cherry farm tucked away in the hills of Venasques. When the bus stopped outside the village, a young boy was waiting to take us to the farm on mule-drawn cart. He invited us to climb up next to him on the front seat, so close to the mule that I got goose bumps. Contrary to most of the children from my village, who were destined for farm work, this was my first trip on a cart. On the way to the farm, as we left the asphalt for a gravel road, the mule suddenly bolted. Without hesitation, the young boy leaped on her back and then pulled himself toward her head. As for me, overcome by panic and barely daring to open my eyes, I had clung to my mother's left arm. Wrapping his legs firmly around the mule's neck, the boy seized her leather head strap with one hand, while he jammed the fingers of his other hand into her nostrils. Then, to my astonishment, he released his legs and slid off, hanging in midair from the head of the runaway animal! The mule immediately decided to trade her fury for a lighter grip on her nostrils and quickly came to a halt. Instantly, the boy had become my hero. In my panic, I had planted my nails in my mother's left arm.

At the farm, we rejoined the Steltzers, who had preceded us into hiding by a few days. Like them, my mother was expected to work, picking cherries in exchange for room and board for the two of us. We would share our lodging with the Steltzers and sleep in a shack in the back of the cherry orchard. I remember the small bedroom with a single window carved into the thick concrete wall, the blinding sunlight that entered the room through the slanted shadow. I remember, too, the ticks in the bed. They did not seem to bother my mother, although she had been horrified when she had found ticks in our bed at home two years earlier. More than that was needed to spoil our sense of security at the cherry farm.

I went with my mother to see the cherry trees on the rocky slope, and for the first time in my life I picked cherries straight from the tree. I made a wish, as was customarily done before eating the first fruit of the season. Since one had to eat carefully, however, to avoid the worms, I had developed a ritual. Holding the stem and slowly rotating the cherry a full turn, I inspected the skin in the bright sunlight for the slightest imperfection that signaled a guest inside. In those days, one did not throw away fruit with worms, but rather ate the cherry around the intruder. If the skin was perfect (this did not happen often), one could enjoy the entire cherry at once. To this day, I instinctively inspect and turn each cherry a full turn before eating it, although no worm can survive modern pesticides.

That afternoon, I indulged in as many cherries as my stomach could hold, and I recall my fascination for the sap that had burst out of the bark and begun to harden on its way down the trunk. I could scrape it off and shape it between my fingers. It gave off a particular sweet aroma that I remember to this day.

The next morning, I awoke to the sound of an argument outside our bedroom. My eyes blinded by the bright summer sunlight, I recognized Madame Steltzer's shrieking voice and her foreign accent. "You can leave your things at the store; they can wait," she scolded my mother. "If a misfortune were to happen to you, what would become of the child?" Several times earlier, my mother had received this warning from friends. Like others, Madame Steltzer did not use explicit language because she felt it held the power to precipitate a tragedy. She counted on the ambiguity of the word "misfortune" to confuse bad luck. Unconvinced, my mother took her own counsel and decided to go back to our store in Le Pontet anyway. Probably shaken by Madame Steltzer's argument, however, she suggested that I stay at the farm until her return.

Absorbed by the new surroundings and filled with admiration for the heroic boy who had stopped the runaway mule, to her surprise, I agreed to wait for her at the farm. She had never left me alone overnight before, and every time she had tried to do so, I had vehemently refused. But this day was different. The boy stood next to me when my mother left, because she had suggested that he take care of me in her absence. I felt torn between my pride in being his friend and my sadness at seeing her leave. As soon as she was gone, however, I worried and cried. I was not yet eight years old, and she was all I had.

She was to return the next day, but she never did. Instead, she fell into the hands of the Nazis and disappeared from my life. I am alive today because, instead of accompanying her, I chose to stay with the boy who was stronger than the enraged mule. Because of him, I also feel a lingering sense of loss. I do not remember his face, and I do not remember his name. I have no memory either of the day my mother was supposed to return to the cherry farm. But I do remember many of the days of nurturing that preceded that day in June 1944, and I have never forgotten the few merciful people who protected me from the worst.

For a long time, I kept these memories to myself, hidden behind a wall of silence. Although my story remained alive in me, I did not have the courage to confront the facts and talk to those who had been its witnesses. Secure that I could retrieve the past just for the asking, I kept it locked inside. But, as time went by, I started forgetting the things I once knew. Entire fragments of my past drifted away in the stream of time; surprisingly, though, other pieces remained etched in my memory with the precision of a laser beam, regardless of how essential—or unimportant—they may have been. It is the terror of complete oblivion, the death of my memories, that brought me to Venasques, trying to remember.

Now, standing in the middle of a cherry orchard on that hot summer day in 1990, my memories fail me. Maybe it was all a dream. Having searched all around, I cannot find the exact place where my mother and I separated forever. I cannot locate among the familiar trees the place where I was standing when her image began to dissipate. I cannot remember her last look, her face, her last words, her last hug. I just remember her walking away from me, disappearing into the distance. She was wearing her bright taffeta dress with big white buttons. I watch her turn beyond the old portal and walk away forever. It is this sight of her that I came to recover after so many years. Her last loving attention to me was to use a safety pin to mend a tear in the pocket of my summer shirt. I remember fingering the safety pin after she left, holding on to it as if she were hanging on to the other end.

In this cherry orchard, I began my trip back in time, determined to break through the forty-six-year wall of silence surrounding my mother. Fearful of losing her memory, I decided to tell her story. Now, I had to find out what had happened to her. I also needed to locate the people who had helped me survive and pay them my tribute at last.

Months of relentless writing triggered a whirl of emotions. I found myself crying—and smiling—at my memories, and I could not break away. Like the variegated handkerchiefs in a magic trick, one memory wove into the next in an endless stream of colors. The recollection of one special moment unleashed an entire rainbow.

2 | *The Waltz of Names*

*Nevertheless, Sarah, your wife, shall bear you a son; and
you shall name him Isaac; and I will maintain My
covenant with him as an everlasting covenant with his
offspring to come.*

> —Genesis 17:19

*Sarah said, "God has brought me laughter,[1] everyone who
hears will laugh with me."*

> —Genesis 21:6

The 1930s–March 1, 1940

I was born in Avignon one hour before midnight on June 28,
1936, a Sunday.

Most of my knowledge about my parents' origins comes from
the stories my mother told me before her arrest, from old documents that had rested for many years in a box of old photographs,
and from my father after his return from captivity.

According to his passport stamp, my father, Meijlech Schöps, alias Lewendel, crossed the eastern border of France on May 19, 1930, at the age of twenty-nine, as an immigrant from Poland. He was making his way to work at the farm of Monsieur Alcide Rolland in Puymeras, a small village in a southern French district, the *département* of Vaucluse. He was born at the beginning of this century in Ozanna, a tiny village of forty-three inhabitants near Lezaisk,[2] the son of Pessli Schöps and Isaac Lewendel. He had received the last name of his mother, and not that of his father, because their Jewish wedding was not officially recognized in the area of Lezaisk where they had settled. My father's parents were poor and gave him no education except that of the Jewish heder, a religious school run by the rabbi. My father could read Hebrew straight, from the side, and upside down, because the numerous students in the heder who could not afford to own books had to circle around the few more fortunate ones. At the Avignon synagogue, I often saw him read the Torah from the side. He was somewhat familiar with the Polish language because of the petty trade he was engaged in, but he spoke Yiddish at home.

I was between ten and thirteen years old when I heard most of my father's anecdotes, which were at the center of the conversations at friends' parties. Eager to share their own experiences, all the participants echoed the typically Jewish afflictions of my father's stories. Strangely enough, my friends and I suspected our parents of paranoia.

Poverty and anti-Semitism were endemic in my father's area of Poland. Because of the Numerus Clausus, a quota law against the Jews, their attendance at Polish schools was restricted, and they were excluded from entire segments of the economy, thus reducing their options to trade and small business. But even if my father had been allowed to attend school, this probably would have made little difference, since he had to earn a living from an early age. Anti-Semitism was rampant in the Polish population, and beating Jews after a good drinking party was part of the way of life. In order to avoid the beatings when venturing outside the shtetl, the little Jewish town, to make a living, my father had to learn a few rules: do not rock the boat, do not go where you do not have to be, and pay for your protection.

Continuous wars made matters worse for the Jews. For generations, the area of Poland where my father and his relatives lived had been a bone of contention between the Austro-Hungarian Empire and Russia. The villages bounced between the warring sides, as the moving border reflected military fortunes and misfortunes. When the Russians had the upper hand, unrestrained hordes of soldiers indulged in "spontaneous" pogroms, helped by the local Catholic population. The theme of the Russian occupiers was simple: The Austrians have beaten our Jews when they invaded our area; now we are beating theirs. The same scenario would be repeated when the Austrians had the upper hand. Both sides displaced entire Jewish villages and resettled their respective populations to further their future claims on these territories. Long columns of Jews on foot herded by soldiers to unknown destinations were a common sight in those days. They were coming from the south and were moved to the north, or vice versa, depending on who was controlling the area. Men and women, old and young, sick and healthy were all equal in their misery. The local Polish population celebrated, while their Jewish counterparts retreated into prayers—a sad rehearsal for things to come during the Nazi era.

In this stormy part of the world, income was low and amenities were scarce. My father's family survived on small trade with the Polish farmers and villagers. In those days, salt, a rare commodity, was used as a currency to acquire goods or zlotys, Polish currency. Winters were particularly harsh, and ice on the river had to be broken in order to fetch a few buckets of water for home use. Since his mother had died when he was ten, my father, who was the youngest child, remained alone with my grandfather after the departure of his older brothers and sisters, some to Palestine and others to America. My grandfather, Isaac Lewendel, soon became ill and totally dependent on his sixteen-year-old son.

During the last weeks of his life, my grandfather became extremely demanding. Since my father was exhausted from a day's work, he tied a string between his own arm and his father's so his father could wake him if needed during the night. My father told me this story when I was around twelve, and from it I sensed the deep resentment he felt. He never mentioned his mother in any of his stories, and it was quite obvious that my father had received little nurturing from his own parents.

My cousin Chipele remembers my father in his mid-twenties. He used to stay with her family when he came to Lezaisk for business. She was not yet ten years old at the time. "You know," she says, "he was alone," meaning that he was single and his parents had passed away. And she adds that her entire family used to look up to my father and his business activity with deep respect because he was an honest man.

The misery of the shtetl and Catholic hostility had combined to squeeze my father—and many other Jews—out of Poland like toothpaste out of a tube. For those Jews capable of tearing themselves away from the tight web of Jewish life in Poland, the "liberal French tradition" promised relief from oppression and poverty. My father believed in that promise enough to undertake the journey to France, a country that offered the hope of a better life and seemed to be more secular, since it had detached itself politically from Catholicism at the end of the previous century. In comparison to Poland, France would be safer for Jews.

Upon setting foot in France, however, my father found himself on unfamiliar ground. Unlike in Poland, there were few shtetls in France. In Avignon, for instance, Jews were scattered among the local population. Although a large group of Jews had gathered around rue des Rosiers in Paris, voluntarily recreating the Polish shtetl in the middle of the French capital, that was the exception.

Not only was peasant work very demanding for my father, given his small size and lack of physical fitness, but his low wages did not allow him to become independent, as he had dreamed. Less than a year later, after looking for a better job, he was hired as an apprentice painter in Carpentras, where he found the work easier and the pay better. My father loved to tell how he was appreciated by his employer, since being useful and having a purpose were the highest forms of ethics practiced at home. In fact, as a teenager, I had to justify to my father every one of my actions by providing an acceptable answer to his question, "Why do you want to do that?" since everything had to have a reason—and a good one. For him, doing the right thing was a recipe for longevity.

My mother, Sarah Goldstein, the daughter of Hersh Goldstein and Ruchli Lewendel, was born in 1904 in the small village of Lipsko, not far from Przemyśl. I have little firm knowledge about her family, as if it did not really exist. She was one of seven or eight children, mostly girls. The Goldsteins had made their home in Przemyśl, a lively and solidly Jewish town of thirty-five thousand in the southeastern part of today's Poland. Being a fur trader, as it is stated on my parents' wedding certificate, her father made a good living. Encouraged by her progressive parents, who insisted on education for their daughters, my mother became a certified accountant. As in other upper-class Polish families, my mother learned and spoke French as a distinctive display of a higher culture. The photographs of her family radiate the elegance of the early 1930s, and the picture of my mother in the middle of a mandolin orchestra suggests a musical education. This 1934 picture celebrates the fifteenth anniversary of Canzonetta, the mandolin club of Przemyśl.

By 1935, at the age of thirty-four, my father had amassed enough money to marry, as expected of a Jew. Before leaving Poland five years earlier, he had set his eyes on the Goldstein sisters, who were his cousins, since their mother, Ruchli, was also born a Lewendel. Marrying second cousins was customary among Polish Jews, because that eliminated the risk of marrying a woman who was not Jewish according to Orthodox rules. In agreement with the Goldsteins of Przemyśl, my father called upon their next available daughter. This is how Sarah Goldstein arrived in

Avignon on August 10, 1935, to become Sarah Lewendel on September 29, 1935. In their wedding photograph, my father, full of pride and elegance, wears a dark suit and a bow tie. My mother, with her high heels and her flowery hat, is much taller than he, since he was only four foot eleven.

After the wedding, my parents settled in a small village near Avignon, Le Pontet, which its inhabitants preferred to call a town. Le Pontet ("the little bridge") was named after the bridge over the Sorgue, a small river crossing the main road in the middle of the village. My parents opened a store next to that road, Route Nationale Numéro Sept (National Highway Number Seven), which was the main artery linking the southeast of France to Paris. The small storefront was set back from the main street at the end of a yard, and a huge plane tree provided much-needed shade during the hot Provence summers. Perhaps this is why there were plane trees everywhere in the area—in the fields, in the yards, and along the country roads—all leaning in the same direction because of the mistral, a cold wintry wind blowing from the north.

I was soon born in Avignon at the municipal maternity ward, being "my own cousin," since I am related to myself through both my mother and my father. My mother kept telling everyone who was ready to listen that I had to be brought into the world with forceps on a Sunday, one hour before midnight, as if this were irrefutable proof of my uncommon significance. I was registered in the French birth registers as Isaac Lewendel for two reasons. Being a "Bible scholar," my father symbolically named me Isaac, since my mother was named Sarah after Isaac's mother in the Bible. Also, it is customary to give a Jewish boy the name of his deceased grandfather. However, my parents immediately started calling me Jacques outside the house and Jacky at home, because these names sounded less Jewish and more French than Isaac. This is how I got my second and third identities. My father also began calling himself Max outside the house, because his real first name was too conspicuously Jewish. However, for friends and family he remained Meijlech, the Yiddish pronunciation for Melech, which means "king" in Hebrew. My mother did not change her name because of Sarah Bernhardt, the famous French actress, but she was called "Madame Levandel" outside the house, and not "Lewendel" as in the legal documents. All this may sound confusing, but we danced the waltz of names with mastery and knew what to call whom when.

Two months after my birth, on September 9, 1936, I became French by declaration of my parents in front of a justice of the peace in Avignon,[3] in accordance with the French law on nationality of August 10, 1927. Although my parents were not yet eligible for French citizenship, I became their first step toward integration.

My mother, who adapted quickly, named our store Minime Prix (minimum price) and ordered beautiful letterhead that said:

> Minime Prix
> Bonneterie et Mercerie
> Maison Levandel
> Rue de la République
> Le Pontet (Vaucluse)

With the typically French spelling of our last name, the letterhead was to last for years.

My mother was typically Jewish; she believed that the importance of one's child was directly proportional to the hardship he caused. She was to tell—and retell—with pride all the little miseries I inflicted on her as if they were the proof of the brilliant destiny in store for me. Not to disappoint her, I made sure to leave a trail of misdeeds, which I started at a young age. Until the last of my parents' friends passed away, it was common knowledge that I had urinated in the face of Docteur André, the local physician, as he was examining me as a baby. Everybody hailed my precocious independence and smiled at this early mark of disrespect for the local medical legend. You must understand that Docteur André had an unquestioned power over the fate of all the children in the village, and hence full authority over their parents. His mysterious prestige was more effective than his treatments, for the state of the village medical art was closer to voodoo than to real science. If you were afflicted with whooping cough (and I was), you were sent to the cooking gas plant in Avignon to inhale the air laden with coal particles. I remember several of the bus trips we took to the gas factory when I was three, because I was impressed by the huge installation of black tanks and pipes, and the smell of coal in the air. If you got strep throat (and I did), you were told to apply iodine to your larynx with cotton. To be effective, it was said, the iodine had to be placed so deep in the throat that it would trigger a vomiting reflex. Of course, my mother did not believe all these remedies would work without her traditional chicken soup, and I got my share of that too. To ensure the best results, my mother fed me until I had eaten the last drop. On chicken soup, there was no compromise. Her techniques apparently worked, since I am still around.

My deeds, and misdeeds, were always portrayed as little miracles. Many times over, I heard the famous story about a traveling salesman and his suitcase at the Avignon train station. We were all waiting for the train; he was leaving town, and we were expecting a visitor. Since I was three years old and unruly, my parents had seated me on the man's suitcase so that they could keep an eye on me. I was so captivated by the hustle and bustle in the huge train station that I forgot to ask for the toilet. Since I had already graduated from diapers, my light cotton shorts were unable to hold my mess, which soiled the suitcase. When the train arrived, my mother picked me up, and everybody realized at the same time what had happened. My parents, their friends, and of course the salesman all were staring at the suitcase. After a brief hesitation, but fearful of missing his train, the salesman ran to find a seat, carrying my gift with him on top of his suitcase. Our party left for the nearby Café de la Gare, where my mother cleaned me up. In the meantime, everyone had a good laugh. In the following years, a visiting family friend could easily buy himself a place in heaven by describing once again the face of the traveling salesman. The last time I heard this story was at my wedding in 1967.

In their attitude toward their newfound country, my parents embodied the typical Jewish dilemma. On the one hand, they had faith in this land of opportunity; on the other, they had to remain on their guard. Having already broken away from the Orthodox interpretation of the Jewish religion before they left the Polish shtetl, my parents were awkwardly striving to behave like the French. Inside, however, they remained ferociously Jewish, and deeply suspicious of Catholics and Catholicism.

During the days before Easter 1939, the local baker had manufactured Easter eggs, bunnies, and bells out of chocolate. According to Catholic tradition, the bells were to "fly to Rome" on Easter day. Barely three, I salivated with envy at the piles of chocolate, but, deeply aware of the Catholic symbolism of these chocolate artifacts, my parents steadfastly refused to let me even taste the broken pieces that were sold at a discount. To this day, I remember my fit of anger. My father put me into my crib because I had refused to eat, pretending to be sick. I remember looking for sympathy through the bars of the crib as I cried my lungs out. So much for my attempt to assimilate by eating "their" chocolate!

To affirm our connection to the Jewish community, we regularly went to the Avignon synagogue, "the temple," as the Jews referred to it. The rabbi and the notables sat with the holy books and scrolls on a stage at the center of the circular synagogue, and the audience sat against the circular wall. Contrary to Catholic practice, the circular arrangement of worshipers around the rabbi and the sacred books encourages debate, questioning, and differing interpretations of the religious texts. But, as is customary in Orthodox Judaism, the women were seated upstairs in the balcony.

The 1939 Yom Kippur service was traumatic for me. While the men were singing the ritual prayers of atonement, I was ignoring the service and frantically pushing a little toy car on the floor near the center of the temple. To my great chagrin, the *shaames* (synagogue caretaker) confiscated my little toy because the rattling noise was inappropriate for the occasion. My mother immediately came down from the balcony to defend me. "What do you want from the poor child?" she demanded of the *shaames*. Without waiting for an answer, she added, "He is only three!" Obviously, the *shaames* was out of line, and my mother did not hesitate to tell him so.

My parents tried hard to impart to me the moral values and honesty befitting a Jewish boy, for they said that Jews must be "a light to the goyim," the other peoples or non-Jews. Ill at ease in confinement, I used to wander away from home into the neighborhood. Sometimes, I went to play with Paulette Lagriffe, daughter of the owners of the Café de la Paix on our side of the road. One day, I returned home with the girl's doll, claiming that she had given it to me. In spite of my strong protests, my parents, who were not fooled, obliged me to return the doll by myself. I felt angry and frustrated because they had made me aware of a boundary I was not allowed to cross. But this did not stop me from trying to cross other boundaries to affirm my independence.

I stayed at the store with my mother, while my father started selling merchandise elsewhere to augment our income. Once a week, every small rural town and village had a regular outdoor market that catered to the local population who could not afford to leave their farms to shop in the bigger cities. On that day, merchants would converge on the village and set up their stalls on the village square. My father, who could not yet afford to own a car, had to ride a special bus with an upper deck, where he used to load his goods, mostly work clothes and underwear for the peasants. In one of our old photographs, he is standing stiffly near the special market bus.

With time, business grew and so did our revenue, and my father bought a used Talbot limousine. Recently, I found an old photograph of my father standing in front of his merchandise display and holding out a pair of pants for sale. The old Talbot was proudly fitted into the picture. As indicated by the glass partition between the driver and the passengers' seats in the back, the Talbot's previous owner must have been a wealthy person. Initially my father, who did not know how to drive, had to hire a driver. Since in those days it took months to obtain a driver's license, my father finally obtained one and became independent.

I remember how, when I was three and a half years old, I anxiously awaited my father's return from the market and how I ran to him as soon as I saw the car stop next to the sidewalk in front of our yard. I was crazy about him and his car, and he usually held me on the driver's seat as we went for a ride.

I often heard the story of how, when I was three, I escaped from my mother at a vacation place, Buis-les-Baronnies, trying to follow my father, who was going back to work. My mother temporarily closed our store during the summer of 1939, and we were vacationing in a mountain area so that I could "get as much fresh air as possible" while my father kept working. At the end of a short visit, since I was not allowed to return with him in the huge car, I quietly followed him down the road where the car had disappeared. When my mother, panic-stricken, realized that I was missing, a search was organized in the area with the help of the other vacationers. I was found on the side of a steep ravine, hanging by my clothes on a thorny bush that had stopped my fall after I slipped on the road. To this day, I can still see the bushy side of the ravine and the people reaching for me. For my mother, this "miracle" was added proof of my unusual significance: God was watching over me. Naturally, my excessive liberties were acceptable because of this "divine immunity."

Some time before the war, Chaim Laufbaum, our cousin on my father's side, visited us on his way from Poland to Los Angeles. I remember our photo session in front of the Palais des Papes, the Popes' Palace in Avignon, because I was afraid of the camera on the tripod, and everybody, including Chaim, was trying to keep me quiet. Chaim was the last member of our family to get out of Poland before the Nazi invasion. Since Le Pontet was not a natural stopover on the way to Los Angeles, Chaim had taken the time to pay a visit to my parents as a tribute to their emerging success. Unfortunately, unlike Chaim, Avignon's Jews did not realize the significance of the Nazis' vociferous threats all over Europe; they felt safe under the protection of Prime Minister Eduoard Daladier, the onetime mayor of Carpentras and representative of Vaucluse. Also, obsessed by their determination to succeed, my parents did not pay much attention to the increasing strength of Fascism in France. They did not see the terrible power that could be unleashed against them by a forthcoming alliance between French Fascism and German Nazism.

Although my father volunteered for the military on April 25, 1939, he was not immediately mobilized when the war broke out that year, because he was a foreign national. However, the creation of a Polish legion in the French army soon provided numerous Polish immigrants—my father among them—with the hope for faster French naturalization. He was finally called to the legion on March 1, 1940. I remember being scared when, a few weeks later, he returned on leave in his military uniform, with his calves wrapped from ankle to knee with special support bands as required in his military unit. To mark the event, he had bought me a bright red pedal car, which I could drive on my own. Soon thereafter, he disappeared into World War II, which explains why I am an only child. Among old documents, I found a postcard my father sent us on March 19, 1940. In a hesitant hand, the result of his Jewish village education, he had written in Polish to my mother that he was well but had been separated from his friend Rozman. With a few spelling errors, he had also added for me in French, "Jack, be a good boy!" in reference to my unruliness.

My father's departure for the front left my mother alone to take care of the store, my father's outside business, the car, and me. To "spare the tires" until my father's return, she had the car raised on jacks in a small rented garage close to home; she consolidated my father's business into our little store; and she began searching for a better location where the store could be more profitable. In its current location, the store, recessed inside a small yard and lacking direct access to the sidewalk, was too dark inside, and its unadorned exterior was not appealing enough to generate a good volume of sales. As for me, my mother was to become the center of my life, enveloping me in her warm circle of love.

3 | *Inside My Little Circle*

> *Together with Font-Réaulx, I am preparing a text [of law]*
> *"flavored with little glazed onions."*[1]
>
> > —Raphaël Alibert, Vichy Minister of Justice,
> > to Charles Pomaret, Minister of Internal
> > Affairs, on July 1, 1940, in reference to the
> > Statute of the Jews[2]

Summer 1940–Early 1942

My mother learned from the Red Cross that my father's regiment had been driven into Switzerland by the victorious German army on June 20, 1940, and that he would remain interned by the Swiss government until the end of the hostilities. She used to read me every postcard we received from my father, and at every opportunity she would tell me little stories about him. She would often recall how I ran after him in Buis-les-Baronnies, for example, and how I loved to ride with him in the car, a story that has stayed with me until this day. While my father was gone, my mother did not to wear any makeup, continuing her practice from before the war. "Your father did not approve of it," she used to tell me, as if she expected him to come home any minute.

We often sifted through our old family photographs together. My mother would point at my father in the pictures. I particularly remember those with the old Talbot. The pictures of my mother's relatives were happy ones, but there were no pictures of my father's family. After we finished, my mother would put the photos back into their box and put the box back on a shelf in the kitchen wall closet.

That summer of 1940, my father sent us a little package containing Swiss chocolate. There were two milk chocolate bars and one white chocolate bar. Since sweets had become rare, this was an unexpected treat. A little later, my mother received a Swiss watch with a gold band, which she had to free from customs because of the gold. She proudly showed it around to everybody. "My husband sent it to me from Switzerland," she'd announce.

After his departure, my father's image faded away, as did the pedal car that he had bought for me. I soon learned how to reach maximum speed. Possibly angry about my father's departure or just because of my inner energies, I started simulating car collisions against the huge plane tree in the middle of our front yard. Georges Delorme, my friend next door, and I competed to see who could smash the car and cause the most damage. We were imitating a car crash that we had seen earlier on the main road. When my mother caught us, it was already too late: the little red car was a wreck. She was furious because such a car was "priceless during these difficult times" and, possibly, because she felt that I was destroying my last concrete link to my father. I shamelessly put the responsibility on my friend Georges, and I hope that by now he has forgiven me.

Our tiny kitchen was in the back of the store. I vaguely remember its small size, the location of the faucet, and my mother's ironing board. However, the ceiling lamp, with its adjustable counterweight and old-fashioned shade, remains sharply etched in my memory. On ironing days, my mother used the outlet, which my father had inserted into the lamp socket because we did not have electric outlets on the wall. The ceiling shade stood out against the darkness of the kitchen. By its feeble light I can still see the *attrape-mouches*, the flycatchers, sticky paper spirals that hung from the ceiling and trapped flies in their glue. I can still hear the endless buzz of the flies trying to escape. Economics required leaving a flycatcher hanging until there was no more room on the sticky spiral.

I remember vividly the door between the store and the kitchen because I injured my left thumb while pursuing Jacques Schneider, the fifteen-year-old son of our family friends. Entering through the storefront and exiting through the kitchen, I was frantically chasing him when he slammed the door on my thumb. After a few days I lost my nail. Today my left thumb is shorter than my right one—a memory etched in my body.

Our store was part of a multifamily apartment complex, and the bedrooms, located upstairs, could only be reached through a common area because they were not directly connected to the living areas downstairs. First we went from our day quarters to the first-floor corridor, then climbed the stairs to the second-floor corridor to reach the door to our bedroom. My mother was particularly concerned with the neighbor's wife, Madame Moutte, who lived across the hall and hated all Jews and foreigners. She made a habit of sweeping the dirt from her bedroom under the door of our bedroom. For as long as we lived there, she always made sure to find a way to pester us. After Madame Moutte died in 1970, her husband apologized to my father for the harassment that his wife had inflicted on us.

One of my friends, René Gaffet, the son of Madame Gaffet and Monsieur André, the local shoemaker, lived in our building at the back end of the main corridor. The shoemaker, whose name was André Mazoyer, was not René's real father. The villagers used to whisper that "Monsieur André," as the shoemaker preferred to be called, was "living with *her* out of wedlock." That was enough to set them apart from the tribe. René and I used to play together for hours, and at times his parents did not know how to get rid of me. One evening, René was getting a bath in a small tub after we had eaten fire-grilled corn on the cob and messed ourselves up (although corn was normally reserved for chickens and Italians, food restrictions had rendered us less demanding). My friend's father pulled an egg out from under his son in the tub and told me, "After you eat corn, you must go and take a bath so that the egg can come out; otherwise, the egg will remain stuck." I ran to my mother and urgently insisted on taking a bath to release the egg. She gently calmed me down while she prepared the hot water.

Since no one had an indoor toilet, all the tenants had to share a wooden outhouse in the backyard at the end of the corridor next to the Gaffets' room. There was a big round hole in the wooden floor and a little inside hook to hold the door shut. I still remember my first visit to the wooden booth when I was no more than two years old. I had granted my mother the exclusive honor of holding me so that I wouldn't fall into the hole.

As the memory of my father faded away, my ties to my mother strengthened and her circle around me tightened. In the years that followed, I seldom lost sight of her, at least not willingly. I felt I was at the center of her life because she was always around when I needed her, except on two occasions. The first time was when Jacques Saltzman, my Jewish friend, stayed for a sleepover. My mother had gone out in the morning to run errands while we were sleeping, and she had locked the bedroom door from the outside for safety. When we woke up, my friend and I perversely pretended that we badly needed to go to the bathroom. We both defecated on the greenish Persian rug beside the bed. My mother was furious, but this was my way of protesting being left alone. The second time she did not respond to my call was when I vainly waited for her to come back to the cherry farm after she had been taken away by the Nazis on June 6, 1944. This time was to last forever.

From these precious few years with her, I retain a strong feeling of having been loved and a deep emotional bond between her and me. Her faith that I could do no wrong was the source of my inner strength and confidence. I certainly was what we call today a "spoiled brat"—but I was a cute one, according to the pictures. The early ones show me with long hair and a big lock on the top. I was pretentiously well groomed. In the later photos, I had lost the lock and long blond hair because I was supposed to look like a boy in kindergarten. It befell Monsieur Gleyzes, the village barber, to cut my baby hair and transform me into a little boy against my will. I was unhappy.

My pictures were taken during elaborate photo sessions in Monsieur Chateauneuf's studio in Avignon. At regular intervals, my mother decided that it was time to take a new set of pictures because it was essential to document some "major" event and send the photos to her relatives in Poland. Every one of the sessions started with proper dressing for the occasion and then riding the bus to Avignon, while she watched to make sure that I did not mess up her preparations. Once in the studio, I was rechecked and recombed, and every fold in my clothes was straightened before handing me over to Monsieur Chateauneuf as he was staging the photo session. Obviously, the elaborate scenery had to be different from previous times, and how could he have forgotten which one he had already used? Then there was the ritual of "Look at the little bird who is going to come out of the camera!" "Hold a minute, Monsieur Chateauneuf! He just closed his eyes!" and "Let us do it again!" until my mother was satisfied that the pictures would be at least as good as the real thing. My pictures then joined the rest of our family pictures in the box on the wall-closet shelf.

I was never short of good ideas, and my mother was kind enough always to take things the right way. On one occasion, when I was about four, I decided to imitate the grown-ups. After dressing me neatly for one of the traditional photo sessions, my mother was upstairs finishing her dressing. While I was left alone downstairs, I decided to polish my shoes like she used to do. There was only one problem: the shoe polish was black, and I was dressed in white from head to toe. When my mother saw me, she invoked the Almighty as if I were His responsibility: "*Reboyne Shel Oylem* [Master of the Universe]! What has come over him?" At the time, she was furious, but later she would tell and retell the story to customers, neighbors, and friends alike—whether they wanted to hear it or not—so that they would realize how "clever" I was.

At this early age, my mother started teaching me simple arithmetic, and she even let me count the money in the cash register. Using her knowledge of French, she also taught me how to read and write. After she realized that I was copying her store accounting book, she gave me my own used copy of a 1937 *agenda*, a kind of appointment book. I found it recently and recognized her handwriting, regular, rhythmic and well formed. The *agenda* was full of repetitive patterns that I had written in the empty spaces: letters, words, numbers, and pictures written over my mother's notes dating from 1937. The word *papa* recurs over several pages. So do the word *maman* and names of family friends. Eight copies of one domino piece cover an entire page. I did the drawing on the day I received the domino game as a gift from Ménaché, the traveling salesman, who lingered to socialize after making his sale. I had also drawn several pictures of houses on wheels, probably depicting the Gypsies who regularly passed by our house on the Route Nationale Numéro Sept. After the war, I would discover that numerous Gypsies had been deported in total silence to the concentration camps. According to a personal communication of Mr. Hayez, director of the archives of Vaucluse,[3] "regrouping" measures were taken by the Prefecture of Vaucluse Division of Foreigners against the Gypsies. However, no mention is made in the archives of their eventual deportation to the death camps. Denis Peschanski notes that the only Gypsies who were deported from France came from the northern region of France and were shipped from Malines in Belgium.[4] The end of the war apparently spoiled the Nazis' designs for most of the Gypsies of France.

While sifting through those pages left untouched for so many years, I was transported back in time. It was 1941, and I was sitting at the kitchen table and applying myself under my mother's watchful eye. I was using a black accounting pencil that would turn violet when I moistened the lead. Later, when I was allowed to use blue ink and a pen, I left on the first few pages ink spots and smears that can testify to my uncertain beginnings. These early encouragements largely account for my future interest in mathematics and engineering.

The original *agenda* entries contained financial transactions that my mother had performed. On April 14, 1937, a payment of 200 francs had been made for "the car" that had been purchased on installment (the Talbot, I presume). The last payment of 150 francs was scheduled for May 15, 1937, to Monsieur Gilhermet. Merchandise purchased for the store on December 9, 1936, was to be paid for on February 15, 1937; the amount: 1,100 francs.

Every page of my 1937 *agenda* included not only the day and date, but also a dedication to a Catholic celebration or saint, as is customary in France. Even today, calendars sold by the post office still print that dedication. Strangely enough, the *agenda* starts on the first of January with the celebration of "the circumcision," without explicitly mentioning Jesus. Most Catholics were unaware of this link. Ironically, the French were celebrating the Jewishness of Jesus as the country was preparing to help the Nazis turn the Jews into ashes.

When I went to the public kindergarten at the age of five, I already knew a lot of the school material because of my mother's nurturing, but I had some difficulties with the required discipline, and I loved recess. In the classroom, I was seated near a little girl, Jacqueline Boude, who lived on the outskirts of the village. One day she told me that her parents wanted her to buy a pair of cotton socks from my mother. I proposed to bring the socks the next day. Fortunately for me, in those days, the textile restrictions did not allow much choice: either you got socks or you didn't. My mother was elated at my initiative. She wrapped the socks up and sent them with me to school. The next day I brought home the money that Jacqueline's mother had sent in payment. This was my first business transaction, and our neighbors heard the story from my mother seven thousand times over. When she was singing my praises, my mother called me by my fourth name, "mein Jackele" (Yiddish for "my little Jack"), and gave me a hearty hug.

During the summer of 1941, the Jewish significance of the war touched me personally for the first time. The village clerk came to register us and to inventory our possessions. When the civil servant arrived, I was playing in the store. My mother's anger at the clerk surprised me, as she was a calm person. She objected to the inventory, reminding him that my father "had fallen prisoner of war while serving France" and that we had "always been faithful residents." To no avail, he insisted that the inventory was necessary and that he was only following orders.

Many years later, I found out that the Vichy government had just enacted a law ordering prefects to perform a census of the Jews.[5] Violation of that law would be punished by fine and imprisonment, and the prefects could impose special camp detentions. A second law immediately followed, requiring the Jews to register and record their assets so that they could easily be tracked and their property confiscated when the time came.[6] The purpose of this law was to "eliminate all Jewish influence from the national economy." Trustees could be appointed to "every industrial, commercial or craftsman's enterprise . . . all movable property or title . . . belonging to the Jews." From the enactment of the economic laws until the end of the war, hundreds of Vaucluse Jews lost their assets to zealous administrators faithful to the Vichy regime.[7] This massive action taken by Vichy against the Jews is captured in the following letter that Henri Chavin, general secretary of the police, addressed to the French prefects on July 19, 1941.

> **I am honored to send you herein my instructions announced by my telegrams of June 13 and 23 concerning the census, mandated by the law of June 2, 1941, of all Jews.**
>
> **I call your special attention to how important it is that this census, a measure of public order, be carried out carefully and supervised with all the means at your disposal and especially**

with the help of the lists that my encoded telegram of June 23 ordered you to establish.

    I am sending you in the same mail enough forms for individual declaration so that all Jews, French and foreign, in your department can make the declaration required by the law.

    It is your responsibility to distribute these forms in the towns of your department according to the approximate number of Jews who reside there.[8]

After the clerk left our store, my mother explained to me why it was unfair to us to do what he was doing, underscoring that my father was doing his duty in the French military. She spoke to me as if I understood the whole thing and was able to repair the injustice. This is my first memory of my mother's deep distress, which filled me with worry.

We went to various places "to settle this issue" (which I did not comprehend). At one point, we took the local train to Avignon and visited the office of Maître Vallabrègue, a French lawyer of Jewish descent. To be admitted to his office, my mother rang the doorbell in the street, and the heavy dark green wooden gate was opened. On our way to the office, we passed through a beautiful courtyard planted with flowers, bushes, and trees, its tall walls covered with ivy vines. What a huge desk and what an impressive library! I stared endlessly at the rows of books behind the tall glass doors. On our way back to the train station, my mother declared that there was nothing to worry about because Maître Vallabrègue had told her so.

We did not buy train tickets on the way back because cheating the authorities is a French precept. Since we were already feeling the pinch of the war, my mother was counting on an acquaintance at the station's checkout gate who would "close his eyes." When we arrived at Le Pontet, my hair and shirt were full of coal particles carried by the thick coal smoke from the engine, because I had watched the landscape through an open window.

In retrospect, the Census of the Jews had a crucial impact on our fate, since it was a powerful instrument that would track us wherever we might go. Could my mother have avoided being registered in 1941? When the law was enacted, everyone in Le Pontet already knew that we were Jewish, since we had lived in Le Pontet since 1935, we did not go to church, and my parents did not take the precaution of hiding our identity. The only way to avoid the census would have been to leave the area and seek counterfeit documents, which was not an easy task for many of the foreign-born Jews.

The census incident was my first foray outside my little circle through a crack in its wall. The Census of the Jews has remained a persistent scar for fifty years. I still remember, as if it were yesterday, the little city bureaucrat with his thick mustache, his round enamel-rimmed glasses, and the traditional beret on his head. As the cracks multiplied, I was to find myself facing reality more often with little room to hide.

Recently, I found out that we had been duly registered not once, as I thought, but three times: on July 1, 1941; August 27, 1943; and May 13 1944.[9] Obviously, the zealous bureaucrats did not wait for the letter from General Secretary Chavin. They registered us immediately after the prefect of Avignon received his encoded telegram on June 23, 1941.

During the 1941 census, the prefect of Avignon recorded 1,474 Jews—1,016 French Jews and 458 foreign Jews—for the department of Vaucluse under his jurisdiction.[10]

The winter of 1941 was the coldest the area had ever experienced. Three feet of snow paralyzed all traffic. We had to dig a passage through the yard between the storefront and the street, and I could barely raise my head above the snow level. This snowstorm was unusual because it rarely freezes in Provence during the winter. Buckets of coal had to be carried home by hand. The harsh winter weather added one more strain to the economic difficulties that my mother was already facing. Although the budget was stretched to make ends meet, my mother never complained about it. She always tried to find solutions. She would remodel old clothes after cutting off the worn areas and carefully examine shoes before deciding whether to resole them or throw them away.

At the end of winter, we moved to a new store across the street. My mother had signed a lease for several years. We did not have to change the letterhead since the new store was on the same street, but we had a new rubber stamp handmade in Avignon with the same words as the letterhead. Our new store was one of two adjacent storefronts that had previously been combined into one large grocery store, Les Docks Vauclusiens. Each side had full living quarters. Probably because of food scarcity and financial hardship, the owner, Madame Magnan, had decided to consolidate her operation into one store and lease the second one out to my mother. Before we moved in, our storefront was repainted with our logo, *Minime Prix*. Imbert, the mason, blocked the interior door between the two stores. Our side had a strong smell of wine, for the owner used to sell local wine straight out of the barrel. The wine overflow that had deeply penetrated the floor tiles was to resist scrubbings in the years to come.

We now had one grocery store on each side of our store. The compressed Docks Vauclusiens was on our left, and a second grocery store, Les Coopérateurs de Provence, owned by Monsieur and Madame Meffre, was on our right.

Our new store was larger than the old one. Before our move, my mother had new shelves built all along the walls. That gave the store a brand-new appearance, except for the old counter that we had brought from across the street. The living quarters were attached to the store, so there was no more need to pass through a common area to go to our bedrooms. The kitchen was in the back of the store, and the bedrooms upstairs. Using a huge wooden ladder, I could go up to the attic from the second floor. I loved the low ceiling and the massive crossbeams I could touch with my fingers. I enjoyed playing with old, useless objects left by the previous owner. However, my mother did not particularly like my looks when I came down with black dust on my knees, spiderwebs in my hair, and often a scratch on my skin or a tear in my clothes.

Many years later, when my wife and I visited the attic, I found it much smaller than I had remembered. The beams, which at the time I could reach only with the tips of my fingers, were now at the height of my chest. A dim light filtered through the dusty windows, making everything look fuzzy, just like it did when I was a child. Rusted nails along the wooden beams offered their support to large spiderwebs spanning the open spaces. The smell of old, abandoned things was all around, just as before. Our old kitchen table had been set against one wall, leaving little space below the roof. Under the blanket of white dust, I could recognize the familiar treasures that had awaited me for so many years: my mother's old kitchen utensils—her hand-operated vegetable blender, rusted and squeaky, and a few aluminum pots, some with wooden handles and some with metal ones—and a Chinese porcelain box containing a few rings and pins. The kitchen utensils, particularly the hand blender, brought back the memory of our trip to Berton et Sicard's, the Avignon hardware store, which in spite of the war was still carrying prewar-quality products. Next to the utensils, I even found my old 1941 *agenda* lying on a corner of our old kitchen table. All my childhood memories suddenly came alive in front of me. On these yellowed pages were my first written words, my first drawings, my mother's nurturing—all had been waiting for me, patiently locked in my old *agenda*. Leafing through its pages brought a few precious moments back. It was as if I had stepped into a time machine.

On the day of our move in 1942, I convinced my mother to let me go to my first movie. *The Bengal Lancers* was playing at Monsieur Gros's cinema next to the Sporting Bar. Completely overtaken by the story of the film, I was too young, at the age of six, to distinguish between reality and fiction. When I went to bed in our new home, the movie caused my worst nightmare ever. It was so real that, even after I woke up, I still saw a huge horse peering over my bed. My mother, who was unpacking downstairs, came to my rescue and cuddled me back to sleep.

Soon after our move, my mother announced that she had to

sell the Talbot, which had been sitting idle. Since it now looked like it would not be used anytime soon, and we were paying for it to be garaged, selling the car would enable my mother to generate cash for additional merchandise.

The move to our new store coincided with my growing awareness about the difficulties facing us as Jews. I began to worry about my own safety. Perhaps it was because I was becoming a little older and more open to the world, or perhaps because of my mother's anxiety, but I became more attentive to the news on the radio and in the newspapers. It was during this time, too, that my mother lost contact with her family in Przemyśl. She had begun to worry when the regular letters and postcards ceased arriving from Poland. We had no idea, of course, that the Germans had started concentrating the Jews into the ghetto of Przemyśl, tripling or quadrupling the original population, and preparing them for extermination. My mother thought just the opposite. "Certainly," she said, "they have fled from the war zone into a safer area."

What safer area? Most of the Jews of Przemyśl perished in the concentration camps, among them my mother's family, the Goldsteins. In 1950, only about 100 Jews remained in Przemyśl out of an original Jewish population of 35,000.[11] Of all my relatives, other than my father, just two cousins on my father's side were able to survive the Holocaust in Europe. Leon Lewendel-Laufbaum and his sister, Chipele, had been sent by their parents from Kraków into the Soviet Union ahead of the German army. Leon was arrested by the Communists and sent to Uzbekistan. Longing for her parents and trying to elude Soviet arrest, Chipele roamed the area close to the border between Russia and German-occupied Poland in the hope of returning to Kraków. She wanted to cross the River San, which separated Germans and Soviets in the middle of Przemyśl, but the Soviets would not let her approach the river. When the Germans attacked the Soviet Union in June 1941 and crossed the border, she finally gave up her attempts to rejoin her parents. She spent the rest of the war evading both

Germans and Soviets with the help of the underground Zionist movement and distant relatives in Ukraine.

When Chipele returned to Poland after the war, she found out that her parents, who had remained in Kraków, had been murdered by the Nazis, and there was no trace of the rest of the family. The Lewendels, the Laufbaums, and the Goldsteins had vanished from the face of the earth, which is why I grew up without grandparents, uncles and aunts, cousins, or distant relatives.

4 | *Maréchal, Here We Are!*

*His Holiness . . . orders and commands that the Jews of
one or the other sex, who currently live or will live in the
cities of Avignon and Carpentras, and in the Comtat
Venaissin, or will arrive from any location or province,
will be obliged to wear the mark of yellow color, which
distinguishes them from the others, and that they must
always wear it, at any time and place, inside as well as
outside the Jewish reservations, and inside their houses
as well as outside; that is to say, that the men must wear
the hat, all of yellow color, without a veil or any ribbon on
top, and that the women must also wear the yellow mark
openly on their head, without covering it with a handker-
chief, or anything which could hide it, under the penalty,
for the ones as well as for the others, of a fine of 50
crowns for each violation and other arbitraries.*

—Edict concerning the Jews by Pope Benoit
XIV, February 2, 1733[1]

Spring 1942–Fall 1942

Since the defeat of the French army in 1940, France was par-
titioned into two parts. The northern part was occupied and controlled by the Germans, and its capital was Paris. The south was

called the "free" zone because it was controlled and governed by the French. Its capital was Vichy, and its leader Maréchal Philippe Pétain. The "line of demarcation" between north and south was a border between "pride and infamy," for Pétain was trying to sell the idea that he would keep French honor alive in spite of the German occupation of the northern part of France. There was a minimal German presence in the south, and that part of the country kept a semblance of French autonomy. One way the French stressed they were their own masters was to exceed German hopes and behavior, much to the delight of the Germans.

As far as the Jews were concerned, the Vichy government was competing with the Germans in setting up a legal framework for their persecution. Le Statut des Juifs, the Statute of the Jews, a collection of independent French measures against the Jews, was enacted on October 3, 1940, and kept alive by frequent updates and additional restrictions until the Allied landing (the last decree is dated June 5, 1944).[2] The statute provided a constitutional basis for consigning the Jews in France, in both the occupied and the "free" zone, to a subordinate position. It included a definition of the Jews that was used as a criterion for their exclusion from French society, and it provided the basis for their later deportation. France was well on its way to its own Final Solution. Not only was the Vichy government in total agreement with the Nazis about the need to rid the country of Jewish influence, but their definition of who was Jewish was even stricter than the German one. Their only concern was that they did not like the idea of deporting those Jews of French nationality. This concern helped delay the fatal outcome for French-born Jews, who sustained a 14 percent death rate during the war compared to 28 percent for their foreign-born counterparts.[3] But the feeble protection offered to the French Jews ironically helped to seal the fate of the foreign Jews.

The UGIF (Union Générale des Israélites de France, or General Union of the Israelites of France) was created on November 29, 1941, by Law No. 5047 to "assure the representation of the

Jews with the public authorities, particularly for questions of public aid, medical assistance, and social reconversion." But, in fact, the UGIF soon became an instrument in the hands of Vichy to enforce the Statut des Juifs. It would be used against the Jews to expedite their extermination.

French collaboration would not have been effective without an arm of repression. The Police for Jewish Affairs (Police aux Question Juives) was created by the Vichy government in the autumn of 1941, and the Service d'Ordre Légionnaire (SOL) on February 4, 1942. On January 5, 1943, the French Militia (la Milice Française) became the autonomous successor of the SOL; composed of volunteers who openly proclaimed their Nazi beliefs, it served as a political police force. Its members directed and executed raids and arrests against suspected resisters and later against the Jews. The militiamen acted as if they had been anointed by the Nazi victors. They despised the regular police, whom they deemed "too soft" (in fact, my mother had some friendly customers from among the regular village police). Later, the villagers would not distinguish among the various branches of repression. Those who collaborated were all called *miliciens* (militiamen), even those who had joined the German police.

The demarcation line between German and Vichy territory was a common subject of conversation, and I imagined it drawn directly on the ground to divide the country. My mother frequently invited to our kitchen refugees who had been able to sneak across the line using counterfeit documents or bribery. In every refugee's story, there was a unique trick that had provided the person with a safe passage to the south. I remember one visitor who proudly recounted how the police did not notice that his and his wife's identity cards were counterfeit, and he showed us how he had used authentic cards but changed the photographs. Another person, who had a name that could pass for French and had managed to avoid the *JUIF* stamp that marked him as a Jew, was able to cross safely to the "free" zone. These stories made it clear to us that the demarcation line was well guarded.

The refugees from the north also talked at length about the mandatory wearing of the Star of David. A German ordinance had provided the legal ground for using the yellow star to single out the Jews:

Eighth Ordinance of May 29, 1942, concerning the measures against the Jews:

According to the full powers granted to me by the Führer and Commander-in-Chief of the Wermacht, I order the following:

1. Jews above the age of six are forbidden to appear in public without wearing the Jewish star.

2. The Jewish star is a star with six vertices having the size of the palm of a hand and black edges. It is made out of yellow fabric and carries the label "Jew" in black characters. It must be worn well in evidence on the left side of the chest permanently sewn on the garment.[4]

My mother and I never had to wear the star since the Vichy government refused to implement this German ordinance in the "free" zone—one of its rare acts of real independence.

Some of the Jewish refugees were ordered to live in transit camps and camps for foreign workers, according to the law of October 4, 1940 (law on foreign nationals of Jewish race), which authorized the prefects to intern them.[5] Some of the camps had been established before the war for the concentration and internment of refugees from the Spanish Civil War. The conditions in the camps were miserable, and the Jewish internees were regularly delivered to the Nazis by the French authorities for deportation to the east. Michael Marrus and Robert Paxton estimate that between 2,000 and 3,000 people died (from malnutrition, poor sanitary conditions, brutality, suicide) in the French camps. A camp for foreign workers was established near the train station in our village. Some of our foreign customers lived in that camp, GTE (Groupement de Travailleurs Etrangers) No. 148. Under the sponsorship of French friends and with the approval of the authorities, other refugees were lucky enough to trade the severe camp regimen for a more clement assigned residence in a town or a village.

My mother befriended some of these foreign workers who came to our store. I remember her engaged in an intense conversation in Polish with one of them. After the man left, I started repeating some of the words I had heard, and my mother marveled again at my brains. So she started teaching me a few expressions and words. "Dobrze Panie" meant "Good day, sir." "Gencouye Panie" meant "Thank you, sir." "Pinionsze" meant "money." I also learned the word "ulica," or "street." This is the way I remember these expressions, although I was recently apprised that they are written and sound somewhat differently: *Dzien Dobry Panu, Dziekuye Panu, Pienadze.*

There was an overweight Czech woman who used to come to the store. She spoke German to my mother, while my mother answered in Yiddish. I was always intrigued by the woman's enormous size and by what secret would be hidden underneath her black dress. So, pretending to play, rolling back and forth on the floor, I peeked. After she left, I proudly reported to my mother that the lady did not wear any panties.

Wherever refugees lived, in the village or in the camp, having crossed into the "free" zone was of crucial importance. The demarcation line between Vichy and the north seemed to offer magical protection against the terrible things that rumor claimed were beginning to happen in the north. There, the deportation of Jews to the east had started in March 1942. On July 16 and 17 of that year, 12,884 Jews were rounded up at the Vélodrome d'Hiver, the winter bike stadium in Paris. The Jews of Avignon outwardly dismissed such events as things happening only in the occupied zone. "Here in the 'free' zone we are safe," they would claim, citing Jewish escapees who had succeeded in crossing to the south. But I could feel their worry nevertheless. When talking about the arrests and about how Jews were being concentrated in the north, they whispered "on account of the child," and my mother evaded my questions when I asked.

MARÉCHAL, HERE WE ARE!

Unfortunately, this feeling of relative safety was not to last long for the Jews who had fled Nazi persecution in the north and established themselves in the "nonoccupied" zone. On August 5, 1942, the Vichy government sent a secret instruction to the prefects concerning foreign Jews (Dispatch No. 2.765 Pol. 9):

> The Secretary of State [Le Conseiller d'Etat, secrétaire général pour la Police] informs you that the Israelites of German, Austrian, Czech, Polish, Esthonian, Letton, Danzig, Saar, Soviet, and Russian origin who entered France after January 1, 1936, . . . will be transported into the occupied zone before September 15, 1942, with the exception of:
> 1. People more than sixty years old
> 2. Children younger than eighteen
> 3. War veterans . . . their spouses or children
>
> Send me before August 16 two copies of an alphabetical list of the Jews with vital statistics. . . . An ordering number must precede each name. . . . Reiterate that it is appropriate to suspend any foreign emigration even for these already possessing a visa. . . . These instructions have a rigorously private character.[6]

Upon receipt of this dispatch signed by Henri Cado, the deputy secretary general of the police, the prefect of Avignon took immediate action. He ordered the establishment of a list that included 108 names, numbered from 1 to 108 as instructed.[7] A few days later, fearing that too many Jews would escape the roundup, the exceptions allowed on August 5 were canceled (Secret Telegram No. 12519; August 18, 1942)[8] and replaced by a very limited number of cases. For instance, children were no longer able to stay behind when their parents were deported. This directive, however, was not uniformly enforced. Cado also expanded the eligibility for deportation to single Jewish males who had entered France between 1933 and 1935 (Secret Telegrams Nos. 12520 and 12524; August 18, 1942).[9] As a result, three names (Nos. 109, 110, and 111) were added by the Avignon police to the original list of 108 names. Given that the census of 1941 had brought up 1,474 Jews, 458 of them foreigners, 111 names represent a small percentage of the foreign Jews in the *département*. Our family friend Pinchas Estryn was included as No. 109 and arrested several times during that period, but each time he managed to be released through bribery. My mother, who had entered France in 1935, was not targeted by this measure.

All the preparations for the arrests were conducted in relative secrecy, but the Vichy government could not avoid leaks, especially after the beginning of August, when the French police started delivering Jews to the Germans from the camps of foreigners in the "free" zone. To no avail, protests were expressed to Maréchal Pétain by members of the high clergy, among them the archbishop of Toulouse, Jules Géraud Saliège (in a pastoral letter read in church on August 23, 1942); the head of the Protestant Federation of France, Pastor Marc Boegner (in a letter to Maréchal Pétain on August 20, 1942); and the archbishop of Lyon, Cardinal Gerlier (in a letter to Maréchal Pétain on August 19, 1942).[10] Based on intelligence gathered by General Charles de Gaulle in London, *Le Peuple*, a Swiss newspaper, published on August 7, 1942, in Geneva, an exact account of and a protest against Pierre Laval's decision to "deliver the so-called foreign Jews into the hands of the Germans."[11] On August 24, 1942, the regional prefects received the final roundup orders (Secret Telegram No. 12882):

> **Following my telegram 12464 of August 18, [I] confirm that arrests and regrouping of foreign Jews ordered by dispatch of August 5 and associated telegrams will take place on August 26. It will be your responsibility to set the starting time of these operations in the way most appropriate to you. However, I am bringing to your attention the <u>advantage of conducting them at dawn around 4 or 5 A.M.</u> [My emphasis]**
>
> **Signed: CADO[12]**

Concerned about public opinion, the French Ministry of Information imposed censorship on the newspapers. The "free"-zone operation against the foreign Jews was not to be mentioned (Instruction 663).[13]

In spite of the protests, many people on the lists were arrested by the French Gendarmerie, a branch of the military serving as a civilian police force. They were shipped under surveillance to the border with the occupied zone and delivered straight into the hands of the Nazis. They were being "regrouped" by the French police into the camp at Drancy commanded by the French police chief Laurent. As a result, 57 out of the 111 people on the Avignon list were deported to Auschwitz in the four weeks following the instructions to the prefects (convoys 29 to 37 from Drancy to Auschwitz). For example, Leopold Freundlich, age twenty-two, was deported on November 6, 1942 (convoy 42), but his parents and his brother were never caught. Max Stark, age thirty, who was on the additional list, escaped the initial arrest but was deported almost two years later on May 20, 1944 (convoy 74).[14]

My twelve-year-old son, Ilan, recently helped me identify the 57 names of the deportees by searching for each of the 111 names in the *Memorial to the Jews Deported from France.* Ilan was thoroughly shaken by the 80,000 names in the *Memorial,* since this was his first encounter with the magnitude of the Holocaust. He was particularly sensitive to the presence of young children in the convoys, whom he identified by their birthdates. After reading the names of Jean Rojman, less than two years old, Micha Goldstein, less than two years old, and Annie Ritscher, less than one year old, Ilan could no longer bear the task. He let me finish the search alone.

On the evening of August 26, 1942, the French administration arrested 6,500 foreign Jews, scattered all over the southern provinces. By comparison, 12,884 Parisian Jews were arrested on July 16 and 17, 1942. It must have been easier to find the Jews concentrated in Paris. During this entire "free"-zone operation, which lasted until November 1942, 11,100 Jews were deported: 7,100 from their homes, public places, and camps for foreign workers, and 4,000 from transit camps. They were delivered to the Nazis by the Vichy government from an area *unoccupied by the Germans.*[15] The governments of France and of three other countries—Hungary, Slovakia, and Bulgaria—are the only ones in Europe who delivered Jews, bound and gagged, from a nonoccupied zone straight into the hands of the Nazis on the other side of the border.[16] In 1941, after its conquest from the Russians, Hungary shipped the Jews from the area of Galicia, as did Slovakia in 1942 from its nonoccupied territory and Bulgaria in February 1943 from its recently acquired territories in Macedonia. These were limited actions; France alone delivered Jews continuously from 1940 until the end of the war.

The partial results of the operation in Avignon and the *département* of Vaucluse is typical of the entire "free"-zone operation, which called for the "regrouping" of the Jews, as Cado designates it in Telegram No. 12519. The Germans, who had expected 25,000 Jews, were disappointed with Deputy Secretary General Cado and his boss, René Bousquet, who had delivered less than half the number of Jews promised. An October 1, 1942, report by the SEC (Sections d'Enquête et de Controle)[17] of Toulouse explains the poor results:

> **The Jews who benefit from leaks that occurred in the prefectorates, and even in Vichy, were able to escape and hide in farmers' homes and therefore avoid being caught during the roundups of August 25 and 26, 1942. These Jews are so much more protected because they are assured to be warned in time.**[18]

On October 1, 1942, Henri Piton, the prefect of Avignon, was able to report to his bosses in Vichy that everything was back to normal in spite of some initial difficulties:

> The measures taken against the foreign Jews have raised
> some emotions among the population, which generally was
> moved by the fate of the regrouped individuals. The attitude of
> the Church on this question was not without influence on pub-
> lic opinion.
>
> However, the selfish preoccupations of everyone speedily
> overcame the aforementioned reaction that has become at the
> present time nothing more than an ordinary memory.[19]

As in other regions of France, remarkable actions by individual members of the clergy took place in the Vaucluse despite general indifference. For instance, Reverend Roche, the rector of
Saint-Joseph High School in Avignon, provided an alibi for one of
his teachers, Robert Maddaléna, enabling him to carry out clandestine actions. Using the high school building and some Avignon
convents, they gave shelter to numerous Jews and other hunted
people.

In his report to Laval on October 7, 1942, the regional prefect
of Marseille, whose territory covered the Vaucluse and five other
départements, seemed more moved than Piton, his subordinate
from Avignon.

> Not that the Jews are viewed with favor. Far from it. They are
> on the contrary violently criticized for their desire for lucre
> and their black-market practices, but opinion is almost unani-
> mous that they should have been stricken only by economic
> and social measures which separated them from positions
> where they were not wanted, and not by bullying policies
> which, in attacking women and children, cannot fail to shock
> popular sentiment profoundly.[20]

Every Jew in Vichy France was aware of the events of the
summer of 1942. Some of those who had not been targeted by the
operation of August 26 started making arrangements for hiding.
Others rationalized the issue away. "We will be protected by our
country," claimed French Jews. "We are safe because Germans
and Turks are allies," said Turkish Jews. Central European Jews

who had come to France before the war were sure that "France will not renege on its hospitality." It was just a question of time before all of them would have to run for their lives.

Although the deportations from the camps in the "free" zone had been documented in 1946,[21] over 11,000 "foreign Jews" deported by the Vichy authorities in 1942 were forgotten by history for decades until they were rediscovered by Robert Paxton and Michael Marrus in 1981.[22] Aimé Autrand, the historian of this period, who worked for the archives of Avignon until his retirement in 1965, never even mentioned these people in his book about the war, let alone what happened to them.[23] Indeed, Autrand reports that for the entire duration of the war there were only 83 "racial deportations" out of the official census of 1,500 Jews in the *département* of Vaucluse, representing 5.5 percent of the Jewish population, an unusually low percentage compared to 25 percent for the entire nation. In his account, the first deportations of Jews take place in 1943 after the Germans occupied the "free" zone. Since those deported in 1942 were refugees who had only recently arrived in the area, they were not considered part of the community, and their betrayal apparently evoked little notice or remorse. In fact, Vichy Prime Minister Laval reportedly said to the German chief of the Service for Jewish Questions, Theo Dannecker: "The only Jews we have are *your* Jews. We will send them back to you when you please" (my emphasis).[24] Laval did not hide his profound contempt for this "garbage shipped to us by the Germans themselves," as he described the "foreign Jews" during the Vichy cabinet meeting of July 3, 1942.

The official Vichy documents avoided mentioning the real purpose of the "regrouping" of these Jews or any concern about it. Officially, this operation was presented as providing workers for the German war effort. But the presence of children and the elderly among the deportees raised the suspicion of the French population and indicated that something other than work was taking place.

The recapture of the "foreign Jews" by the Nazis represents a crucial turning point in German attitude. As early as the end of

1940, many of these Jews had been expelled from the territories controlled by the Germans, who had hoped to pressure the big powers to find a place for the Jews outside Europe. Now the Nazis were reclaiming these Jews in order to reduce them to ashes. They were also demanding the other Jews, those with French nationality.

In 1942, not only were individual "foreign Jews" arrested and deported to Auschwitz, but entire families, both parents and children, were taken as well, because these Jews were more expendable. Since they were arrested so early in the war, it is likely that none of them survived. Who then will speak for the Ajgengolds, the Bechers, the Eisemanns, the Feins, the Goldbergs, the Goldsteins, the Jeruchemsons, the Josephs, the Niedwiechis, the Strumers, the Schachters, and the Ziedelmanns? Who will tell their story? Who will find their murderers?

As it was delivering the Jews to the Germans, Vichy was parading. As he had promised during his first visit on December 4, 1940, Maréchal Pétain returned to Avignon on October 10, 1942. He passed by Le Pontet on this occasion. Long before his arrival, people started lining up on the side of the street, eager to see their hero. They kept asking one another, "Is he coming? Is he coming?" Taken in by the atmosphere of celebration, I badly wanted to go, but my mother was hesitant, because Pétain was "not good for us." As usual, I finally prevailed, though I do not remember her being next to me in the street. To get a better look, I sneaked between the people to get to the edge of the sidewalk. For his security, Pétain was preceded by a convoy of gendarmes. When he finally appeared, the crowd cheered and sang "Maréchal, nous voilà!" (Marshal, here we are!). He was comfortably seated in a large white convertible, waving to the crowd. Only when the last car disappeared toward the city of Sorgues did the crowd disperse in small groups, recounting what they had just witnessed as if to assure one another that they had recorded the historic event correctly.

The school principal had a mast and a flag erected in a hurry, and from that day on we assembled every morning in the schoolyard, raised the flag, and sang the song of praise to the Maréchal, the "hero of Verdun," as the teachers said. The song went like this:

> *Maréchal, here we are!*
> *In front of you,*
> *The savior of France,*
> *We are vowing,*
> *We, your boys,*
> *To march and to follow in your steps.*

Everyone participated eagerly, and the teachers led the way. I did not sing with the same enthusiasm, though, because I felt that my mother did not like Maréchal Pétain. Our teachers paced around us to make sure that we were properly lined up around the flag and that they had our attention. When the attention of a child wandered away to the locust tree or a bird on the roof, a tap from the teacher nursed him back to singing. The occasional visit of a village official multiplied the energy level of our song without the need for the teachers' intervention. On wintry days, the cacophony resounded inside the classrooms.

The link of Pétain to Verdun was a reminder that he had saved France and the French by heroically standing up to the Germans during the World War I battle for Verdun. This reference to Pétain's heroism at Verdun allowed the French to cover up their embarrassment at their 1940 defeat. It was also a subtle hint that his collaboration with the Nazis was another form of his courage.

Even as a child, it would have been difficult to ignore the importance of Maréchal Pétain because of his visit, our daily song at school, and his ubiquitous picture. He was on the stamps, he was on the coins, he was on the bills—he was everywhere. He had even replaced Marianne (the female personification of the French Republic) and Mercury on everything official.

5 | The "Foreign" Jews of 1942

The only thing necessary for the triumph of evil is for good men to do nothing.

—Attributed to Edmund Burke

With my memories racing in my mind, I became determined to find as many survivors of the 111 Avignon Jews deported in 1942 as possible. I focused on the younger ones, who could still be alive. After much searching (and some luck), I was privileged to meet some of them, people who helped me reconstruct the past.

Anna Rochwerger, age thirty-seven, and her son Bernard, eight, had settled in the small town of Apt after Bernard's father, Gerson Rochwerger, forty, had been arrested in 1941 in Nice and interned in the camp of Les Milles. Anna was sent to Auschwitz on September 7, 1942, in convoy 29, but Bernard did not appear on any deportation list. On January 12, 1992, I met Bernard on his home in Avignon after locating him in the telephone directory. He had escaped deportation because, when the police came to arrest his mother, he had accepted separation from her and had stayed behind with relatives. His mother had preferred separation to the frightening alternative. The police did not seem to have applied the directives of Vichy to the letter, since Bernard should not have benefited from exemption 2 of August 5, 1942 (regarding unaccompanied children below the age of eighteen),[1] which had been canceled a few days before the roundups (Telegram No. 12518). A few weeks later, his uncle, Abraham Borensztein, clandestinely took him across the border to Switzerland. Luckily, Bernard was interned in the Swiss camp of Moudon, where he remained until the end of the war, but his uncle was expelled back to France the same day, because "he was too old to be a child and too young to be elderly." Faithful to their "neutral destiny," the Swiss representatives in Vichy declared on September 30, 1942:

> **Because of the exceptional character of the current circumstances, the Swiss government is no longer able to welcome on its territory people who generally do not have French nationality and who wish to take refuge on Swiss territory without having applied for a normal visa at a Swiss consulate in France. Orders have been given to drive these people back, excluding a few of the most exceptional cases.[2]**

To better understand this Swiss accommodation of Vichy desires, one needs to remember that Vichy France was offering a transportation corridor free of German control. We now know that the Swiss Federal Council, during its session of August 4, 1942, had decided to collaborate with the Nazis by upholding article 9 of the Swiss government decree of October 1939: "Repel at any cost."[3]

Bernard was allowed to stay in Switzerland because its government was not ready to face the moral implications related to children. Instructions of September and December 1942 list the following cases "for which expulsion would be too harsh a measure":

> **1. Refugees older than 65. The spouse when one of them is at least 65.**
> **2. Unaccompanied children younger than 16.**

3. Parents accompanied by their own children younger than 7; parents accompanied by their own children, one of whom is younger than 7.[4]

Preceding his wife by a few weeks, Gerson Rochwerger was shipped from the camp of Les Milles to Drancy, and deported to Auschwitz by convoy 21 on August 21, 1942. In our interview, Bernard confirmed that his cousin Rose Chvat—No. 31 on the Avignon list—escaped deportation by hiding until the end of the war.

Osias Tieder and his wife, Brucha, both fifty, were arrested in the small village of Sablet and deported from Drancy to Auschwitz by convoys 30 and 33, respectively, but their three children—Sarah, sixteen; Ida, fifteen; and Martin, thirteen—were spared. On January 14, 1992, I found and met Sarah in Paris. Her story of the children's escape provided an additional link to my own story. In May 1940, the Tieders were interned in the camp of Agde in the "free" zone, together with 3,150 Jewish refugees from Belgium. By 1942, Sarah and Martin had become ill as a result of malnourishment and poor medical attention in the camp, and were allowed to join the nearby children's home of Moissac. At the same time, their parents and Ida were allowed to leave the camp to return to Sablet, where they had a friend, Madame Sonja Sokolowski, a Jewish woman from Russia. On August 24, 1942, a call from the village office for verification of their identity made them suspicious, and they sent Ida to seek information from Madame Sokolowski in Avignon. Some time before, her husband had developed a good relationship with Pierre Thomas, a helpful employee of the prefecture of Avignon. This enabled him to obtain critical information about impending measures against the Jews. This is how he learned about the imminent arrest of the Tieders. Having entered France in 1930, the Sokolowskis themselves were not targeted by the measures of August 26, 1942. When Ida returned home with a warning on the afternoon of August 26, 1942, it was too late. Her house had been sealed, and, according to an employee from the village hall, her parents had been arrested by the gendarmes of Vaisons-la-Romaine and sent to the camp of Les Milles near

Marseille. In panic, she returned to Sonja Sokolowski, who arranged for her to go to a clandestine children's home, where she stayed until the end of the war. When she told me her story in Paris, Sarah Tieder was not aware of my connection to Sonja Sokolowski, who had been a friend of my family's since before the war. Learning about her role in the survival of Ida Tieder drew me a little closer to the Jewish refugees of 1942.

Soon after meeting Sarah Tieder, I accidentally encountered the Margolis sisters at a talk in Chicago on May 5, 1992. Esther and Rose Margolis were listed on the August 26, 1942, arrest list (Nos. 72 and 73) but were never deported. To no avail, I had repeatedly tried to locate Esther and Rose, who were respectively twenty-five and twenty-one years old in 1942, by searching the French telephone records. At the Chicago talk, however, the women's accents and their interest in the literature on display prompted my curiosity. Since I have turned into an avid listener and since they were eager to talk, I soon learned that they were the two missing sisters on the list. A few days later, I heard their story during an evening at Rose's house in Skokie, near Chicago.

The Margolises, who were wealthy leather tanners in the Polish city of Łódź, could afford to send their daughter Esther to study in Paris in 1937, while her younger sister Rose remained in Poland. Rose was suffering from mastoiditis, a chronic and painful ear problem that was common among children in those days. Esther made arrangements for her sister to undergo surgery with a famous surgeon in Bordeaux, Professor Portmann, and in 1939 the family was temporarily reunited in France. After the operation, both parents returned to Łódź. Since in those days any surgery was a serious affair, Esther planned to remain in Bordeaux as long as needed for Rose's recovery and then to accompany her sister back home. Fatefully, the Germans attacked Poland on September 1, 1939, and closed its borders before Esther and Rose were able to return.

By sheer coincidence, Esther's and Rose's path crossed that of the Sapirs—Joseph and Szayne, the parents, and Esther and

Jehuda, their children—old acquaintances from Łódź who were now refugees in France. The Sapirs had money and owned a car but knew no French; Esther knew French but had no resources. This is why the Sapirs "adopted" the two Margolis sisters. After a failed attempt to cross the border to Spain, the family made its way to the small town of Bollène in the *département* of Vaucluse. They had heard of a helpful Christian family there. The Margolis sisters and the Sapirs were duly registered as Jews in the village of Bollène. Their names appear on the list of 111 Jews arrested in the summer of 1942.

The Margolis sisters owe their survival to the excessive eagerness of the two French policemen who were supposed to arrest them. On the afternoon of August 25, 1942, the police came to make sure that the Jews on their lists were actually at home, but the presence of the police during a birthday party raised people's suspicion. Rose was quickly smuggled away by the hosts. Esther was out of town, recovering from an appendectomy in the nearby town of Orange. When the two policemen came back at 1:30 in the morning, they found only Szayne Sapir, who faked insanity and mumbled unintelligible words. In fact, she was speaking Yiddish and warning the rest of her family to disappear. The two policemen, afraid of her insanity, left her alone. (Szayne knew the superstition held by the people of Provence, who believe that the devil resides inside the bodies of the mentally ill.) Both Esther Margolis and Szayne Sapir were later saved thanks to the help of two French doctors who provided the police with certificates attesting to their "severe" medical conditions.

When the storm subsided, all gathered at the home of the Devèze family. A sympathetic French policeman volunteered to take the entire party to a smuggler in the city of Perpignan, near the Spanish border. To increase their safety on the train, he hand-cuffed them ostentatiously to suggest that he had arrested them. Esther still relishes the "safest trip in her life" and the sympathy of train passengers for the "poor young children." Unfortunately, the smuggler turned them over to the Perpignan police, and they were interned in the camp of Gurs, where they were temporarily spared because Esther's knowledge of French landed her a job in the camp offices. Unfortunately, this did not help Joseph Sapir, who was sent from Gurs to Drancy as a part of a group of 1,814 men[5] and shipped to Auschwitz on March 4, 1943, by convoy 50.

At the administrative offices in Gurs, Esther Margolis saw Joseph Sapir's name on the list and was able to see him leave. He never came back, but due to Esther's position in the camp offices, the rest of his family and the sisters Margolis were spared. When the camp was dissolved in the spring of 1943, they all made their way back to Bollène, where the Devèze family protected them until the end of the war.

The story of the Sapirs recently took an unexpected turn. Esther (Estelle), the sole survivor of the family, now seventy-two years old, lives in a small apartment in New York. In 1946 and 1947, she traveled to Switzerland and located some of the bank accounts that her father had opened before the war in Basel, Lausanne, Zurich, and Geneva. First she was told she needed the account numbers. Later, after presenting account summaries that she had located, an employee of Crédit Suisse in Basel confirmed the existence of the account, but told her she must provide a death certificate for her father. The Swiss banker was not swayed by the fact that she was unable to provide the document. Disgusted and desperate, Esther had virtually given up on recovering her property. Thanks to Senate hearings in 1996 and the support her testimony generated, however, the bank finally began a restitution process. Thus far, though, it has not yet yielded a red cent. As an ironic footnote, Joseph Sapir's accounts, acknowledged since 1947, do not appear on the list of dormant accounts provided by the Association of Swiss Bankers as a gesture of their newfound candidness.[6] How many more dormant accounts are still hidden in the Swiss coffers?

The name of one person had been crossed off the 1942 arrest list. Mossé (Max) Neumann, born on June 13, 1894, in Germany, had been granted an exemption because he was the UGIF delegate living in Camp No. 148 for foreign workers in Le Pontet. As a UGIF delegate, Neumann was in charge of registering the Jews in the camp and determining the needy among them. In that capacity, he actually made these Jews more vulnerable by providing their names to the Nazis. Max Neumann's name does not appear on the list of any of the convoys from Drancy to Auschwitz. He was spared from deportation in exchange for keeping an eye on his peers. Neumann was dismissed on March 10, 1943,[7] as a result of an order to "reduce the number UGIF delegates to 1% of the number of Jews," issued on January 29, 1943, by the Commissaire Général aux Questions Juives (Chief Commissioner for Jewish Questions), Darquier de Pellepoix.[8] Ordered to return the UGIF identity card that was his sole protection, Neumann disappeared into anonymity. He was sighted in the area of Avignon during and after the war.

I remember well the numerous Jewish refugees from the occupied zone who came to our store to visit my mother. Some of them lived in Le Pontet, others in the neighboring villages. Their numbers rapidly swelled, then they faded from my memory shortly after their arrival, never to reappear. The explanation now seems simple: some were arrested and sent to their deaths, and others went into hiding.

Sarah Tieder, Bernard Rochwerger, Pinchas Estryn, the sisters Margolis, and Madame Sokolowski have made the "foreign Jews of 1942" emerge from a clouded fresco in my childhood memory. Meeting these survivors has sharpened my image of the refugees of 1942, and I have become connected to them, one by one, as if I had shared their fate. Both the dead and the living—they reminded me so much of myself.

As the Jews of 1942 disappeared, my mother and I were to be the only Jews left in my memory of Le Pontet for the two years following that tragic summer. My mother undoubtedly knew what had happened to the Jewish refugees from the occupied zone. Did she realize the significance of these events? If so, why did she seem so unaffected?

6 | Les Français parlent aux Français

Through a conversation with two young Frenchmen who have just arrived in this country after doing good work for us in France, I learn that the continued reference in BBC broadcasts to the persecution of the Jews tends to be resented by the French, who themselves have so many relatives imprisoned in German prison camps or concentration camps.

—Special Operations Executive Storrs to Political Warfare Executive Gilgud, January 2, 1943[1]

November 1942–Early Summer 1943

One day, while playing on the floor of our store as I usually did, my attention was attracted by a steady rumbling on the Route Nationale Numéro Sept. A constant vibration coming from the ground accompanied the rumbling. I stood up and went to the glass door. There were trucks loaded with soldiers and trucks towing cannons. Some of the trucks were huge, their loads covered with tarpaulins. A few smaller cars with soldiers in tidy uniforms were trying in vain to pass the other vehicles. I stood for hours staring at the continuous flow of the German military moving south. I was fascinated because I had never seen such an impressive parade, but I did not go out on the sidewalk because I was scared. This lasted for days. A few weeks later, the German convoys, which by now had reached the Mediterranean coast, started going in all directions, tightening their grip on the country. The Germans had some unusual trucks with three wheels, two in the back and one in front. One of them flipped over next to our house, bringing the entire German column to a stop. In our area, the Germans established their quarters in the French military camp of the Seventh Engineering Regiment near our train station, next to the Route Nationale Numéro Sept railroad crossing. As their numbers increased, the Germans moved into the girls' school near the church. The girls' classes were combined with the boys' classes, and the forced mixing of genders caused a patriotic furor among the residents, who had never seen "such a shame." That was the talk of the day in our store, but popular furor did not seem to affect the victorious march of the Germans.

Prompted by the Allied landing in North Africa on November 8, 1942, the Germans occupied the "free" zone on November 11, 1942. Initially, the huge mechanized convoys of German soldiers headed south to strengthen the occupation of Vichy territory and to establish fortifications along the Mediterranean coast. The long convoys of displaced Gypsies passed by more frequently, but this time they were headed to the north. I was unmoved, because the displacement of these strange people did not violate my world's order. Little did I realize that the Nazis had started "cleaning up" the area of "subhumans." Like the Jews, the Gypsies were targeted for extermination by the Nazis as "impure."

My mother purchased a used LMT radio from before the war, *un appareil de TSF*,[2] as it was called then. As soon as we got the radio, I became glued to it, fascinated by the "talking box." The official French radio broadcasts were filled with anti-American, anti-British, and anti-Semitic propaganda. They attempted to brainwash the population, and claimed that the Germans and the Vichy government were fighting a conspiracy led by the Jews, the Bolsheviks, and the Anglo-American capitalists. Although I did not understand the official rhetoric, the Vichy government's hatred of the Jews and the Americans was pretty obvious to me. This hatred was also printed in a pamphlet that I found in the street and kept with me for many years. It was folded in two, and on the outside it looked like a regular dollar bill. On the inside, it said: "This bill was signed by the Jew Morgenthau" (the American secretary of the treasury), and "This bill has paid for the Jewish-American war," hinting that the Jews had conspired to cause the war. The Nazis were picking up on a traditional anti-Semitic pattern by accusing the Jews of being behind every possible evil plot.

The official propaganda against the Jews made me feel uneasy, and I was elated when we started listening to the Free France broadcasts from London on the short waves. The broadcasts were preceded by a short musical station identification, repeated many times, which always started with the motto "Les Français parlent aux Français!" ("The French people are talking to the French people!"). This immediately triggered a continuous jamming, which made the broadcasts difficult to understand. People were exhorted to "resist occupation" and not to believe "the lies of the Vichy traitors." Strange encoded messages were interspersed with the broadcasts: "The carrots are cooked!" or "Uncle Henri got a flat tire on his bike!"

Before the invasion of the south, the Germans had enacted a measure prohibiting the Jews from owning a radio:

> **Decree of August 13, 1941, concerning the seizure of TSF appliances belonging to Jews:**
>
> **According to the full powers granted to me by the Führer and Commander-in-Chief of the Wermacht, I order the following:**

1. **It is forbidden for Jews to have radio receivers in their possession.**

2. **The Jews having TSF receivers in their possession are required to surrender them before September 1, 1941, in exchange for a receipt from the mayor (local police authority) of their current or permanent home.**[3]

Although one could have expected the law to take effect under the occupation, it was largely ignored in the southern zone. Nevertheless, the Jews were exhorted to obey it by the official newspaper of the UGIF (issue of September 1943). In the evening, when we gathered around the radio, we lowered the volume to avoid discovery by unexpected visitors. Secrecy was essential because of the constant fear of denunciations by *lettre anonyme*, an anonymous letter. This was an easy way of settling accounts with neighbors. The authorities probably knew that they could not blindly trust the massive influx of denunciation mail, but, once in a while, they were lucky enough to catch a big fish among the tiny ones in the daily fry. Interrogations were frequent and ostentatious to keep the threat alive. The denunciations were a usual topic of conversation in our store, and my mother listened intently. The customers brought a constant stream of rumors and news about who had been targeted by a denunciation, who had been arrested, and who was the likely squealer. They did not show much sympathy for the victim, however, and always stated the rumored reason for the denunciation as if there could be no doubt about it. They usually cited the black market or sympathy for the Resistance.

I became interested in the newspapers as well as the radio, and I read the headlines written in big letters. One day, after I finished the headlines, I went to the newspaper store two houses down and asked for "tomorrow's newspaper." The people at the store were amused and my mother delighted. "How clever he is!" she said, leaving them little room to disagree.

My mother kept in touch with the other Jews in the area, and

I began to realize that there were different kinds. The most common were the ones who spoke French with an accent and to whom my mother spoke Yiddish. They also tried to teach me Yiddish. Later, I understood that these were the Ashkenazi Jews from Central Europe. The second kind also spoke French with an accent, but my mother spoke French to them because they did not know Yiddish. These were the Sephardic Jews who had recently arrived from countries around the Mediterranean Sea. My mother also spoke French to the third kind, but they had no accent when they spoke French. They had been in France for generations, and they did not sell goods in the marketplaces or in small stores. One of these families, the Alphandérys, owned a large farm in the area and produced honey. Vallabrègue, the lawyer, was another.

The French Jews looked down on the foreign Jews, Ashkenazi or Sephardic, because—so they said—the rude and primitive behavior of the foreign Jews encouraged anti-Semitism. The Ashkenazi Jews, in turn, considered themselves more advanced than their Sephardic counterparts. In competition with Gentile anti-Semitism, the Jews had set up their own internal hierarchy. The three groups never really mingled except in the synagogue.

We kept in touch with Jews from Central Europe living in the area, and once in a while we paid them a visit. I remember Monsieur Rosenthal, the shoemaker from Avignon, and his wife. He was always unshaven and wore black-rimmed round glasses. He sat in his tiny workshop with a shoe form firmly anchored between his knees, surrounded by his tools and large sheets of leather hanging on the wall. Dyes and waxes, nails and thread were scattered over his tiny table in front of him, and small shreds of leather lay on the floor. There was barely room for us to sit. I watched the simple tools in his hands, cutting blades and brushes, caressing the shoe sole, because in those days the sole was more important than the top. While he, his wife, and my mother were conducting a lively discussion in Yiddish, he was able to drive nails through the sole, cut the excess leather, and dye the side of the leather to match the top.

Monsieur Rosenthal would prepare the sole and the shoe with contact glue, then let the glue dry for a few minutes before pressing the sole onto the shoe. After the sole was in place, he would fill his mouth with nails. Pushing the nails out one at a time with his tongue, he used his mouth like a third hand, speedily nailing the sole around the edge. With his mouth full of nails, he was still able to take part in the conversation by using facial expressions, eloquent gestures, and occasional sounds. I loved the smell of the contact glue and the odor of the melted wax permeating the workshop. Sometimes, I sensed that I was the subject of their conversation.

We also took the bus to Beaucaire to visit the Schneiders, whose son, Jacques, had earlier smashed my thumb in our kitchen doorframe. Beaucaire is a small town south of Avignon across the Rhône past the River Durance. We had to change buses twice, and because of the poor transportation, we had to stay overnight.

After the German invasion of the south, I do not remember that we ever attended a religious service at the synagogue. Our Judaism had been reduced to as much as Jewish food possible, casual visits to our Jewish friends, and a good dose of suspicion toward the Gentile world. In the last, we were not about to be disappointed.

In early January 1943, my mother's identity card was stamped at the offices of the Gendarmerie with the word "Juif" (Jew) as required by law. This was the result of the instructions sent to the prefects by Henri Cado, deputy secretary general of the police, on December 18, 1942:

> **The law No. 1077 of December 11, 1942, requires that in the month following its enactment, every person of Jewish race according to the terms of the law of June 2, 1941, will be required to have the stamp "JUIF" stamped on his food-rationing card and on his identity card (or on the document taking its place) . . .**

> The term "JUIF" must be stamped in one-centimeter-high characters on the portion of the card (or the title) and of the food-rationing card where the vital statistics of the interested party are recorded. To that effect, you are required to take all measures necessary to equip the appropriate services with a wet stamp necessary for the stamping of the term under consideration.[4]

The Gendarmerie, not sparing any expense, acquired a special stamp just for the few of us. In 1991, a French archive employee was kind enough to forward a photocopy of my mother's stamped identity card. Under profession was listed "merchant for the account of her husband," and under children, "Isaac Lewendel."

Everyone needed a food-rationing card. Ours were stamped with the word "Juif" so that we could be controlled through our stomachs. I remember the stamp because I saw it frequently when we went to the grocery store or to the bakery, but my mother did not dwell on it at home. My card was also stamped *J1*, meaning the youngest age bracket; there also were *J2* and *J3* for older kids.

Food-rationing coupons were allocated on a regular basis according to age, but they covered only part of our needs. Until textiles became rationed too, my mother had a privileged position, since we could exchange some of our merchandise for butter, chickens, and eggs. She had to collect the coupons from our customers, and I helped glue them on master sheets, which we gave to our suppliers in exchange for new merchandise. It was my job to camouflage, in the middle of the sheets, counterfeit food and textile coupons, which began to appear at that time. Women's silk stockings disappeared from our shelves and were replaced by artificial fiber, rayon and *fibrane*. When the artificial fibers disappeared too, bottles of tan dye burst on the market. The bottles were equipped with a brush that women could use to dye their skin and create the illusion of silk stockings. Clearly, there was a limit to what the French would accept, and they were not yet ready to give up the look of their women's legs. At least the dyed "stockings" did not run.

People would often reminisce about the "good old days before the war," and the quality of every product was always compared to the prewar quality. "This is the quality of before the war," said the merchant. "This is worse than the quality before the war," said the haggler. Of course, our merchandise was always as good as before the war.

Our customers were mostly women. They all bought the same corduroy pants and flannel shirts for their men, young or old. They chose dresses for themselves according to their ages: mixed colors for the young and black for the old. As they advanced in age, the colors of their clothes turned to purple and black because women were expected to fade away ahead of time. Trying to look younger was sinful, because women beyond the age of forty were supposed to look their age. One older villager did not fit the pattern: her face was heavily made up, and she used to wear red and green clothes. Everyone claimed she was crazy. If she had not been deranged, she would have been depraved.

Since our store had no fixed hours, my mother divided her time between the store and the kitchen from dawn to darkness. When she had to run an errand or visit someone, a terse note on the store's front window would specify her return time, and that was enough. When she was not attending to a customer, arranging new merchandise on the shelves, putting some order in the accounting, or rearranging the displays, she was in the kitchen cleaning, cooking, or writing letters. Since she was always busy, she had Monsieur Crumière, the handyman, install a door chime on the top of the store door to make sure that no customer alone in the store would be excessively tempted by the merchandise. The chime was made of five copper tubes of different lengths, hanging on strings next to one another. Monsieur Crumière moved the chime up, moved it down, tried it one way, then another, until it was hung high enough to prevent the tubes and the strings from becoming tangled when the door was opened but low enough to create an avalanche of musical warnings. As soon as the chime rang, my mother would keep an eye on the store visitor through the open kitchen door until she could get there. If she couldn't drop what she was doing in the kitchen, she would talk to the person from a distance to make her presence felt or she would send me out to the store. My mother was justified in her suspicions, because a woman's bike had recently disappeared right in front of our store while the customer was making her choice inside. Bicycle thefts were frequent, everyone claimed, because, after repainting them, it was easy to use them under the nose of the victims.

I used to spend a lot of time in our store. At times, I would sort and redistribute loose buttons that had fallen off the button cards. My mother accumulated them in a large box. I put them back into the appropriate box one by one by matching them to the sample attached in front of the box. Sometimes the sample itself had fallen off too. I also enjoyed rearranging the boxes of zippers and socks. When I was not helping, I was drawing and writing in my old *agenda* at the desk in the back of the store. This is where my mother would also take care of the bills and the accounting.

Our kitchen at the end of the store had two impressive pieces of equipment. A huge (for my size) coal stove stood against the wall. It included a large range, a deep oven, and a container to heat water; a faucet on the right front side was connected to the hot water container. When my mother ordered a new load of coal, she would stack it near the kitchen under the stairway going up to the bedrooms. The smell of coal emanating from our storage area reminded me of my trip to the gas factory in Avignon to heal my cough. Toward the end of 1942, when coal became so rare that we could no longer exchange it for textiles, my mother made a deal to buy discarded wooden beams that were buried under the rubble of an old silk factory, near the quartier de Fond Rose. Monsieur Crumière borrowed a horse and a cart to carry the wood.

The other piece of equipment was a hand water pump near the kitchen sink. The water pipe came straight out of the tile floor. The pump had to be primed with a little water, so we always had to set aside some water to start the pump next time. Sometimes the pump dried up, and Monsieur Crumière was called in to repair it. When he came with his toolbox, he acted very important. He was able to fix all kinds of problems: sewage plugs, doorknobs, locks, and hinges. He also supplied us with black-market soap, which he made at home. The soap was very good, and everyone agreed it almost looked like the large cubes of real Marseille soap. Monsieur Crumière's fingers were yellow from cigarette smoking, and he smelled like medicine.

The handyman was also the one who found and installed a secondhand ceramic toilet bowl for us. My mother wanted the toilet inside the large closet under the stairs to the bedrooms. He improvised a door—without lock or knob—that one could close from inside using a simple metal hook. In one day, we had jumped straight into the twentieth century, except that we had no running water. That was easily solved by always keeping a bucket of water ready.

Monsieur Crumière was also indispensable for extracting the separated base of a broken lightbulb or replacing bad bulbs in our store, because the ceiling was too high for us to reach. It was often my job to buy new bulbs at Monsieur Rieux's drugstore. "Buy two of them, sixty candles each," my mother would say (in those days, people used the word "candle" instead of "watt"). "Also bring mothballs for the merchandise!" she added. Mothballs were as necessary as the sticky flycatcher rolls hanging from the ceiling, and one could find both at Monsieur Rieux's drugstore, which was on the other side of Le Pontet on the way to the train station. I liked the smell of the drugstore, and I can still remember the mix of chemicals in the air. I did not mind waiting in the drugstore because I enjoyed watching Monsieur Rieux mix paint for a customer or fill a can with putty to repair a loose windowpane, while Madame Rieux was preparing clothespins or a broom for a housewife. I also loved to listen to the free advice Monsieur Rieux provided his customers. His experience was obvious, since he always had an answer. After I came back home with the bulbs, Monsieur Crumière could resume his repairs, and I was proud of my contribution.

One day, my mother fired Monsieur Crumiére, and he was told never to come back again. Since I had been absorbed in a drawing, I asked my mother what had happened. She told me that he had misbehaved with her and that was it. She was embarrassed by my question. Being curious and uninhibited, as many young children are, I stretched my mother's modesty on more than one occasion.

To overcome food scarcity, my mother had to dig deeper in her bag of Jewish Polish recipes from back home. In the midst of her frantic preoccupation with food, I do recollect the peaceful moments that followed some strikes of good luck. I loved the omelets that my mother would prepare. Extending the egg with a little milk, water, and flour would puff the omelet and create the illusion of plenty. Sometimes, a little more flour, a few rare potatoes, and onions would turn into kreplach, Jewish ravioli. I watched my mother make them from scratch: thin layers of dough, little spoonfuls of filling, discs of dough cut out with a drinking glass and sealed by pressing the wetted edges together. The residual dough was reshaped and the process restarted until no dough was left unused. What a feast when the hot kreplach soup was served!

Cauliflower "mushrooms" were another delicacy. One egg, a little water, and a little flour served as batter. My mother used to steam the cauliflower ahead of time. I still remember the chunks of cauliflower dipped in the batter and fried with their stems up in the hot pan. I could not wait for them. When they were ready, they looked like big mushrooms with their white stems and brown caps.

When things went our way, my mother could accomplish a miracle with a small but well-cared-for chicken, a few vegetables, onion, one egg, and a little flour. The flour and the egg turned into noodles made on our kitchen table. The chicken and the vegetables produced an aromatic broth. The ribbons of noodles, long and short, wide and narrow, rejoined the boned chicken in the soup, but the meal was not complete until we had the delicious stuffed chicken neck. My mother prepared it by pulling the skin off the neck bones. Then she sewed one side of the skin and stuffed it with a mixture of potatoes, fried onions, flour, and meat. Finally, she carefully closed and sewed the other side. The stuffed neck was gently dipped in the soup, then fried in a hot pan.

The Puttos, an Italian immigrant family who owned a dairy farm, provided us with milk and, sometimes, the much rarer butter. Every time they came to our house, the strong smell of their stable emanated from their bodies and lingered long after they had left. When they brought butter, we were caught in a dilemma: eating the butter all at once was irresponsible, but if we kept it for too long it would get rancid. So my mother would slowly boil the butter, then cool it down in a jar. This process preserved the butter and allowed us to make it last longer, but the melted butter lost its smooth texture and felt somewhat granular on the tongue. She would rejuvenate our stale bread by grilling it on the hot top of the coal oven and spreading it with the preserved butter. I still salivate at the thought of those bread slices, charred at the edges by the red-hot oven and covered with the preserved butter, and I can still smell the distinctive toasting smell that pervaded the house. When milk was available, I enjoyed a bowl of café au lait with the toast.

With time, *végétaline*, a disgusting white shortening, replaced oil and butter, and we brewed coffee made of roasted barley. To maintain the illusion of real coffee, my mother extended the roasted barley with chicory, as she had done with the rarer coffee, although barley and chicory were now equally available.

Rice pudding was another treat. It was made with milk, sugar, rice, eggs, and raisins. The milk was boiled beforehand with a large vanilla bean that was used many times. After each use it would be returned to its narrow glass tube with a tiny cork to keep its aroma from dissipating. My mother would fold the egg yolks straight into the rice mixture, but the egg whites first had to be beaten until they were fluffy. This always took her a long time, since she did it by hand with two forks. Only the baker owned an electric mixer. The pudding did not come out of our oven evenly, but that didn't matter. It was light and sweet, and did not last very long.

Our most elaborate kitchen appliance was the manual food mill, which we had bought at Berton et Sicard's. It was ideal for mashing potatoes, but my mother used it primarily to puree vegetables for soup, since I could not stand all the wartime vegetables: turnips, Jerusalem artichokes, rutabagas, cabbage, and the like. Because the vegetables were stringy, it was necessary to add broth every few minutes and to turn the crank in the opposite direction to unclog the strainer.

My mother kept our food more or less kosher. She never served meat with tasty milk sauces or snails in garlic like our neighbors did when they had a lucky break. She never objected, however, when Madame Meffre or Madame Brun called me over for a taste. Today I savor the spicy food of Provence. At the same time, however, my yearning for the plain food of my mother's kitchen is one of my few remaining connections to her.

My mother discovered that Lucienne, the local hairdresser, had a steady supply of large German round rye and potato bread loaves because she was going with a German officer. My mother, who was able to trade counterfeit textile coupons for rare garments, traded the garments for the rarer German bread. One day, while picking up a loaf of bread, we found the hairdresser in tears, and a few months later a blond baby boy with clear blue eyes was born in infamy. We ceased picking up new loaves at that time because the German officer had been sent to the Russian front. To this day, I have a strong craving for that dark German bread, but I have never been able to find one that tastes the way I remember.

When things got tougher, I had to overcome my deep disgust for cabbage. I always felt like vomiting. But my mother fed me patiently and helped me to overcome my profound revulsion at the cabbage soup she placed in front of me.

Since I did not look healthy despite my mother's ministrations, I was forced to ingest a mix of raw egg yolk, lemon juice, sugar, and a spoonful of *fortifiant*. The *fortifiant*, a dark brown liquid with a strange taste, was aimed at generating appetite, and hence it was highly recommended for skinny children. She adjusted the sweetness of the brew until I got it down. It tasted awful, but I surely preferred my mother's mixture to the commonly used cod liver oil, which supposedly had similar virtues.

Food became so rare that even the mice had a hard time. At school, I was seated next to Robert Fage, the son of the baker Auguste Fage. Robert always came to school with a piece of fresh bread that he hoarded in his desk until he finished it bit by bit. At night, the mice had a banquet with the crumbs scattered at the bottom of his desk drawer. When we started class in the morning, they would escape through the empty inkwell hole on Robert's side of the desk. One day, the mice ate half of his French grammar book, probably because the previous day he had eaten his bread without leaving enough crumbs. Robert and I were good friends and used to play together. Sometimes, he would share with me a piece of quince bread that his father had baked specially for him. The whole quince, cored and sweetened, was covered with French bread dough before baking it in the huge oven. While waiting for the delicacy, Robert and I watched the moving circles of dough in the electric kneading trough. Periodically, the baker would check the loaves in the oven and slide some of them out on his long wooden paddle. Our faces were a dancing reflection of the red flames inside the oven. Finally, our quince bread was ready. Waiting for it to cool down was torture to my stomach, but the first few bites were worth all the torment.

When Robert was playing outside, his paternal grandmother, *la mère* Fage, would call him from her house in such a shrieking bad soprano voice that the neighbors would close their windows, even on a summer day. In Provence, older, more respected people are called "la mère Dumas" or "le père Roux" instead of "Madame Dumas" or "Monsieur Roux" as a sign of deference. I recall that neither Robert's father nor his mother ever called him for supper; they left that for his grandmother, because their voices did not measure up to hers. While it was Auguste Fage who baked the bread, his wife and his mother sold it to the villagers in exchange for counterfeit or real food coupons. They were unable or unwilling to distinguish between the two kinds of coupons, although the difference was obvious, even to me. One day, my mother found a large piece of rope inside our bread. It had probably fallen off a bag into the flour. We did not return the bread because it was not wise to alienate the baker. The French merchants' reluctance to take back defective merchandise was aggravated by the food restrictions.

We Jews are raised with the belief that the mind triumphs over the body, and that good triumphs over evil. From an early age, we are discouraged from being physical, because that would make us too much like the goyim, the Gentiles. We become convinced that an arsenal of wit, ingenuity, and honesty is all that a Jew needs to sail through life safely. There is no need to strengthen our bodies; our brains will do the job. We are so convinced of the superiority of mind over muscle that we develop an uncontrollable nausea at the thought of a physical Jew. The Lewendels were no exception. To fulfill this Jewish fate, I was a successful student at the Ecole Primaire, or grammar school, and that was good. However, in my first week of first grade, I punched the nose of a classmate who had gotten on my nerves. As soon as my mother got wind of the incident, she hired a bigger boy from fourth grade to serve as my bodyguard in exchange for a brand-new, handmade comb. My mother could not bear the sight of her "clever Jackele" turning into a Christian right in front of her eyes. Behaving like Goliath was not proper for a young Jewish boy.

Like the other male teachers, Monsieur Roux, the first-grade teacher, maintained strict discipline. He often inflicted corporal punishment using a long, thin bamboo rod. When we did not behave according to his taste, we had to hold the fingers of our right hand up, and he used the tip of his long rod to whip them from a distance. Punching my classmate's nose made me eligible for the bamboo rod. When my mother brought the comb to my bodyguard, she also went to Monsieur Roux and did what no other parent had ever dared to do: she asked him who had allowed him to brutalize her "innocent Jacky." Objecting to corporal punishment at school was a bold act in 1942.

Madame Castagnier, my second- and third-grade teacher, was more supportive than Monsieur Roux was. She proposed that I skip second grade. Since she taught both grades in the same classroom, she remained my teacher. When she was sick, Monsieur Parpillon, the sixth-grade teacher, substituted for her. We used to call him Monsieur *Papillon*, which made us giggle, since *papillon* means "butterfly" in French. I hated Monsieur Parpillon because he used to call me the "rag peddler," a demeaning reference to my mother's business. It may have been a sarcastic reference to my well-publicized kindergarten business deal as well.

Most of the villagers were poor. They owned tiny farms or worked on someone else's farm. Since their homes were generally not educational incubators, most of the students were no competition for me. As a result, I had an important status in the school, and I regularly helped students from higher grades with their math difficulties. Drilling was the favorite teaching method, and reciting the material by heart was the culmination of any good teaching. We recited everything—math, science, history, literature, and geography. Our teachers invented rap much before its time, and the multiplication tables were their favorite morning singsong. I also had a good memory and learned poems by heart just by listening to the teacher. To this day, I remember "The Wild Mare" by Guy de Maupassant. This indomitable mare was uncapturable, but it was finally overcome by the dry heat of the desert. Evoking the migrating dunes, Maupassant writes, "The sand buried her corpse under a moving shroud."

In contrast to my mother's attention to my studies, many parents used their children as free labor before and after school. For instance, Pampignolli, the son of Italian farmers, used to feed the cows before coming to school, which explains why he often had hay in his hair and on his shirt. One day he proudly came to school with his hair full of brillantine, an oily substance grown-ups used to make their hair shiny like that of Tino Rossi, the popular movie star and singer whose picture was on the posters. He had stolen the brillantine from his older sister, and it was dripping all over his shoulders. Saint-Léger, the son of a factory worker, always got the worst grades when the teacher announced the monthly scores. The students sat in grade-descending order, with those having the worst grades sitting farthest away from the teacher and toward the back of the classroom. Saint-Léger claimed that he loved to be the worst student because he got to sit near the door and be the first one on the playground at recess. I was always seated in the front row next to the teacher.

In early 1943, I became more independent. After school, I started roaming around the village with my friends, looking for interesting things and places. We played around *le lavoir*, the village washhouse, constructed for the housewives next to the River Sorgue. The cold river water had been diverted through the washing basin. The women used to bring laundry in huge baskets and take a spot on either side of the basin. Although a roof protected them from rain and sun, there was no relief from the mistral, the cold winter wind. The laundry was left to dry on the wires outside the washhouse. The *lavoir* served as the village information exchange, the heartbeat of gossip. When the conversation was too sensitive, we children were told to take a hike.

From there, we went to play in the bushes near the river behind the washhouse. We used to catch mayflies, which we tied by one leg and flew at the end of a yard of leather thread. It was easy to locate the bugs on the branches by following their characteristic scent. We had also built a cabin next to the river by bending and tying together the branches of the tallest bushes, and we used to spend hours inside. During the summer, we discovered the pleasure of roasting lizards in an old pot over an improvised fire. In the beginning, we lost a few lizards until we learned how to avoid catching them by the tail. We were amazed how they could leave part of their tail in our fingers, and we were mesmerized by the detached tail that wriggled in our hand. After the roasting, we conducted proper funerals for the victims. One of the boys officiated as the vicar, since the lizards were good Catholics. I used to dig the grave or pretend to be part of the family, since there was no need for a rabbi. Although it was just a boys' game inspired by war and we knew nothing about the crematoria in the concentration camps, in retrospect our cruel game leaves a chilling memory.

We usually did not admit girls to our clubhouse, but we made an exception for a little British refugee, because we found her entertaining. She claimed that babies are brought by storks because her mother had told her so. We sensed she was wrong because of the insinuations of older children, but we knew nothing concrete. Nevertheless, we giggled as if we were much wiser, and we had a lot of fun at her expense.

We loved to play backstage in the movie theater owned by our neighbor Monsieur Gros. Although the entrance to the theater was next to his coffee shop, facing the Route Nationale, one could get to the stage through a back entrance on the Route de Vedène. We played at hide-and-seek under the stage and behind the huge curtains. One could reach the floodlights by climbing a wooden staircase leading to an upper ramp, but Monsieur Gros would chase us away when we pushed our luck.

Next to the backstage entrance were the backyard of the bakery and its flour warehouse. Robert Fage and I would climb on top of the bags of flour piled up in the warehouse. We'd roll down, bouncing from bag to bag. The smell of the flour penetrated the air as the bag released a fine dust. I was not a pretty sight when I returned home.

Sometimes, we watched the smith fit the horseshoes of huge beasts of burden. He heated the shoe in the smithy while pumping air onto the coal with an enormous hand bellows. When the shoe became red hot, he seized it with pliers and quickly applied it to the horse's hoof to adjust the fit. Then, he nailed the shoes with square nails while the heavy smoke carried the acrid smell of burned horn into the street.

My friends and I particularly enjoyed watching Monsieur Imbert, the welder across the street from Monsieur Chanu's gas station. Many cars on the road were already equipped in the rear with big containers called "gasogène." They generated a gas that car engines could use instead of gasoline, because gasoline had now become rare. I vividly remember that there were two kinds of systems: one kind was fed with a grayish, stonelike material; the other with charcoal. While writing these lines, my intense need to validate my memories enticed me to look into my chemistry books, and I was elated to find that indeed there are two kinds of processes. Some gas generators produced acetylene using carbide and water, while others generated "water" gas by injecting steam over burning charcoal. Both flammable gases were used to fuel the car engines.

Before our eyes, Monsieur Imbert converted the old Rosengart pickup truck of Semillard, the butcher and coal supplier, to *gasogène*. But he put the *gasogène* tank on the side of the Rosengart because Semillard needed the space in the back of his truck. We watched the operation in silence to avoid being chased away by Monsieur Imbert. Many villagers stopped to comment on the transformation of the truck. Monsieur Chanu, however, did not like it because he was in the process of losing his last customer in the village. While tidying his gas station on the other side of the street, Monsieur Chanu watched from the corner of his eye.

We carried our mischief everywhere in the village. Monsieur Guimbert used to bring the produce from his farm to the grocery stores with a cart and a mule that he parked on Town Hall Square. While he was making a delivery to the grocery store nearby, we untied the mule's paunch belt. As soon as the beast moved, the cart would tip back, and all Monsieur Guimbert's melons would roll across the square. We did not stick around to see his face.

The horse carriage belonging to Guendon, the street sweeper and garbage collector, was another vehicle of interest to us children. We were impressed by the way Guendon controlled the huge white horse by voice commands while he was emptying the garbage cans into the deep cart. Guendon constituted the entire streets and sanitation department, and that made him the lowest-ranking municipal employee, far below the second municipal guard, Raybaud, who in turn had little authority compared to his boss, Tessier. Guendon's thankless work was taken for granted by the villagers, but there was little doubt he would remain on the job for life. Since only the children deigned to recognize him, he let us play around the cart and even tolerated our excesses.

In the summer I could not resist the appeal of the sweet berries luring me from the branches of the mulberry trees in the church garden. The tree was full of silkworms and their cocoons. The old curate probably picked the cocoons and sold them to the silk factory on the edge of our village. When the vicar, Souchon, and his curate were away on duty, my friends and I used to climb over the metal fence and fill boxes with the forbidden fruit. A funeral was a good opportunity, because everyone would follow the vicar and the curate in their procession from the church to the cemetery, and that could take hours. Nevertheless, I was scared because, unlike my friends, I was not accustomed to the church surroundings. Once our boxes were full, we ran away to our club-house near the river, where we had a banquet.

My mother discovered my incursions into the church orchard one day when I returned home with heat stroke, a terrible headache, and a box full of mulberries. But her compassion over-came her anger. I was enlarging my little circle with my frequent expeditions outside our home, but my mother still remained my center of gravity. Because I was her only companion, she shared with me the thoughts she would have shared with an adult. My insatiable curiosity drew us together as partners and strength-ened my bond with her.

7 | *David and Goliath*

*David replied to the Philistines, . . . "And this whole
assembly shall know that the Lord can give victory without sword or spear. For the battle is the Lord's, and He
will deliver you into our hands." When the Philistine
began to advance toward him again, David quickly ran
up to the battle line to face the Philistine. David put his
hand into the bag; he took out a stone and slung it. It
struck the Philistine in his forehead; the stone sank into
his forehead, and he fell face down on the ground. Thus
David bested the Philistine with sling and stone; he
struck him down and killed him. David had no sword.*

—1 Samuel 17:45–50

May 1940–Summer 1943

Immediately after the French defeat, the "Jewish question"
became one of the central themes of the Vichy government, and a
plan of attack with two essential elements was drawn up. First,
the Jews needed to be identified, marked, and dispossessed in
order to eliminate them from the economy. Second, they needed

to be severed from the French nation. Minister of Justice Alibert started working with an anti-Semitic passion on the Statute of the Jews, a legal framework that would provide a solution to the first problem. Salivating with anticipation at the thought of his own legacy, he claimed to be "preparing a text [of law] flavored with little, candied onions."[1]

The Vichy government was examining the second issue. The foreign Jews did not belong to France and therefore could be easily eliminated. Although a large number of Jews who had immigrated to France after World War I had recently been naturalized, this privilege could easily be revoked without much public outcry. The French Jews, however, presented the Vichy government with a more difficult problem; they would be left for last.

On July 22, 1940, a few weeks after the armistice was signed, the Vichy government decreed that the Jews' French citizenship, which they had acquired since the enactment of the law on French nationality of August 10, 1927, would be reviewed.[2] As a result, 7,000 Jews would become subject to denaturalization. It would take several years to examine all the cases. For instance, the Gronner family was denaturalized on October 28, 1942, by decree of Maréchal Pétain and Minister of Justice Joseph Barthelemy.[3] All denaturalization decrees were published in the *Journal Officiel*, a government publication in which legislative measures were listed.

Although the nationality laws made it clear that French citizenship was a favor, not a right, and could therefore be withheld, its annulment had to be submitted to the court.[4] Therefore, the French government was acting arbitrarily, in defiance of the law and of its own legal practices.

Under this hostile set of circumstances and in the most unlikely of times, my mother decided to apply for French citizenship for herself and for my father, who had been a prisoner in Switzerland for six months. She was trying to use the system in order to blend in. As the application below shows, my mother did not know that my citizenship was being challenged.

Le Pontet, December 11, 1940

Monsieur the Guardian of the Seals,

The named below:

1—LEWENDEL Meilech, born on May 3, 1901, in Ozanna (Poland)
  • who entered France on May 18, 1930, and has resided here since then.
  • Having volunteered to serve France even before the war started (statement of the mayor of Le Pontet dated April 25, 1939) and currently interned as war prisoner in the camp of Thöringen (Switzerland).
  • Father of a son, Isaac LEWENDEL, born in Avignon on June 28, 1936, and declared French on September 9, 1936.
  • In possession of identity card No. 39CS80263 valid until September 15, 1942.

2—GOLDSTEIN Sara, born on March 1, 1904, in Lipsko (Poland).
  • In possession of a renewal receipt for her identity card No. 34AC19267.
  • Domiciled in Le Pontet near Avignon (Vaucluse) since 1936.

Are honored to request of your benevolence the benefit of French nationality, attaching to support their request:

  1. birth certificate of Meilech LEWENDEL
  2. wedding certificate
  3. certificate of good behavior and morals of Meilech LEWENDEL
  4. certificate of good behavior and morals of Sara GOLDSTEIN
  5. certificate of residence of Meilech LEWENDEL
  6. certificate of residence of Sara GOLDSTEIN
  7. medical certificate
  8. statement of volunteering to the French military
  9. statement of French nationality of the son

Identity cards and passports that Madame Goldstein cannot part with are kept at the disposal of the competent services.

(Signed Sara Levandel-Goldstein and Meilech Lewandel)

As can be expected, the government took no action on my mother's citizenship request. Moreover, my own French citizenship had been revoked. Indeed, the law of July 22, 1940, included what looks like a deliberate ambiguity: Although its title announced "the revision of naturalizations," the text of the law itself mentioned "the revision of all acquisitions of French nationality," which is a much broader category. Indeed, the term naturalization applies exclusively to individuals born abroad, while acquisition of nationality also includes foreigners married to French nationals as well as children born in France to foreign parents.[5]

The government had won rounds one and two—denaturalization and denial of citizenship—and my mother was now ready for round three. According to a recent finding at the Ministry of Social Affairs and Integration, on August 11, 1942, my mother for the second time arranged for me to receive the French nationality for which I was still eligible by birth, according to article 3 of the law of August 10, 1927, which had not yet been repealed.[6] Armed with a power of attorney signed on June 1, 1942, by my father at the French consulate in Lugano (Switzerland), she found in Avignon Judge Jean Chambon a man courageous enough to confront the system even after the Vichy government had started enacting its policy of arbitrary denaturalizations on July 22, 1940. Between the arrests in Paris on July 16 and 17, 1942, and the deportation of foreign Jews from the "free" zone on August 26, 1942, my mother had become conscious of the liability borne by foreign Jews and tried to protect me with French citizenship. With the help of Judge Jean Chambon, she was now successful and had won round three.

This would be a fragile victory in my mother's paper war against the French government. The government was ready to

counterattack, and in early summer 1943, my mother's gains—
and those of thousands of other Jews—were wiped out in an
instant by the bureaucrats of hatred. Indeed, surrendering to
German pressure, the French government was finally ready to
facilitate the elimination of these Jews, and at the same time to
give up its most sacred symbol of sovereignty, the act of granting
French nationality. The minister of justice issued a blanket
instruction canceling all citizenships acquired by Jews since
August 10, 1927.

MINISTRY OF JUSTICE

The Head of the Government,
The Council having been heard,
decrees:

Article 1—Are annulled under the law and from the date
of the publication of the present decree all naturalization
decrees which occurred since August 10, 1927, in favor of foreigners considered as Jews according to the law of June 2,
1941.

Article 2—There may be exceptions to the dispositions of
the preceding article in favor of people who may request them
and who fulfill one of the conditions allowed by Article 3 of the
law of June 2, 1941, legislating the Statute of the Jews and
from whom French nationality has not already been taken
away.

Article 3—Under penalty of foreclosure of the present
decree, the request for an exception and the documents
deemed necessary by the applicant must be sent to the
Chancellery within three months of the date of the publication
of the present decree.

Article 4—The dispositions of Article 1 of the present
decree are not applicable to war prisoners who are presently
captive.

Article 5—Will be punished with a jail term of six months
to two years and with a fine of 10,000 to 100,000 francs any
person who, after being stripped of French nationality by the

application of the preceding rules, will have claimed the qualification of French citizenship or will have used a document or any act in which this qualification is recognized.

Article 6—The present decree will be published in the <u>Journal Officiel</u> and executed as law.

Pierre Laval
The Guardian of the Seal,
Minister,
Secretary of State for Justice[7]

The Vichy government had won round four. At the same time, it had also won the document war against the Jews, since no Jew could now escape the stripping of French nationality. All Jews of foreign origin had now become equal in defeat. In addition, the mind-set created by government harassment rendered them defenseless in the face of administrative arbitrariness. Perhaps this war was not meant to be won by these Jews. In the end, my mother's joust with the Vichy government was pointless as far as her own fate was concerned, since by June 6, 1944, the day of her arrest, there was no longer a distinction between French and foreign Jews. Furthermore, the illusion of her possible victory may have masked her awareness of imminent demise.

8 | *He Is Not Like the Rest of Us*

At the shout of horseman and bowman, the whole city
flees. They enter the thickets, they clamber the rocks.
The whole city is deserted, not a man remains there.

—Jeremiah 4:29

Early Summer 1943–June 4, 1944

Théophile Delorme, the mayor who had been duly elected before the war, resigned on April 15, 1943, because of his conscience. At least this is what was said in our store. Or did he smell the odor of the coming defeat? Apparently, his conscience had not bothered him too much when he ordered the village clerk to register us as Jews and inventory our assets, enabling the German and French Nazis to capture and dispossess us. Nor did his conscience bother him when the stamp on our food-rationing cards branded us as Jews every day of the week. Awareness of the impending German defeat only made his choice easier. Whatever his motivation may have been for resigning, if he was able to do so under the German occupation, he could have done so that much

81

easier before the Germans arrived. Delorme's actions show us that civil servants had some latitude in deciding whether to collaborate or to leave the administration.

A new and more willing mayor, Victor Cisterni, was appointed together with new and more willing citizens—Gabert, Goutarel, Coudurier, Hébrard, and Raoux—who were ready to collaborate and to fill empty spots on the city council left by resignations. Gabert, Goutarel, and Coudurier were reelected after the war, showing that the distance between collaboration and respectability was not so great after all. The villagers, who did not particularly like Cisterni, mentioned his name with a mix of respect and fear—respect for his reputation for being tough and fear of his pro-German sympathies.

In one of his first jobs, Cisterni sponsored a letter of recommendation to the prefect of Vaucluse in Avignon attesting to the character of my mother.

Le Pontet, July 29 1943

**From the Mayor of Le Pontet to
Monsieur the Prefect of Vaucluse**

The woman LEWENDEL, née Goldstein, Sara, born on March 1, 1904, in Lipsko, of Polish nationality, entered France on August 10, 1935, to rejoin her husband, LEWENDEL, Meijlech, established in France since 1929 [sic], and who practiced the trade of haberdashery, principally at fairs and in open markets of the region.

The child from their wedding, Isaac, born on June 28, 1936, is French following a declaration in front of the Justice of Peace.

The husband of the interested party, called into the Polish military in 1940, is currently interned in Switzerland. His wife receives a military allocation plus a supplement for a child. She manages the business of her husband, established in Le Pontet, and she claims an income of 1,000 francs per month.

Her conduct, her morality, and her attitude from the

**national point of view have yielded no unfavorable observa-
tion.** [My emphasis]

(City seal)[1]

The letter was the usual supporting document in an application for the renewal of my mother's identity card, opened on July
30, 1943.[2] Oddly, the letter names no official and has no signature,
as was customary in the French administration. But it looked like
the author of the letter, unable (or unwilling) to predict the future
turn of events, was careful not to leave any tracks. Or was it sheer
embarrassment? In the file, the mayor's recommendation,
"Deserves to obtain satisfaction," made us eligible for a new *JUIF*
stamp and a new census. Vichy's generosity toward the Jews
knew no limit! In fact, by offering a semblance of legality to the
Jews, the government was luring them into a trap. My mother's
application for an identity card made us more vulnerable to future
tracking and arrest.

At the beginning of Cisterni's tenure, we were again registered as Jews to make sure that we were still around and had not
been lost.[3] Cisterni also ordered the names of Jews to be posted
at the entrance to their homes, but he never forced us to comply.

By the fall of 1943, the official anti-Semitic propaganda had
already penetrated the village fabric. The daily salute to the flag,
the praise to the Maréchal, the scorn of the "enemies of France
and the Jews," and the teachers' speeches made me wish the earth
would swallow me up. Schoolmates started shouting "sale Juif!"
(dirty Jew!) in my direction, and I reacted by denying my
Jewishness. "Liar!" they said. "We saw the Jewish stamp on your
food-rationing card!" Obviously, the Jew-branding technique was
working; there was nowhere to hide.

I discovered at this time that my penis was not like everyone
else's, because none of the Catholic children were circumcised.
When I asked my mother about it, she became embarrassed and
explained that this was the sign of a special covenant with God
made at the birth of a Jewish baby boy. I angrily replied that I did

not want to have any special covenant. I was also furious because my mother refused to let me write to Santa Claus and order my Christmas presents. "Jewish children don't get Christmas presents," she told me. Everybody and everything seemed to be turning against me: my schoolmates, the Jewish stamp on my food-rationing card, my circumcision, my mother, and even Santa Claus! As usual, my mother compromised and bought me a gift: the *Fables of La Fontaine*, a seventeenth-century rendering of the fables of Aesop. She explained that Christmas was not such a big deal because Santa Claus did not really exist. (This is how I got a head start in life over my Catholic schoolmates, who still believed in Santa Claus.) I felt secure on her lap, and together, though slowly, we began reading the fables. I was fascinated by the fox who could talk a piece of cheese out of the mouth of the vain crow who could not sing, and amazed by the stupidity of the frogs who rejected an inert tree trunk as a king and instead got a hungry stork who swallowed them alive.

During the winter of 1943, we had to cope with young neighbors who regularly yelled anti-Semitic slogans under our window and drew Stars of David on our back door. One day, after my mother realized that the harassment would not stop, she poured cold water on their backs. Immediately, their parents came to protest the rude treatment. From then on, my mother always kept two full buckets of water in our bedroom. I liked when my mother fought back, and I was proud to be her ally.

My schoolmate Robert Fage, who had been a good friend, was one of these children. The Fages exemplified the ambivalence of many French people around us. Despite his slogans and taunts at us, Robert was treated like a hero because he had dared to sing the outlawed French anthem, "La Marseillaise," amid the patrons of the Sporting Bar, at the risk of being fingered by the Militia.

Among themselves at the café, people loved to call the Germans by derogatory names: *Fritz* or *Fridolins*, *Boches* and *Chleus*. *Fritz* and its derivative, *Fridolin*, obviously originate from a common German first name (in a morbid parallel, the Nazis called every Jewish woman Sara). *Chleu* may originate from a primitive North African tribe name. *Boche* comes from *caboche,* or hard head; hence it stands for a thickheaded person, a stupid man. Because of their hatred of the Germans, it is surprising that the Fages saw nothing wrong with their son sharing the French anti-Semitic tradition with the German Nazis.

The Fages, like many French, hated the Germans in part because they were responsible for the war shortages. In Marcel Ophuls's 1970 documentary *Le Chagrin et la pitié (The Sorrow and the Pity),* a pharmacist from the city of Clermont-Ferrand mentions in a postwar interview that he joined the Resistance because "the Germans had taken the butter and the steaks off the French tables." Were butter and steaks the only things that counted?

Most of the villagers were either hostile or indifferent to us. This was painful because village life was a tightly knit fabric. The villagers could satisfy all their daily needs in the village, and they went to Avignon only when they had an unusual need, like a food mill from Berton et Sicard. I got my hair cut by Norbert's father and my shoes repaired by René's father. We bought bread from Robert's parents and groceries at Claude's parents' store. They in turn bought clothes from my mother. As the anti-Semitic Vichy propaganda invaded every fiber of the village life and our merchandise dwindled, many of the villagers cut the threads connecting us to them. My mother lost a lot of business, and I started losing my friends.

However, the Vernets, our neighbors in the back, were genuinely kind to us. *La mère* Vernet was a gentle lady with her gray hair tied in a bun on the top of her head. Her husband worked at the gunpowder factory on the road to Sorgues. René, her oldest son, was married and a policeman. Gaston, her twenty-year-old son, lived at home. Like all other young adults, he was supposed to serve in the Chantiers de Jeunesse (Youth Labor Camps), which had been set up after the defeat to replace military service for the 1940 class of twenty-year-olds. The youth camps were scattered all over France; one of them was in the neighboring town of

Cavaillon. In 1943, the Germans seized the opportunity of taking some of the recruits to Germany to aid in the war effort. Some would go, others would join the Resistance. Gaston would avoid the labor service thanks to the complicity of Docteur André, who provided him with a medical exemption. This was his and his family's way to exercise passive resistance.

Gaston often crossed the street to visit us, and he would teach me card tricks and mathematical riddles. He showed me how to guess the pair of cards that he had chosen among ten pairs on the table. I also learned how to split an eight-liter can of wine into two exact halves, using only the eight-liter can and two additional empty cans, one five-liter can and one three-liter can. He teased my brain with all kinds of riddles, and my mother proudly watched as I came up with the correct answers.

Monsieur and Madame Meffre, the owners of the grocery store next door, Les Coopérateurs de Provence, were decent people too. Monsieur Meffre had a large stomach and a red nose, a sure sign that he used to spend a lot of time with "his head under the tap [of the wine barrel]," as they say in a famous French song. Since he owned his own vineyard in the nearby village of Saint-Saturnin, his personal wine cellar could escape government control. The Meffres often advised my mother to leave the area for her safety.

Every day, an old man, wearing a long black dirty robe down to his shoes, used to walk behind our house from the direction of the quartier des Agassins. Then he would come back the same way. He wore the long robe because he was incontinent, and the villagers called him "lou pissaïre," which is the local patois for "the pisser." The children used to run after him and throw stones in his direction, but the stones never reached him. Afraid to get too close, they ran away before they got within range. If a child was careless and did not keep his distance, *lou pissaïre* would take a run at him, brandishing his cane. The adults tolerated their children's game, however, and even encouraged it, "because he is not like the rest of us." The villagers disliked everything and everyone different.

The collaborating assistant of the collaborating mayor, Cisterni, decided that it was essential to provide decent lodging for the German officers. This is why two officers of the SS were sent to our house "to occupy [our] empty rooms." They were two well-groomed young men. My mother became scared because she knew that the SS were the worst kind of Nazis. Obviously, this was a vicious attempt to invite the cats into the birdcage. Surprisingly, the young Nazi officers in their black uniforms accepted my mother's explanation that the rooms were filled with equipment and merchandise, and that there must have been some mistake. They became convinced after my mother took them upstairs to inspect the rooms. As soon as they left, my mother went to the village hall to see the mayor's assistant, the one with the mustache and the beret. He was the same bureaucrat who had visited our home two years earlier during the first Census of the Jews. She angrily accused him of playing into the Nazis' hands. Did she think that keeping the Nazis next door would help?

Wearing his traditional long black cassock and a miter on his head, Souchon, the local vicar, used to plod daily from the church at one end of the village to the cemetery at the other end. He had to pass either in front of our house or behind it. I was puzzled by the vicar's attire and looked at him intently when he was passing by. He never said anything to me and behaved as if he did not notice me. In time, he started looking the other way. He was popular with the Catholic residents who regularly attended mass in large numbers. Today, I wonder what he used to talk about in his sermons during mass. Did he say that our punishment fit the crime because "the Jews slew Him and did not believe in Him"?[4] Did he skip John 8:44, "Ye [Jews] are of your father the devil, and the lust of your father ye will do," and other New Testament passages that vilify the Jews, or did he make a point to read them? Did he tell the Christians to be helpful and compassionate toward the Jews, or did he tell them not to worry? Did he ever look into his mirror and talk to his maker about the anti-Semitism of his parishioners? Or did he keep silent? The archbishop of Avignon,

Jean Avril, did not provide him with a good example: he had a leaning toward the right-wing notables and, therefore, did not like the Jews.

On Sundays, the parishioners crowded in front of the church at the end of the services. They were dressed in "Sunday clothes" and seemed not to want to go back home. Engaged in endless dialogue, they lingered in small groups. Since I did not dare to get too close, I have no idea what they were saying, but the fact that I was excluded made me feel uncomfortable.

My mother was becoming tenser and silently hugged me for longer periods of time. Without any explanation, I could sense her mounting worry. Often, I felt that she was silently watching over me in my sleep, because she was quietly sitting at my side when I woke up in the morning. Panic struck me every few days when the Gestapo and the Militia would visit our neighbor Gros, the restaurant owner, for mysterious meetings. A black Traction Avant, a front-wheel-drive Citroën limousine, would regularly stop near the sidewalk in back of our house. Three or four men in leather jackets with distinctive felt hats and leather briefcases would step purposefully out of the limousine and disappear into the backstage entrance of Monsieur Gros's theater. They never went in through the front door. I used to watch their arrival from our window, but my mother would gently pull me away. Since they never came in through the front door, rumor had it that they were discreetly meeting with Monsieur Gros, who was said to be a Nazi informant. According to the village gossip, his brother-in-law on his wife's side lived in Paris and was connected to the Gestapo. This put an end to my playing backstage in Monsieur Gros's theater.

A large retreating unit of the Italian army arrived in our village. With it came the rumor that the Italians were losing on the Italian front. The French villagers joked about the military prowess of the Italians, whom they did not like. They claimed that when an Italian baby boy is born, the midwife performs a test to find out his future by pressing on his stomach. If he cries he will grow to be a tenor, and if he fills his diaper he will become a soldier. What an irony in the face of the unequivocally French collapse of 1940!

The local French authorities issued orders to the population to surrender all copper objects to support German ammunition production. The beautiful copper trim around the counter of the Sporting Bar next door was soon replaced by an aluminum one. The Vichy government had stopped issuing bronze coins and replaced them with aluminum coins stamped with the symbols of the Vichy government, the face of Pétain on one side and the Francisque, the traditional double-edged ax, on the other. The Vichyist slogan "Travail, Famille, Patrie" (Work, Family, Fatherland) replaced the Republican "Liberté, Egalité, Fraternité" (Liberty, Equality, Fraternity). My mother started withdrawing from circulation all the bronze coins that passed by the cash register and amassed them in boxes that she stacked inside our kitchen wall closet next to the box of family pictures. I was in charge of counting the money and writing the amounts on the boxes. My mother and I were enthusiastic accomplices in this modest sabotage of the German war effort.

The Germans didn't stop with copper. They wanted steel too. They pulled the abandoned streetcar tracks out of the Route Nationale to help the war effort. The streetcar to Avignon had stopped servicing Le Pontet in 1937, but the tracks had been left in the asphalt.

As the situation became tougher for the Germans at the front, there were rumors of Jewish arrests closer to home. Soon they were happening all around us, and our Jewish friends urged my mother to go into hiding. One of them, Madame Sokolowski, was especially insistent that we leave immediately. Her husband and five children had already left, and she reminded my mother that Jews we knew had already been arrested in Marseille, Arles, and Nimes. She also said that Rosenthal, the shoemaker from Avignon, and Schneider, the merchant from Beaucaire, had fled to safety. After she left, I asked my mother why we should not listen to her advice. She said, "Those who give advice do not pay for the consequences." I was not yet seven and did not understand what she meant. She then explained that she could not leave the store, which was our sole source of income. We were trapped by the Nazis, like the monkey who wants to eat a banana hidden by a hunter in a small hole in a tree. The opening of the hole is wide enough for the hand without the banana, but too small once the hand is clenched on the fruit. As soon as the monkey grabs the banana, it gets caught because it does not want to release the food. Our meager resources and my mother's network kept us alive as long as we remained the Nazis' prisoners.

I did not know at that time that, one year earlier, Madame Sokolowski had saved Ida Tieder, whose mother had been arrested near Bollène during the French hunt for foreign Jews that took place on August 26, 1942. After recently talking to Ida Tieder's sister, Sarah, and to Madame Sokolowski's eldest daughter, Claire, I realized that Madame Sokolowski instinctively knew how to interpret the valuable information she had, and she made it available to others. Unfortunately, my mother did not trust Madame Sokolowski's good judgment.

Others also sensed the gravity of the situation. For example, a delegate of the Oeuvre de Secours aux Enfants (OSE)[5] reported on how the train station in Avignon was particularly dangerous for Jews:

> **It looks like this town is particularly targeted. The train station of Avignon has become a real rat trap. All the Jews who are imprudent enough to transit there are taken down the trains and shipped elsewhere. . . . Recently, with much difficulty, we have succeeded in saving there twenty-seven children who had to transit through the station, and this was made possible thanks to the help of French people.[6]**

The French Resistance was becoming more active and effective, and sabotage occurred all over the area. There were explosions at the Poudrerie, the gunpowder factory in the village of Sorgues, and at various factories in the area. These acts of sabotage were the talk of the day among the pupils at my school. As usual, people were propagating stories about the "heroic *résistants*" that no one could verify. There were even occasional rumors that the Germans had summarily executed resisters in Avignon. Since I never saw the resisters, they provided me with no concrete protection, but I trusted them because they were opposing the Germans and the French Nazis. During these days, Monsieur Beccarud, the village carpenter, was one of the people caught trying to sabotage the central train depot. The news of his arrest by the Germans flashed through the village, and he was looked upon as a hero. He was the first *résistant* whom I knew personally.[7]

At the beginning of 1944, the Germans blocked the main road in several locations by cementing antitank obstacles in the middle of the asphalt, obliging every vehicle to slow down to almost a halt while maneuvering around the concrete blocks. It had become obvious that the Germans were preparing for an invasion. This German state of mind is confirmed by a letter of the Sicherheitsdienst (Security Services or Gestapo) of Avignon on behalf of their loyal French helpers.

SECURITY POLICE—SD   **Avignon, February 22, 1944**

FOREIGN SERVICE AGENCY AVIGNON

To Liaison Staff 761
Division Sergeant Major Höhr
AVIGNON

In Re: Nomination of agents and secretbearers, who in case of Anglo-American landing will need special identification cards.

Special identification cards are needed for the following people:
>   **56861   Karl UHL, 16 Rue Flammarion, Avignon**
>   **56872   Laurent Joseph IDLAS, Ave. St. Jean, Avignon**
>   **56883   Pierre TERRIER, 5 Boulevard des Villas,**
>   **Avignon**

56894	Victoire ANDRE, 10 Place des 3 Pilats, Avignon
56505	Simone PILLET, Rue de la République, Avignon
56516	Titien FEROLDI, Caserne des Passagers, Avignon
56527	Jean POUTET, L'Isle-sur-Sorgue
56538	René Yves Louis LE FLEN, Orange
56549	Yves THEMAR, 71 Rue Joseph Vernet, Avignon
56510	Vahan SARKISSEF, 31 Avenue Monclar, Avignon
56611	Robert CONRAD, 18 Impasse Moline, Avignon

Signed

SS-Lieutenant and

Agency Leader[8]

The London radio broadcasts intensified, bringing better news about the Allies from the various fronts. The optimism of the broadcasts did not make me feel more secure. The "French people [were] speaking to the French people," but no one was speaking to the Jews.

We stopped going to Avignon. We also lost our free access to the peasants who sold food on the black market, because the Germans put a checkpoint at a small bridge on the Route de Vedène. In the spring of 1944, the noose tightened around us, and more Jews were arrested in neighboring towns. Although raids against the Jews had occurred every few weeks in 1943, one of our Jewish friends brought us the news of a particularly large roundup in Avignon at the end of March 1944. She mentioned that the Palombos and their three children had been arrested; two of them were roughly my age.[9] Other names were mentioned as well. The raids were supervised by the German police and executed by French *miliciens* in plain clothes. My mother was trembling, but for me the arrest of the Jews was somewhat abstract because I did not know the people arrested. Those I knew well—the Sokolowskis, the Kurlandczyks, and the Schneiders—had already left. However, my constant fear was real and vivid. Our Jewish friends, as well as a few Gentiles, kept warning us that roundups were happening regularly and pressed us to leave. "What will you do," they said, "if a *misfortune* happens to you?" I was constantly afraid, but my mother was not listening.

One day, my mother invited a German soldier into our house. She led him from the store into our kitchen. I started arguing with her in French so that the German would not understand, telling her that we should stay away from him. My mother explained that he was a Pole who had been forcibly enrolled in the German army, that he had a son like me in Poland, and hence he was harmless. I did not believe that German soldiers had families because they were the "bad guys." The soldier visited us several times and started taking an interest in me, but his interest in my mother made me terribly jealous of him. In addition, Lucienne the hairdresser's notorious love affair with a German officer may have roused my suspicion. Or did I catch some subtle messages between him and my mother? Since his uniform looked like the one my father wore when he came home on leave at the beginning of the war, it even crossed my mind that this might be my father who had joined the German army. Fortunately, the German soldier disappeared as abruptly as he had appeared, and I never asked any questions about him.

Despite the arrests and the fear, we still had moments of calm normality. I loved taking my baths outside. To economize on coal, my mother would set a large basin of water in the sun on the sidewalk behind our house. Around eleven o'clock, the water was steaming hot, and my mother would give me a bath. Every time she would tell the story of our trips to the sea, when I was three. She and my father used to take me to the seashore seventy kilometers away to heal my bowlegs and strengthen them. Frightened by the waves, I hysterically refused to get into the water at first. On our next trip to the beach, my parents solved the problem by filling with seawater a basin similar to the one in which I took my bath. Of course, when it was time to return home, I loved the water so much that I refused to leave voluntarily.

My mother tried to establish connections to members of the local establishment who would always welcome a warm pair of socks or a rare cotton shirt from under the counter of our store. I remember when we were invited by Mademoiselle Roman for a tea at her large estate in the district of Saint-Tronquet, within walking distance of our village. She served tea on a lawn table in her sunroom, which faced a large yard. As far as I could see, huge oak trees and bushes filled the landscape. Sometimes I could catch a glimpse of the tall wall that seemed to shield us from our usual insecurities. Outside the window, I could see many birds on the branches of the trees. For the occasion, Mademoiselle Roman had taken out her fanciest china and the silver spoons that had been in her family for generations. Taken by the atmosphere, I tried to act like everyone else. There was a problem, though, because Mademoiselle Roman had no sugar, just saccharin. Normally, tea had to be sipped with a piece of sugar in one's mouth. This is the way Madame Sokolowski used to do it when my mother invited her for tea in our kitchen and sugar was available. Since Mademoiselle Roman had no sugar, I mixed the tea and sweetener with the silver spoon but did not like the taste.

The traditional horse races in early May 1944 were held at the Roberty racetrack "in spite of the situation." For the races, my mother wore her blue shirt with large white polka dots and a dark blue skirt. Before wearing the skirt, she "dry cleaned" it. First, she poured a little black coffee in a soup plate. Then she dipped a clothes brush into the coffee and repeatedly brushed the skirt from top to bottom with it. The skirt was like new! She hugged me intensely, and I can still remember her smell—a light scent of sweat, cologne, and cosmetics.

At one o'clock, like everyone else, we set off to the racetrack. Since the track was within walking distance, we strolled with the crowd along the sides of the Route de Vedène, which was crowded with cars, trucks, buses, bikes, and horse carriages, all heading for the races. It was slightly hot, as usual for May. The elegance of men and women, the race announcers, the horses being led to the track, the false starts, the drama of the races, the tense moments before the finish—all these made me forget reality. Here, no one knew that we were Jewish. The presence of German officers was the only cloud, but they were too busy watching the horses with their binoculars to pay any attention to us.

In the middle of May, Allied bombardment caused an abrupt change in our lives. We had been told at school and by posters in the streets that we would be warned by sirens in case of imminent bombing, and that we should get away from the road and from the buildings. A sequence of three short siren bursts meant the beginning of an alert, and a long wailing siren meant the end of danger. The first time the sirens were triggered in the middle of the day, people did nothing but stand outside. We could hear the distant rumbling of the bombers, and as the rumbling intensified, the planes passed over our heads. They looked like little shiny stars in the middle of the bright blue summer sky. Soon, loud clicking, like hundreds of metal chains hitting each other, covered the rumbling. Less than a minute later, staggering explosions surrounded us. All the bombs sounded as if they had landed next door, and thick clouds of dust rose up and hid everything. Everyone started running. The next thing that I remember is my mother and I lying among hundreds of people behind the church. We were in a ditch. Tucked against my mother, I had hidden my face in the grass. We, the only Jews in the village, had taken refuge next to the church, but we would have chosen the synagogue, had there been one in our village.

The bombardment did not feel or sound like it does in the movies. The heavy smoke smelled like dust and fire. The explosions were much more violent than I expected. The earth trembled under my body, and I could feel the shock wave of the explosions on my neck and chest, as if the bombing were happening inside my shirt. Burying my head in the grass had no effect. There was nowhere to hide. My mother had reached the limits of her power and could do nothing more to help me.

This bombing scenario was repeated several times, because our village was located along the Route Nationale Numéro Sept, the only strategic road from Marseille to Paris. During subsequent bombardments, we ran away from the main road when we first heard the siren instead of staring at the sky to see what would happen.

The bombing destroyed roads and buildings. Deep craters spotted the area, and people estimated the weight of the bombs depending on the crater sizes. The two largest craters were next to each other on the Route Nationale Numéro Sept, in the middle of the commercial area of the district of Le Pigeonnier. The craters were centered in the middle of the road between the stores, and they were exactly as wide as the road. On either side of the road, all that remained standing were the building facades; the backs of the houses had been blown away. I could see the rubble beyond the fronts of the disemboweled stores and the deep blue sky through the paneless second-floor windows. My teacher, Madame Castagnier, was wounded in the face during the bombing of Le Pigeonnier.

To hit the German soldiers in their stomachs, the Americans had also targeted the herd of cattle the Germans kept in the neighboring woods of Roberty behind the church. Many people died at Roberty. A schoolmate who lived next to the woods told me gruesome details of finding dismembered bodies. The Americans also targeted La Rotonde, the central train depot near Avignon.

During every air raid, the planes used to drop packets of thin paper strips covered with aluminum. The packets descended slowly, creating the illusion of many more attacking planes and confusing the antiaircraft guns.[10] I used to collect these packets and treasure them as if they were a precious, personal message from the Americans. Yet I was confused because the American bombs were so threatening.

Unfortunately, the bombardment and military pressure did not stop the roundup of the Jews. Our third registration, on May

14, 1944, was another indication that the Nazi police and the French administration were still working hand in hand to eliminate the Jews. By then, the picture had apparently become clear in my mother's mind. All Jews were threatened, and she and I would not be able to elude the hunters.

As a result, on June 4, 1944, we finally made our way toward a hiding place. My mother told me that we would look at the hiding place, which our Jewish friends, the Steltzers, had proposed to share with us, and then we would see. The Stelzers felt indebted to my mother for the financial help she had extended to them after they had emigrated from Poland to our area, and they also respected her for her education. Madame Steltzer, frantic with worry for the last few months, had been instrumental in convincing my reluctant mother to leave.

My mother lowered and locked the iron curtain at the front of the store as she always did before a long trip, and we boarded the bus to Carpentras at the station near our house. She was carrying her large purse. In Carpentras, we were to transfer to a shuttle bus serving small villages, among them Venasques. As the road snaked along the mountainside, the potholes threatened to dismantle the body of the old bus. When the bus came to a stop near the sole bistro of Venasques, the sun was at its zenith and a mule-drawn cart was waiting to take us to the farm. A young boy was standing near the mule, firmly holding onto the leather strap attached to the metal bit in the mule's mouth. He waited until we had climbed onto the cart seat, then he took his seat near us. With a pull of the reins, the mule trotted away and soon left the asphalt road for a small dirt road winding between the sparse farmsteads. The mule trotted steadily along the row of cypresses, the monotonous chirp of the cicadas masking the rhythmic crackle of the mule's hooves on the gravel. Suddenly, without a warning, the mule stood on her hind legs, tilting the carriage backward.

This small incident and the prowess of the young boy who was able to control the enraged mule made a fateful difference between my mother's destiny and mine, sending her to her death and keeping me for life. I impulsively chose to stay behind at the cherry farm, forever waiting for her return. In the years that followed, I bore a heavy burden because of this decision I had made so lightly. How could I allow myself to grieve for a loss I had inflicted upon myself? How could I account for such a frivolous decision? How could I talk about my betrayal of my mother?

9 | Claire

I, a stranger and afraid
In a world I never made.

—A. E. Housman, *Last Poems*

Early June 1944

I remember Monsieur and Madame Steltzer and their three daughters—Esther, Genie, and Claire—well. Claire was by far the most unruly. Monsieur and Madame Steltzer were our Jewish friends who lived in Carpentras near the mountain area of Haute-Provence. Instead of giving my mother advice, they were ready to help. Using his network of acquaintances, Monsieur Steltzer had arranged for our stay at the cherry farm and our trip in the mule cart.

When my mother did not come back to work in the cherry orchard on June 6 as agreed, we all became worried, each for a different reason. The farmers were worried because they were afraid and did not know what to do with me. I was worried because everyone else was worried, because the Steltzers could not answer my questions, and because my mother had never been so late before. "I want to go home," I insisted. "My mom must be there." The Steltzers were worried because they had one more problem on their hands. So they relied on Claire for the answers, because, in spite of her fifteen years, she was the most resourceful of all. She immediately took me by bus from the cherry farm back home to Le Pontet. At the same time, the rest of the Steltzers decided to return for a few days to their home in Carpentras, to be safer in case my mother had been caught and forced to talk. The security of home provided a psychological shield with little real value since the Nazis were looking for the Jews at their home addresses.

When Claire and I arrived in Le Pontet, we went straight to the store. The iron curtain was ajar, too closed for this time of the day and too open for comfort. I ran into the store through the open space under the iron curtain, while Claire went to talk with our Christian neighbor, the owner of Les Docks Vauclusiens next door.

During the previous few months, our store had still looked normal, although there was little variety. Monotonous merchandise had been lined up in straight piles on the wooden shelves that we had ordered from the local carpenter, Beccarud, before he got caught. Buttons and zippers, pants and dresses, socks and handkerchiefs, shirts and sweaters had been available for sale, some in exchange for textile-rationing coupons, but mostly on the black market.

Now, the shelves and the cash drawer were menacingly empty. In the half-light, I could see that everything was gone. Claire found me in the kitchen staring at a dried and charred omelet inside the open oven of the cold kitchen stove. Obviously, my mother did not get to start her meal. I do not remember how I had gotten to the kitchen in the back of the store. I just recall my loneliness in front of the dried omelet. I remember glimpsing into the kitchen wall closet. My boxes with the bronze coins had vanished. I do not remember resisting Claire, who was trying to get me to leave the place. Forty-seven years later, when she visited me in the United States, Claire recalled that moment. She could not tell me then what she had learned from our Christian neighbor or why we had to speedily disappear from Le Pontet. At a loss for words, she was desperately trying to pull me by the sleeve, but, spellbound by the open oven, I resisted her appeal.

Our stove had been full of life before, always on when needed. In winter, it was hot before I got up in the morning, and its warmth lingered into the evening. My mother used it to cook the bits of chicken that she had received from peasants in exchange for some rayon socks or other clothing. She often skipped her own meals. To economize on scarce coal, my mother and I had to cuddle up closer and closer to the stove. There, my mother used to read me stories before going to bed. Many times I fell asleep before the end and woke up as soon as she stopped talking. There, I learned to forget my fear of lightning in the safety of her arms. There too, by the stove, I felt more secure during the darkness of the *couvre-feux*, the air-raid curfews, when the Germans would shoot at any light they saw. Beside the stove, I did not even fear the frequent bombing as much. Now the stove stood dead, and the kitchen was empty.

I do not remember leaving the kitchen, but I remember Claire hauling me into a truck that she had somehow hurriedly stopped. We rode back to Carpentras, where her parents lived. We were both crying; she knew why, and I was mad with worry. I remember nothing else about my way back.

Back at the Steltzers, I remember standing in the living room, next to the round dining table, facing the closed door to the kitchen. A fabric screen with little red and white squares covered the glass window of the kitchen door, and I could hazily see Claire and her mother on the other side. However, I was able to clearly overhear their emotional dialogue behind the kitchen door. Madame Steltzer was speaking Yiddish, as she did when she was upset, and I overheard her say: "Ikh hat ihr gezugt!" (I had told her so!) Claire was speaking French. My entire world came to an end when Claire said to her hysterical mother: "There is nothing you can do. The Germans did it!" I instinctively understood what she meant. When the door opened, I was thunderstruck.

It took the Steltzers hours to calm me down so that I would be able to listen to them. They made me promises no one could keep. It took days until I let them convince me. Claire took me out for a walk, gently trying to focus my attention away from my despair. We walked up rue Porte de Mazan, past the arcades, and right into Cathedral Square, where a large toy store used to be. She knew she had my emotions under control when I agreed to exchange my tears for a small toy. At that moment, I locked my wound inside me. On that day, I stopped sharing my sadness with others, the beginning of a silence that would last forty-five years. But in my mind I told and retold my memories, and I held on to them so that I would never forget them.

The toy Claire bought was a set of *osselets* (small bones), an aluminum imitation of five small lamb bones used as a game of dexterity. You had to send one bone in the air, and then pick from the table one, two, three, or four bones with one hand, before catching the bone in the air with the same hand. During that time, you kept your other hand behind your back. To make the game more complicated, we invented all kinds of variations while the *osselet* was in the air. The aluminum set was considered much fancier than the real bones. I still cringe at the bargain I made by trading the public expression of my sense of loss and injustice for the set of *osselets*.

In despair, I treasured the safety pin that my mother had pinned on my shirt at the cherry farm in the magic hope that nothing would happen to her as long as I could hold on to it. To this day, I still feel a twinge of sadness when I come upon a safety pin lost in the middle of a busy drawer.

10 | *The Steltzers*

A friend is devoted at all times;
A brother is born to share adversity.

—Proverbs 17:17

A Few Days after June 7, 1944

The Steltzers, who had briefly picked up some business, took me in for a few days until they could find a new safe place for me and for themselves, because they were afraid that my mother would talk under "pressure" (I think they meant torture). My mother's imprudence in returning to the store must have angered the Steltzers, since it shattered their plans and caused them to undertake a panicked search for a new place for themselves and me to hide. I know today that they had strongly objected to my mother's return to the store because of the danger to her as well. However, they never revealed their fright or anger to me. On the contrary, I remember their determination to solve the problem at hand. Monsieur and Madame Steltzer already had their hands full with their many worries—a dry goods store, a fruit and vegetable garden, the Germans, the French *collaborateurs*, and three daughters—when I, unexpectedly, became one more worry.

At the beginning of the war, the Steltzers felt safer in Carpentras because the town was twenty kilometers away from the Route Nationale Numéro Sept. Carpentras had an air of lazy sleepiness typical of small provincial cities that have lost their importance. From Carpentras, one had easy access to Mont Ventoux, which was covered with snow in winter and with fragrant *garrigue*[1] in summer. Since the mountain area was sparsely populated, it did not require heavy military occupation. This made the town relatively safe for Jews. There even was a synagogue near the rue des Juifs, the street of the Jews, the oldest synagogue in Europe, a comforting testimony to the town's once thriving Jewish community.

Monsieur Steltzer had a mustache and frequently wore a *casquette*, a visored cap. Madame Steltzer held her bun in place on the back of her head with a brown comb. Every night she used to drop her false teeth into a glass of water on the kitchen table, a fact that did not make her very talkative, and every morning she would publicly reinsert them to restart her discourse. She kept an eye on the store and on her three daughters: Esther, eighteen; Génie, sixteen; and Claire, fifteen. Esther's foot was malformed since birth, which kept her close to the house and within safe distance. Génie was the tidiest and got much attention from everyone. Claire was independent and by far the most difficult of their worries.

Monsieur Steltzer took care of supplying the store with textiles, buttons, zippers, and genuine cotton thread. To beat the restrictions, he used to travel to the peasants scattered in the back mountains of Carpentras, where he exchanged his merchandise for food and seeds for his garden. Based on mutual need, he had developed a robust symbiotic network with the local peasants.

Monsieur Steltzer had a first name at home: Madame Steltzer called him Moishe (Moses in Yiddish). Outside, he had another first name: the Christians called him Monsieur Maurice. Madame

Steltzer did not seem to have any first name. Her daughters called her *mamme* in Yiddish, and I called her Madame Steltzer. Her husband did not call her at all; he just made sure she heard him by slightly raising his voice. The multiplicity of first names made them comfortably Jewish for me.

Monsieur Steltzer's textile peddling and his peasant exchange network did not endear him to the Polish Jews of Avignon. He reminded them too much of their Polish past, the past they felt they had left in Poland when they emigrated to France in the mid-1930s. They had decided to look like the natives, which meant not associating too much with the lower class. Most of these Jews had become honorable merchants in Avignon. If worst came to worst, they sold goods on market days in neighboring towns, always waiting for the customers to come to them. In contrast, Monsieur Steltzer peddled his goods to the peasants one on one. His bicycling among the Gentiles made him an outsider for the Jews of Avignon, who called him a *bauer*, or peasant, in a derogatory way. It was this behavior, however, a second nature to many Jews, that saved my life as well as the lives of his family members.

Monsieur Steltzer did not know how to read Polish or French, but since he had learned Hebrew at a religious school in Poland, he served for a while as a rabbi for the small Jewish community of Carpentras. Monsieur and Madame Steltzer related differently to their Christian neighbors. He genuinely liked them and sympathized with their hardship, and there was gentleness about him. She deeply hated them and despised their way of life, an attitude rooted in a mix of fear, deep distrust, and a religious way of life. In fact, she would have starved her family rather than eat peasant food, as if the peasants were the reincarnation of the anti-Semitism she thought she had left behind in Poland.

In my recent contacts with Claire, I have learned a little more about her family. In the Jewish emigration wave of the early 1930s, the Steltzers came to France with only their oldest daughter, Esther, leaving their two younger daughters behind in Poland. Génie stayed with Madame Steltzer's well-off, religious sister, while Claire remained with her father's sister, who was poor and uneducated. When they arrived in France, Monsieur Steltzer was working as a migrant farm worker. To save money, he fed himself by eating tomatoes straight from the plants, enhancing their flavor by dipping them in salt. Madame Steltzer worked as a maid in richer households.

In 1937, ten-year-old Génie and nine-year-old Claire rejoined their parents in Carpentras. Since their parents had left them at a young age in Poland, they felt as though they were meeting them for the first time. Claire, who adored her Polish aunt, was devastated when she had to rejoin her parents, and soon it became clear to her that her mother did not hold her aunt in high esteem. She felt her mother's animosity toward her aunt as though it were directed toward her, and maybe it was. This situation did not yield a warm relationship between mother and daughter, and Claire's resentment was still present when she visited me in Chicago many years later.

As the war progressed, the Nazi noose tightened around Carpentras. That made Madame Steltzer very uncomfortable, and she wanted to leave. Also, in early 1944, Claire had repeatedly rejected the blunt sexual advances of Pons, the pharmacist. She was frightened when he told her after a few rejections: "I know that you are Jewish and, if you keep refusing, I will have you hanged on a streetlight!" Gentile hostility toward the Jews compounded Madame Steltzer's worry, and she shared her fears with other Jews. Also, she was angry with my mother, who did not want to leave Le Pontet "because of the store." As Claire reported later, Madame Steltzer had once exploded, telling my mother, "You are a pain in the butt with your store!" Ironically, my mother had become the cause of the Steltzers' return to Carpentras.

Stunned by the disappearance of my mother, I remained a few days with the Steltzers in Carpentras after my return with Claire from Le Pontet. Crammed in between the merchandise, the counter, and the customers, I sat for hours in their store, which, in spite of its smaller size, reminded me so much of ours. The store's glass door opened directly onto rue Porte de Mazan. The sidewalk was so narrow that one person could barely walk there, and people with shopping bags had to walk in the street. Behind the counter, rows of button boxes and zippers were piled up on the shelves. A sample of the buttons inside the box was affixed on the front of the box, so that the customers could choose the button before taking down the box. The zippers were "first class," and the cotton thread was "manufactured by Dolphus." It was obvious that Madame Steltzer and her customers were in tune with each other, because she acted with authority. "I have exactly what you need," she would say with her Jewish accent. Her speech was also strongly affected by her false teeth, which did not fit well, and one could hear a characteristic sucking noise between her words.

Under the pressure of the events and with the insistence of his wife, Monsieur Steltzer decided that we all had to go back into hiding and that, for safety, it would be better for us to separate. In Sarrians, a small village between Carpentras and Orange, he knew a good family who would probably be willing to keep me. He told me, "Of course, you understand that it is necessary, but we will keep in touch with you!" Although Claire disputed her parents' decision to send me alone to Sarrians instead of keeping me with her family, their judgment was final.

Monsieur Steltzer took me on the back seat of his bike and pedaled for several hours through the farmland. Madame Steltzer had repaired the torn pocket of the little shirt I was wearing, but I still kept my mother's safety pin attached to it.

11 | He Who Saves One
Single Life . . .

*The world has angels too few
And heaven is overflowing.*

—Samuel Taylor Coleridge,
"To a Young Lady"

June 11, 1944–End of August 1944

Monsieur Steltzer had chosen Sarrians because its location
would further separate me from Venasques and Le Pontet, making it more difficult to trace my whereabouts. I do not remember
the details of how we got there, but suddenly a farm appeared at
the end of a gravel trail off a small side road two to three kilometers past the small village of Sarrians. Just in front of the house,
the gravel trail broadened to a small yard surrounded by bushes
and cypress fences separating the fields from one another and
from the house. There was a large wooden barn door next to the
living quarters, in the same building. I could not see the neigh-

boring farm or the small road back to Sarrians because of the distance and the vegetation.

Monsieur Steltzer set his foot on the gravel while holding the bike straight until I could get down. He then removed the metal rings that held the bottom of his pants tight to his legs. (It was customary for male bike riders to use these rings to prevent their pants from getting messed up by the black grease of the bike chain or simply being caught in the chain.) As soon as I touched the ground, Monsieur Steltzer told me, "These are Monsieur and Madame Brès," pointing at the two people, roughly his age, who had come out of the smaller door in front of the building. Referring to me, he immediately addressed them. "His mother was just arrested by the Germans," he said. "Can you keep him?" Monsieur Brès accepted without a hesitation. Monsieur Steltzer, who was worried, did not spend much time at the farm and promised that he would come back to see me once in a while. As he left to rejoin his own family, Monsieur and Madame Brès took me inside the house.

Overcome by sadness, I sat quietly at the kitchen table, facing the large fireplace used for cooking and, in winter, for heating. To distract me, Monsieur Brès then took me outside and showed me the surrounding fields. There were several sections separated by cypress hedges to protect the plants from the mistral. In each section, there were different crops: melons, tomatoes, and grapevines. When we came back to the house, all the children had already arrived. Their oldest son, Fernand, was a *sourcier*, a dowser, who had the undisputed ability to find water springs by using his "personal fluid." This is how he was introduced to me. Next was their daughter Mireille, who had a little two- or three-year-old son, Robert. Then came their daughter Magali, who was sixteen years old, and finally, Michel, an adopted Polish child whose parents had died. Michel and I would sleep together, because he was "just [my] age." Everybody was kind to me, but, angry with my mother for abandoning me, I waited for darkness to cry silently in my bed.

The next morning Michel showed me the remains of a British airplane that had fallen fifty feet away from the house during the last bombardment. He knew that this was a British plane because, contrary to the Americans, the British were "not afraid to take more risks and fly low so they could hit the target precisely." The remains of a parachute were entangled inside the charred cockpit. Michel mentioned that the pilot did not survive. I was happy that this one airplane would not frighten me anymore, as had the planes that bombed Le Pontet, but, on the other hand, I knew that the pilots were "on our side."

Because Sarrians was a remote village with little strategic value, the Brès' farm was safe from direct air attacks. However, low-flying British airplanes often passed over us during their missions, and I soon learned how to recognize their Spitfires attacking the German antiaircraft batteries. During the following week, we climbed on the roof of the barn to watch the fires down in the valley caused by the relentless bombings. From the top of the barn we could also judge where the hits had occurred. The bombings were particularly spectacular because of the darkness. One night, the city of Orange caught fire.

I soon learned that the Militia and the German police were operating in the village. A few weeks before my arrival, Albin Durand, a neighboring farmer and a member of the Resistance, had been denounced to the German police. They came at night and burst into his bedroom. He was caught along with an accomplice and interrogated at the farm. To force him to talk about his connections, his legs were cut off with his own electric saw. He was then shot and his farm set on fire. A report obtained by Serge Klarsfeld confirms this story:

> On April 1, 1944, in Sarrians, around 20:30, a formation of German soldiers led by SD[1] agents, surround the farm of Mr. Durand, active member of the Resistance; Mr. Durand and Mr. Diouf, chief of an FFI[2] group, are arrested, tortured, and shot in the yard of the farm. Then, the farm is set on fire. Shortly thereafter, the discovery of Durand's body allowed

the observation that both his legs were cut off above the knees.[3]

The willingness of the Brès family to take me despite the brutal treatment of their neighbors shows that they were fully aware of the fate awaiting me had they refused. They seemed unimpressed by the danger caused by my presence, and the Nazi action against their neighbors did not deter them. Quite the contrary. Although they were ordinary people—perhaps too ordinary for some of their neighbors—they made a conscious decision to follow what they knew in their hearts was right. The Brès had access to the same information as their peers, and yet they acted differently. It is not what they knew that set them apart, but what they did.

The day after my arrival, Monsieur Brès gathered us around the large kitchen table and declared that I had to go to school, because my staying at home could raise suspicion among the neighboring peasants. He told me to keep to myself at school. This was around the twelfth of June, and school would end about the fourteenth of July. Magali was to take me to school the next morning, together with Michel. We had to walk the two or three kilometers to the village because there was no room for a second child on Magali's bike. We arrived at the school before classes began and went straight to the principal, who asked Magali who I was. Surprisingly, the Brès had not thought about that question ahead of time, and Magali was dumfounded. So, I had to improvise. I told him I was cousin from Toulon, which I had chosen because it was several hundred kilometers away and because I had heard on the radio that this German stronghold on the Mediterranean coast had been severely bombed. The principal asked Magali for my school documents, which we did not have, and again she could not answer. So I lied again and said that the documents had been lost when my parents were killed during the last bombardment. And that was the end of questioning at school. On my return to the farm, I got a hero's welcome because I had saved their lives, they said, by my poised lies. When my mother was still around, I had always been open and candid. It would not have occurred to me to lie for my safety because I had not experienced any need to do so before. In just a few days, though, I had become an eight-year-old survivor, a *résistant* by force of circumstance.

The last four weeks of school went easily for me. Having no problem with the material, I was able to do my homework and help the other kids with theirs. All the teachers claimed that the schools in Toulon must be excellent. Michel was also in dire need of help, and sometimes it was faster for me to do his homework than to explain to him how to do it. So his grades improved during the last four weeks of class. I discouraged any attempt of the kids to get too close to me, so that no questions would be asked. Even Michel got strict orders to stay away from me at school, so that we would not risk talking too much. I was also instructed to come straight home and not to wander into the village. I was constantly afraid of being discovered.

The early nighttime hours, just before I fell asleep, were the best hours of the day, because I could be me. When nobody was watching me, I could cry without being asked why. The Brès understood my silence about my mother and never tried to break it. Magali once asked me about the safety pin. When I told her my hope, she burst into tears and hugged me.

Nobody celebrated my eighth birthday on June 28, 1944, because I did not tell anybody that it had come.

The Brès were a poor family with no formal education. They had little food on the table and were constantly struggling. Although they received assistance from the government because of their poverty, the rationing coupons were not sufficient. Nonetheless, they generously shared their food with me. Sensing my embarrassment at being an additional mouth to feed, they even pushed me to take second helpings.

One day, while walking back from school, Michel and I decided to deviate slightly from the small road into an orchard of peach trees beyond the little stream along the road. We could no longer resist those huge yellow peaches, which we had spotted in the preceding days. In my memory, the peaches remain larger than grapefruits. We jumped over the stream, passed through the row of cypresses, and darted toward the closest peach tree. Perched on Michel's shoulders, I had just enough time to pick the two largest yellow peaches I could reach before we had to run away. The owner of the orchard had seen us from a distance. As expected, the irate man came to complain to the Brès and threatened to call the police. Monsieur Brès took him aside, and the case was closed. After the peach tree owner had left, Monsieur Brès talked to me "man to man." He was not angry with me at all, just worried that if I did it again he might not be able to avoid the worst. I learned my lesson, but the peaches were so sweet and juicy!

The Brès' crops were watched carefully by the authorities, and they had to turn their harvest over to the government, since violations were punished severely. At the beginning of July, the wheat that was grown clandestinely started yellowing and was ready for harvest. Magali was supposed to watch for unexpected visitors, while everyone else threshed the grain to separate the bran. Tension was high because we were about to make our own bread without using food-rationing coupons. We obtained a few quarts of seeds, and the mechanism Fernand had improvised to produce flour by cracking the wheat between two stones took a long time and much patience. But when the flour was finally ready, Madame Brès took charge and set to bake two small loaves of bread. They did not turn out the way I had expected. The bread did not rise much because the flour was too rough and chunky, and we probably had not waited long enough for the yeast to work. Nevertheless, eating that bread was like eating cake, and we had a feeling of victory.

I have kept a photograph from those days when we were obsessed with food. We were preparing for a feast because the Brès had been able to obtain a scrawny chicken on the black market. Its feathers were plucked, and the chicken was flamed over a wood fire outside to singe off the pinfeathers. Before cooking the bird, the Brès decided to capture the occasion for posterity, and Fernand took a picture of the chicken with his camera "from before the war." I was given the honor of holding the chicken by the neck in front of the camera. Since I had never held a whole chicken in my hands before, I held it stiffly at arm's length. In the picture, proud as a peacock, I looked as skinny as the chicken.

Michel and I often went to catch crayfish in the little stream near the road, but we stayed away from the peaches. Michel's technique was perfect, and we never came back empty-handed. We used to insert a piece of rotten food in the middle of a bundle of dried vines, which we tied together with a steel wire. After throwing the package into the stream, we would wait a couple of hours before pulling it out. Dozens of crayfish would be entangled in the vines. Every time we brought our harvest back, the Brès would greet us with a warm welcome.

The shoulders of the road next to the little stream were covered with abundant grass because of the constant flow of water. Michel and I often searched for four-leaf clovers amid the regular three-leaf kind. The four-leaf ones were rare and said to bring good luck to the finder. Since my mother had disappeared, I felt that I was in particular need of good luck, and I relentlessly searched the clover patches. Unfortunately, the few four-leaf clovers I found did not work as promised.

Sometime in July, Madame Brès noticed that Michel and I were scratching our heads a little too often. An immediate inspection disclosed the truth—we had lice. The treatment was swift. First, our heads were shaved like eggs. Second, she rubbed our heads with a little kerosene that she had gotten in the village. Then, any residual nits that had remained on our scalps had to be systematically destroyed by crushing them between two nails. The whole family participated in this four-hour operation as if it were a national emergency. At the end, without our hair, Michel and I looked like twins.

Fernand Brès was a reputed dowser. He supposedly could determine the location of underground water by using a forked branch from a willow tree. He would hold one fork firmly in each hand while he walked over the area of interest. If there was water underneath his feet, the central part of the branch was supposed to point downward suddenly, in spite of his grip. He demonstrated the method in the yard and "discovered" a spring hidden under the ground, but we could not confirm anything because the Brès could not afford to dig. Nevertheless, the entire family knew for sure that underneath there was water, which they would harness after the war. In addition to his ability to detect water, Fernand was also able to locate hidden objects. He used a pendulum to "capture the vibrations of the hidden object." When the pendulum was close to the object, it would start oscillating wildly because the "energy [was] highest." Being convinced that I had "the talent," he set to show my powers by hiding an object and letting me find it. Armed with the pendulum, I walked around the room, hoping the pendulum would start oscillating. Initially, nothing happened, but what awe appeared on everyone's face when I found the pipe Monsieur Brès had hidden in a shoe box! Fernand needed no more proof of my talent. However, one thing was clear to me: I had found the pipe because of the strong clues that Fernand was involuntarily giving me through his body language. When I was moving away, his body would stiffen, but as I neared the shoe box he would jump with joy.

I got several visits in Sarrians. Monsieur Steltzer came once as promised, and he brought some fruits and vegetables in a box on the back of his bike. He told me that he and his family had gone into hiding in the small village of Mormoiron near Venasques, and that he probably would not be able to see me often because of the numerous checkpoints on the road. Another visitor was René Vernet, our neighbor from Le Pontet. René was serving in the French police in the village of Bédarrides, about fifteen kilometers away. Since it was easy for a policeman to move around, he came to visit me seven or eight times, and he too would bring food in a box on the back of his bike. I have no idea how René got wind of where I was, but his visits were heartwarming for me. I still remember his black bike leaning against the heavy wooden barn door. He was my "connection back home."

The Brès did not completely fit in their surroundings. In fact, every time Michel and I tried to get too close to some of the neighbors, they would chase us away as if we were contagious. They often mentioned in a demeaning way that the Brès were on welfare. In addition, referring to Michel and me, the Brès took in other children, as if they didn't already have enough trouble.

The Brès did not trust some of their neighbors either, and I had the impression that harboring me was a way of reacting against their surroundings. They were very aware of who was cooperating with the Germans or the Vichy government, and they instructed me as to whom I should avoid. The Brès never went to church as most of their neighbors did. They never strolled into the village as the other families did; someone would go to town only when it was necessary. However, inside the limits of their farm, the Brès were warm to each other and to me in particular. Once in a while a trusting friend would come to Monsieur Brès for advice, treating him with considerable respect, as Monsieur Steltzer had done.

A few weeks after my arrival, a young German soldier visited Monsieur Brès and asked to speak with him privately. He arrived on the gravel road, and we all watched anxiously when Monsieur Brès took him into the living quarters. The men stayed there about fifteen minutes. Panic-stricken, I froze next to Magali, but everything seemed all right when they reemerged from the house. They even shook hands and agreed to meet again the next day. After the German left, Monsieur Brès shared the news with us. The soldier had deserted the German army and wanted to join the Resistance. He had learned that Monsieur Brès had connections with the French underground and was hoping to get help from him. Monsieur Brès denied having any contact, but promised the German he'd try and find leads within a few days. Monsieur Brès was successful in scheduling an appointment between the German and the underground. What would happen, I asked, if the German soldier were bait. The people in the underground would liquidate him, Monsieur Brès replied.

I was scared by the incident but comforted by Monsieur Brès's cool thinking. Unfortunately, this was not the end of it. One evening, the Brès received a warning that the German police would come and arrest the men for a follow-up investigation into the Durand affair. Although the informer suggested that it would be wise to sleep outside, Monsieur Brès refused to leave his home. "Fine," he said, "let them come and take me!" Then he went straight to bed. The same warning came several days in a row, but the police never showed up. As for me, I was not afraid of staying put because Monsieur Brès was so quiet and serene.

At the end of the school year, I graduated as expected and had more time to wander around in the wooded area. Michel and I had become inseparable, but we stayed out of trouble.

Everything seemed temporary because people constantly referred to "before the war" as a comparison with our precarious conditions, or to "after the war" when they were hoping for better times. I, too, had resigned myself not to expect my mother back before the end of the war.

At the beginning of August, I suddenly realized that I had lost the precious safety pin that had been on the pocket of my shirt. I searched for hours and could not find it. I had lost more than a simple safety pin: I had lost my last link to my mother. At the same time, though, better news started reaching us over the radio. The Germans were beginning to tremble, and, according to the broadcasts, their military convoys had started moving north. In the distance, the bombardments intensified. People were talking about the war being over soon. When the war was over, I thought, my mother would surely return.

12 | *The Liberation*

August 16, 1944

On this day in mid-August the entire Brès family and I went together to the village of Sarrians for the first time. The news of liberation by the Allied forces had reached us at lightning speed. When we arrived in town, people had assembled in masses in the tiny village square in front of the city hall, as many people as had stood together during Maréchal Pétain's visit to Le Pontet. They lingered on the village square for hours, talking about the incredible events that had just occurred.

In the early afternoon, it became obvious that something unusual was going on inside city hall. Civilians armed with shotguns were walking in and out through the main entrance. The last time I had seen so many guns, they were in the hands of the Germans. People on the square were talking respectfully about those civilians who had "resisted the forces of occupation." They spoke self-importantly about justice prevailing inside; whether this was bloodthirstiness, a sense of moral duty, or both I am not certain. Over and over again, the armed civilians dragged into city hall men and women whose hands were tied behind their backs. After a while, the prisoners were brought out with their hands still tied behind their backs. The women's hair had been shaved, and the crowd booed them and spit on their faces as they passed. The hair of the male prisoners was not shaved, but their faces were bleeding, and they were walking with extreme pain. They were booed, and the people closest to them would also spit on their faces. The words "traitors," "collabo,"[2] and "tribunal of the people" were often heard when a newcomer on the square would ask about what was happening.

Suddenly, I heard a shot coming from the direction of the village hall door, and a wavering man appeared on the doorstep. Blood was streaming out of a large wound on the side of his head. Wavering back and forth and sideways, he advanced a few steps, then he stopped, followed by an armed civilian with a revolver in his right hand. The wounded man advanced again, crossing the street and moving toward the center of the square, where everyone had assembled. Finally, he collapsed in front of the people closest to him in the square. I heard several people yelling "salaud" (dirty pig). Justice had been served because it was "the will of the people."

Two village personalities, Doctor Pons and his wife, were also brought to a summary trial. She was accused of socializing with the Gestapo and fingering the Brès' neighbor, Albin Durand, while her husband was accused of performing abortions on French women who had sex with the Germans. Since the abortions were viewed as encouraging relations with the occupiers, Pons and his wife were both shot by a firing squad against a wall padded with their own mattress to prevent plaster damage. Shooting them against their own mattress was a morbid reminder that they had supported sinful sex.

Everyone was riveted by what was happening on the village square, and so was I. Everything was all right, I felt, because no one questioned what was taking place. Also, I felt safe in the middle of the crowd. I had never seen such a public spectacle, and I was happy that the "pigs" were "finally going to pay," as everyone was saying. But I was particularly happy for another reason: now my mother and I could finally be reunited.

According to the radio, we had been liberated by the Allies—American, British, and French soldiers. I was puzzled, though, because the armed civilians beating the collaborators were the only liberators I had seen so far. Monsieur Brès explained that the Allies were concentrating their effort on the main roads and that the Germans had fled the area. He also said that the purge of the village collaborators would be done by the *résistants* who were coming out of hiding. The purge lasted several days. Each day the same crowd of onlookers gathered on the village square. We would walk to the village early in the morning and return home late in the afternoon, having witnessed righteousness at work.

Rumors circulated that the Resistance was crushing the retreating German army in the narrow Rhône valley north of Valence. The newspapers told of roadsides littered with incapacitated German armored columns and soldiers' bodies. The villagers punctuated their vivid versions of the same stories with macabre details, as if they themselves had just returned from the theater of operations and had participated personally in inflicting this stinging punishment on the Germans. Their descriptions of the exhausted and disorganized German survivors painfully trudging northward along the roadside sounded as if they had been borrowed from accounts of Napoleon's retreat from Russia.

A big celebration dance was to be held the next Saturday night on the village square. The village band was already rehearsing in the clubroom they had used before the war, and everyone went to hear the rehearsal. I had never heard a band playing happy music before. The ball on Saturday was memorable, and everyone was happy. A few fights broke out between young villagers who had had too much wine. Although Michel and I ran around, playing with schoolmates, I was not sure whether I wanted to be happy or not.

Toward the end of August, Monsieur Steltzer appeared on his bike. He was wearing the same metal rings on the bottom of his pants. Now that the Occupation was over, he had come for a visit, and he told me that he would come back and pick me up soon. I did not want to go back to the Steltzers because I was beginning to feel attached to the Brès family. I particularly liked the caring parents, and I liked my friend Michel and he liked me too. I liked Fernand because he treated me with admiration. I liked his sister Magali, who treated me as her little brother. This is why I was hoping that Monsieur Steltzer would not find his way back. As for my mother, I would manage to find her on her return.

Unfortunately, Monsieur Steltzer knew his geography. He reappeared as promised and took me back to Carpentras. Since I did not have any possessions, he was able to fit me on the rear seat of the bike as he had done a few months earlier. It is my understanding that Monsieur and Madame Brès did not ask for one centime in exchange for what they had done for me. And if they had, who could have paid it anyway?

Although I was sad to leave the Brès family, I felt Monsieur Steltzer was taking me a little closer to the return of my mother. I remember the noise of the tires on the gravel path as we were leaving, and I can still see the facade of the farm shrinking behind us. I remember, too, the warmth and the gentleness of the good people who stood by my side while we were leaving. However, I have forgotten their faces.

While struggling with my memories, later in life, I realize that

I have often forgotten my most significant connections to the good people I was leaving behind me. I could not remember their faces, their eyes, their tears, or their touch at the painful moment when I was parting with them. Yet I remember the smallest details of my arrival and of my life in their households. I have found it difficult, I suppose, to look departure straight in the eye.

13 | Back to the Steltzers

Awake, awake, Jerusalem, clothe yourself with splendor,
O arm of the Lord!
Awake as in days of old,
As in former ages!

—Isaiah 51

End of August 1944–October 1944

When I returned to Carpentras, I learned that the Steltzers had been hiding too, living apart from each other to minimize the chance of all of them being caught. They were helped by French peasants whom Monsieur Steltzer had helped before the war, living proof of the biblical passage, "Cast your bread upon the waters: for thou shalt find it after many days" (Ecclesiastes 11:1). It had not been easy for Monsieur Steltzer to find enough different families to hide them. In addition, Madame Steltzer refused food that was not kosher. This meant that they could eat only a small part of the scarce supply, and certainly no meat. Each of them had had a few close calls at checkpoints because they had to move often, which they never did all together. They always traveled alone or in pairs.

From the Steltzers, I learned that, after my mother's arrest, Esther, Génie, and Claire continued picking cherries at the farm in Venasques for a few more days, but they soon left, fearing detection. In addition, a German garrison was stationed in an old castle behind the hills, and two soldiers who often came to eat fresh cherries for free developed a crush on Esther and Claire. The one who was attracted to Claire's "nice blue eyes" had studied music in Paris before the war. His name was Dieter Wolf.[1] While accompanying Claire to the road, he told her, "You and your sisters do not look like farm girls. If I were in your place, I would leave immediately, because the soldier who is trying to charm your dark-haired sister belongs to the SS, and he is experienced at squeezing information out of people." In spite of his supportive attitude, Claire was so scared that she refused to shake his outstretched hand. After this incident, the three sisters did not return to the cherry orchard. They remained near Mormoiron, where the Steltzers had taken refuge. The entire family had been reunited just a few days before Monsieur Steltzer picked me up from Sarrians. Of course, the daughters were not able to go to school, a situation that caused them irreversible damage. Since they were older than I was, school was not mandatory for them. While staying home would have raised suspicions in my case, it would have been an unnecessary risk for them. In addition, they had to work for food.

Back in Carpentras at the end of German occupation, the Steltzers were immediately able to resume their business because the merchandise was still intact. Their neighbors had kept an eye on the store, and no one had broken in.

The following months at the Steltzers were somewhat confusing for me. I was supposed to be happy because everyone else was happy. I was not afraid anymore, as I had been before they took my mother away, and I could safely run around with the other kids. The Steltzers even used to encourage me to mingle.

But I was ready to trade it all in for those scary times before June 5, 1944, because now I was happy on the outside but empty on the inside. Happy on the inside meant that I was the center of my mother's life, but I obviously was not the center of her life anymore. Happy on the inside meant that I could speak my mind, but now I had clammed up. Happy on the inside meant that I had my mother's unconditional support, but that support was now obviously gone. She had vanished.

Initially, I was not eager to go out and play, as the Steltzers suggested I do. Sensing my sadness, Madame Steltzer would ask me to help in the store. There she would give me a box of odd buttons that had fallen off the standard button cards and ask me to match them with the appropriate sets. Or I would fold socks and rearrange them on the shelves. This was a quiet, absorbing job that reminded me of our store in Le Pontet.

Like the Brès, the Steltzers were nice to me, and they never pushed me to come out of my shell. They just suggested things and made it easy for me to accept or refuse. Their kindness made my separation from the Brès easier for me to accept. However, I never talked about the Brès with the Steltzers. It was obvious that the parents liked me very much, and their three daughters did not show any jealousy toward me.

Since I was skinny, everybody gently tried to make me eat more, which was difficult for me because Madame Steltzer's cooking was bland. She just boiled the food and added salt. I hated her cabbage concoctions and her pink borscht, a red beet soup mixed with sour milk. Worst of all was her soup made of dried chestnuts boiled in milk. Also, I missed my mother's attention during the meals. Sometimes Monsieur Steltzer would leave home with some merchandise and bring home peasant food, provided that Madame Steltzer deemed it kosher enough. He also brought back prunes and grapes, and we sometimes got flavorful goat cheese, covered with wild thyme but too ripe for the market. Since Monsieur Steltzer's food supply was neither sufficient nor steady, Madame Steltzer had to supplement her husband's findings. After tough bargaining in her broken French with the grocery store owner, Madame Steltzer bought imperfect fruit and vegetables at a discount, ignoring her daughters' embarrassment with her behavior.

The dinner table was a forum for family discussion. Since the house was not too spacious, the sisters often argued during meals. Who had taken a sweater? Who had last used a lost comb? Whose turn was it to clean the dishes? Génie was often busy taking care of her looks, Claire was trying to avoid contact with the family, and Esther was always complaining about everything and everyone. Constantly running between the kitchen and the dinner table, Madame Steltzer presided over the meal. When all the food was on the table, she was finally able to participate fully in the family discussions. Madame Steltzer was as hard on her husband as she was on everyone else, except me.

I remember the gentleness of Monsieur Steltzer, who was so crucial to my survival. He generally soothed the parties in the family arguments without taking sides, while Madame Steltzer was more judgmental. He would always come home carrying some food or produce. He always brought news home, too, though he did not seem to have time for small talk. He would tell us about the peasants and about the crops. Once, he mentioned the phylloxera that was threatening the vineyards; another time, the potato bugs. Although there were very few cures to save the crops, he was sensitive to the peasants' problems, and this is why they liked him.

Monsieur Steltzer was sometimes dragged against his best judgment to take sides in a controversy at the dinner table. Then he would express his opinion once, without further nagging. To make his point, he often added some popular wisdom that he had absorbed from the peasants in the area.

I noticed that Monsieur Steltzer loved to eat sour milk and raw onions, as my mother did. Later in life, I became very attentive to the real, deep bonds between people that can hide behind subtle food preferences. One example comes to mind. It happened in 1966 in an Air France Caravelle plane on my way to Rome from

Casablanca, where I had been sent by the Israeli government to organize undercover Jewish emigration out of Morocco. As, for security reasons, I had been trained to avoid casual conversations with strangers, my equally taciturn flight neighbor attracted my attention when he ordered orange juice with his lunch, a typical Israeli habit. I was therefore not surprised when he appeared at the Israeli embassy in Rome, where I had preceded him to swap my identity. "Next time," I said to my stunned colleague, "do not order orange juice with your continental lunch! Drink wine like everyone else!"

In Carpentras, I saw American soldiers for the first time. They were everywhere in the streets and on the roads. Every time they showed up, people would greet them with enthusiasm, and kids would beg for chewing gum. I particularly remember the taste of the cinnamon gum. The Americans were soon joined by the British, who did not use as much chewing gum. But this did not bother older kids, who were after cigarettes. Sometimes, we would run away with condom packages that fell from the soldiers' pockets to show them off at school. They were individually wrapped in a khaki plastic with English inscriptions. The older kids explained, with an air of superiority, how they were supposed to be used, but I did not understand them.

Since rationing was still in force, loaves of soft American bread started appearing in bakeries and on the black market. In spite of the food restrictions, people preferred the crisp French bread to the soft American variety. However, since the Americans were the "liberators," nobody dared criticize their bread openly.

Madame Steltzer invited to dinner a Jewish British soldier who brought us military food rations. This was the tastiest meal ever. I especially remember the soldier whipping a can of cream to top the fresh strawberries that he had brought with him. I think that Madame Steltzer had her daughter Génie in mind when she invited the British soldier. He was even invited to celebrate Yom Kippur in the synagogue at Carpentras. The services reminded me of the last High Holiday service I had attended with my parents, when the *shaames* confiscated my toy car. This time I behaved. The services took on special meaning after the preceding dark years, and one could feel the deep emotions. All the men were wearing their prayer shawls, and all the women were upstairs, as was customary. The cantor was extremely moved when he prayed for the "Jews who had left us," which is traditionally done in the middle of the prayer day. Overcome by emotions, some people in the audience were unable to utter a word. I thought that the people present were thinking a lot about those who were absent. At least I was. Even the kreplach soup that Madame Steltzer had prepared for the dinner at the end of the Yom Kippur fast reminded me of my mother.

After the High Holidays, I began attending school again near the Steltzers' home, where I was to stay for almost the entire school year. Their house was at the end of rue Porte de Mazan. Small stores lined each side of the street. At the city limits, toward Mazan, there were two bars. To the left, two parallel streets climbed up to my school—one small street and one large boulevard. To the right, the ring road started its loop around the city. Everywhere the streets were lined with *platanes,* plane trees, which cast a comfortable shadow on hot summer days.

I remember my classroom, but I cannot recall the teachers or many of the kids. I had difficulty seeing the text on the blackboard because I had drifted into near-sightedness without anybody noticing. But this did not bother me very much because I was able to guess the parts I could not read.

Although the school was only two hundred yards away, it could take me an hour to come back to the Steltzers, depending on which friends I was returning with. After a few weeks, my grasp of the school material had become common knowledge, and schoolmates used the way home to get some coaching for their homework assignments. The little fountain at the bottom of the street close to the Steltzers' house was the rallying point. I charged twenty marbles or four agates for a complete math assignment.

Minor help would go for two or three marbles. The Steltzers were proud to see me already "in business," and I enjoyed my newly acquired standing.

All the boys in my school were Christian, and so were most of my friends. Lucienne Rozman was the only Jewish child of my age, and we played together during and after the religious services. Lucienne's kind parents often invited me for dinner, but their food was as insipid as that of the Steltzers. I felt at home with the Rozmans, who lived in a small apartment above the arcades on the main street. Once in a while, I brought a friend along to dinner.

With time, I enjoyed the strolls on Main Street, and I welcomed Madame Steltzer's requests that I run errands for her. Both sidewalks were covered with old-fashioned arcades filled with stores: bakeries, butcher shops, grocery stores, vegetable stands, cheese and fish stores, shoe and textile merchants, newspaper and stationery stores. To better lure the customers, every store displayed stalls of merchandise on the sidewalk under the arcades. Everything one needed could be found on that street, and a variegated wreath of smells accompanied me on my walk: herbs and vegetables, fresh bakeries and spicy delicatessen, succulent cheeses and the fresh aroma of the sea. The sharp smell of anise from pastis, an aniseed liqueur, wafted from the open door of the bar. The smell of rubber shoe soles, household chemicals, and fresh paint jostled with barbershop perfumes.

I had developed a ritual after school. I had noticed that people who had been taken away by the Germans started coming back. They were listed in alphabetical order in the daily newspapers. When the Steltzers, who did not read French, noticed my interest in this section of the newspaper, they made sure to buy *La Marseillaise*, a daily newspaper for the southeast of France, which they would keep for me until my return from school. Since the apartment was pretty dark, I used to sit near the kitchen window that opened onto the street. From the living quarters upstairs, I could see the street humming with people. Unlike during the Occupation when people spent as little time in the street as possible, there was now a sense of abandonment in aimless strolling along the street.

Children noisily played hopscotch on the pavement. The adults had set up their chairs in the street near their doors. Since the doors were close to one another, conversation and gossip could travel from chair to chair all along the street. While Madame Steltzer was cooking dinner, she discreetly watched me read the list of camp survivors in the newspaper, but she never said a word. This ritual continued for months. I was overwhelmed by anguish as the list of names dwindled and finally vanished from the newspaper. My mother's name never showed up, but I was sure that someday she would be back.

During all this time, in spite of the Steltzers' understanding, I never asked about my mother and what had happened to her. Although Madame Steltzer knew that I longed for my mother's return, she never mentioned the subject to me. With time, I also felt that I was not supposed to ask. Yet, whenever a stranger asked about me, Madame Steltzer would take him aside and talk to him in Yiddish. While listening in, I caught bits and pieces of information about my mother's arrest and her deportation. I also got the impression that deportation was an abstract place, not the end of the road. I refused to connect the fate of my mother to the horror stories that had started to appear in many conversations and in the news. I was afraid of the answer I might get, and since I did not want anyone to destroy my fantasies, silence was the best way to hold on to my dreams. Asking about my mother was like admitting publicly that I missed her, and this admission was like disclosing a deep, dark secret. Every day became temporary, and I started waiting for tomorrow.

14 | *The Soldier's Tale*

THE SOLDIER

(Back in his village)

"Hurray, here we are!" *We're home at last.* "Good
    Morning, Mrs. Gray!"
She is in the garden. "Hello there! How's the world with
    you?"
"She doesn't hear me," *never mind—there's Arthur,*
    "Hey!"
"Hey! Arthur!" *He's mowing the five-acre meadow, a*
    good old friend and true . . .
Eh? What's the matter, he doesn't reply?
    "Arthur, hi! Don't you know me, why
    It's Joseph—Joseph the soldier—Jo!
    You remember him! You know!" . . .
The mower mows on, and on we go.
And there's the school, with the tower and the bell,
Joseph, old Jo, you remember him well!
Here's the mill, the inn, now villagers everywhere.
Men, women and children stand and stare.
    "What's the matter? What's up with the lot of you?
        What's got
    Into you all? Are you afraid of me, or what?
    You know me! All of you there!

Joseph!" *No one speaks*
And then a door slams, and another slams, and more and
more,
And the rusty hinges shriek
As every door
Slams shut. "That's funny, but mother will know.
I'd better go . . ."
She sees him coming, she screams, and runs away.
But then he thinks, "There's my fiancée."
Married!
With two children!
—Stravinsky/Ramuz, *The Soldier's Tale*

October 1944–Spring 1945

One day in October, I came back from school as usual. When I entered the house, a small soldier in uniform was sitting on a chair and speaking Yiddish with Madame Steltzer. No one else was home. When Madame Steltzer announced, "This is your father," it was as if I had been struck by lightning. I could not move. The man—I mean, my father—got up and silently hugged me. My body stiffened. He started crying all over my shirt. The more he cried, the more I stiffened, and the more I stiffened, the more he cried. Revolted by his intrusion, a thousand thoughts raced through my mind. How could a grown-up cry so much and in broad daylight? Why did he care so much about the loss of my mom? Nobody had the right to hug me like my mom used to do!

The episode with my father seemed to last forever. Finally, he dragged me onto his lap and started telling me Bible stories. He realized that my Jewish education was sorely lacking, and catching up was his first priority. After he left, I felt relieved, but I was worried because he said that he would be back. I made sure not to touch the chair he had sat on when he had taken me on his lap. I felt that my father was robbing me of my memories of my mother, and I was not ready to share them with him or with anybody else. This is why I cried that night. Madame Steltzer had called my father Meijlech. My mother had always told me that his name was Max, although the Jews from Poland called him Meijlech.

My father's visits were infrequent because he had to rebuild the business. I thought that was good. He told me, though, that someday he would take me with him. Since he gave me no firm date, I assumed that it would take some time, but I did not show my satisfaction at that thought. The visits, the hugs, and the Bible lessons continued, and I remained stiff. The biblical stories were safe conversation, and I even began liking them. I was struck by my father's biblical knowledge. He knew all the stories by heart. One of the first stories he told me was about Joseph in Egypt. I did not understand how Joseph's brothers could sell him as a slave, because I had not personally experienced sibling jealousy, but I certainly sympathized with Joseph's abandonment and determination to survive. I remember Joseph's dream about the seven fat cows and the seven lean cows, and how the lean ones devoured the fat ones. "It meant that the Egyptians would have seven years of great plenty, followed by seven years of famine," my father explained, "and if the people did not plan carefully and save, they would eat up all their crops and starve during the years of famine. What could the Egyptians have done without the Jews?" This was my father's way of telling me that it is the God-given role of a Jew always to think about tomorrow. The story of Joseph led to a discussion of the exodus from Egypt and the story of Passover. I heard all about the miseries of the Jews at the hands of the Egyptians. My father also told me the tale of Esther, another story of Jewish suffering. My father's predilection for tales of Jewish persecution made me feel uncomfortable. In apparent contrast to other people, the Jews always needed godly interventions to save them from barbarian hands. I wished the Jews had been more self-reliant.

When my father came to visit, he would talk with the Steltzers about his "captivity" in Switzerland. Eager to maintain its traditional status of neutrality, the Swiss government had refused to liberate its internees from the Allied countries. My father tried to escape twice: the first time he had been caught by the Swiss border patrol, but the second time he was successful. He often told about his anti-Semitic Polish camp commander, about his long workdays in the camp, and about his relief when he was allowed to live and work with a kind Swiss Protestant family. He had tears in his eyes when he mentioned that they had a young son, just my age, who reminded him of his lost family life. Although he was not talking to me, I did not like this part of his story, because it reinforced the sadness that dwelled in my family. Happiness seemed forever gone, and I would have preferred him to promise me the stars.

The Steltzers' daughters were all becoming a problem. Esther, the oldest, was always complaining and telling everyone how things should be. She did not yet have a Jewish boyfriend, and that was Madame Steltzer's first problem. Génie was the second problem, because the Jewish soldier did not seem to take the bait in spite of all her efforts, smiles, and innuendos. Claire caused the biggest worry because she was able to manage on her own. Every day she would go out "to see another girlfriend." That worked nicely until the day Madame Steltzer did not find her at the friend's house. Her explanation did not seem to convince her mother, who grounded her for a few days, but she found a solution by volunteering to work in the family vegetable garden whenever there was a need. Claire was happy again.

The vegetable garden was a rented plot on the outskirts of the city. One had to take the outer ring road around the city for about three hundred meters, following a gravel esplanade that was the site of the Provence bowling games. On bright summer days, the shade of the *platanes* enabled the best shots. While commenting on the game, spectators and players alike enjoyed a double pastis, which is why most older men in the area had ruddy noses and cheeks. The Steltzers' garden plot was at the end of the esplanade. Being practical, the Steltzers grew vegetables and fruits but no flowers.

One day at the end of spring, I overheard a fateful conversation. Claire was speaking in French, her mother in Yiddish. Madame Steltzer said, "Your waist is becoming larger!" Claire responded, "Mother!" Without paying any attention to me because I was "too young to understand," Madame Steltzer began nervously sizing her daughter's waist several times a day. I made sure not to disclose my deep curiosity and pretended to be absorbed in my homework or to play with a toy. One day, her mother finally said it, "My God, Claire, you are pregnant!" Claire burst into tears. Her mother asked, "Who did that to you?" It was young Goumarre, the son of a Catholic paint store owner. "Did he do it in the vegetable garden?" Madame Steltzer asked. When Claire nodded, her mother became hysterical, and a flow of Yiddish imprecations rolled out of her mouth. Monsieur Steltzer tried to calm her, but on that day there was no small talk at the Steltzers' dinner table.

The next morning Claire left for Avignon, alone and penniless. A friend of the family found her wandering aimlessly and kept her for a few days until things cooled down back home. Many Jews from Carpentras and Avignon got involved. Some gave moderating advice and others reignited the fire. Finally, the Steltzers resigned themselves to contemplating a wedding. Where to hold the wedding was a bone of contention. The Goumarres wanted a church wedding, and Madame Steltzer wanted a civil one. Finally, they both got what they wanted, but Madame Steltzer did not go to the church. While Madame Steltzer was devastated by the whole matter, Monsieur Steltzer considered it one more act of God.

Toward the end of the school year, my father said that he could now care for me and took me with him to Le Pontet. I was still stiff when he touched me, but I had become used to it.

I remember all the Steltzers and their care for me. I remember Claire in particular. But I do not remember saying good-bye to any of them. Once again, I have forgotten the parting moments.

15 | *Back to Normal*

We had to leave the job half-finished.

—Aloïs Brunner, the fugitive Drancy camp
commander, to *Kronen Zeitung*, Damascus,
December 19, 1987

July 1945–September 1945

In July 1945 I made my first visit to my home since June 7, 1944, a little more than a year earlier. I stood silently in the middle of the store. The counter, the wall paint, and the desk were the same as during my last visit. Even the wine marks on the floor tiles had not gone away. But the empty shelves had been restocked with merchandise, much like they were when my mother was still around. I went to the kitchen and found the same appliances and the same furniture. The armchair where I had cuddled up with her was still there, just below the electric meter. However, the dried omelet in the oven was gone, and fresh food was stacked in the wall closet. I went upstairs and found the same beds, the same closets, the same ladder to the attic. Some rooms had been replenished with stocks of merchandise. Everything was back to normal, it seemed, except that I had had to trade my mother for my father.

Despite its contents, the house felt empty. While I kept searching for clues, I found in the wall closet our old box of photographs, which the Nazis had neglected to take away. The pictures of my mother and me put a little warmth back into the cold house, and I used them as an occasional refuge. They helped me keep my early years alive inside by preserving my memories.

My father tried hard, but my stiffness would not go away. He prepared food, took care of the house, attended to the store, and got my clothes cleaned and repaired. He made sure that I ate what he had prepared, but I preferred *tartines*, bread spread with a thick layer of butter and sprinkled with a lot of grated bittersweet chocolate. Because of the food restrictions still in force, my father did not want me to take my *tartines* outside lest people become envious. Often, he would prepare sour milk by leaving fresh milk to cure spontaneously in a few drinking glasses. To protect the milk from the omnipresent flies, he would set the glasses on a tray and put the tray in the kitchen wall closet. Sour milk was one of his favorite foods, which he would eat with boiled potatoes and raw onion. Every time he prepared it, he unknowingly brought back sweet memories for me, because my mother had done it the exact same way. Although neither of them ever succeeded in convincing me to taste the sour milk, I felt some comfort in the subtle linkage between the two of them, a link that came all the way from their native Poland.

Many of our Jewish friends from the past had "returned," as people used to say in those days. They visited my father as they had formerly visited my mother. There was no need to ask where the Sokolowskis, the Schneiders, and the Kurlandczyks had been before their return, because everyone had heard their stories of hiding, their narrow escapes, and their machinations to survive. There was no need, either, to inquire where David Ehrenfreund, the dentist, had returned from, because he had remained silent since his return, and everyone knew why. Part of him, it seemed, had not come back. "It will take him a long time to recover from that hell," people whispered behind his back.

The visitors often came early in the afternoon, when customers were rare, and sat around the table in the kitchen. My father's captivity in Switzerland was usually the main topic of discussion, and the visitors would also tell about their own experiences. In their memories, good and evil were clear and distinct: there were good people who had helped them and anti-Semites ready to deliver them to the Nazis. All would conclude their stories with loaded sighs, careful not to touch on painful subjects in front of me. The day of Beracha's visit, however, was a notable exception. My father had just described the German armored trains crossing into the Tessin district, close to the Italian border, where he had spent some of his internment in 1944. The Swiss train story seemed to bring to the surface the painful past of Beracha, who ignored my father's hints to watch his words in front of me. He went on to tell about his own arrest, "on June 6, 1944, the same day as Madame Levandel." He described in vivid detail the brutality of the police and his determination to escape at the first opportunity, which presented itself in the sealed train car after leaving Avignon en route for deportation. "Together with another man, I jumped from the moving train through a hole in the car wall," said Beracha, possessed by his own words and still shaken by emotion. "In spite of our urging," he added in disbelief, "Madame Levandel refused to join us because her handbag could not pass through the hole." Angrily, my father, who clearly did not believe Beracha, finally stopped him, as he engaged in a gruesome description of the concentration camps he had avoided by his escape. Beracha's visit and my mother's refusal to jump from the train left me with a bitter doubt about her determination to return home.

I used to watch my father shave with the "Swiss razor" that he had brought from "captivity." After frothing the lather with his brush, he would cover most of his face with it and then begin to shave. I felt more at ease when his face was covered with the shaving cream. After shaving, he ritually sharpened the razor blade "for next time," using the leather sharpening belt that came with the razor.

My father watched my language, which had become somewhat dirty because of my newfound friends, and I became very careful when I was around him. He did everything that he was supposed to do, but he never talked with me about my mother and did not seem to pay attention to my sadness. I felt as if she existed only in my heart. When I did something wrong, he would get angry with me, but it wasn't a good, constructive kind of anger like my mother had. When she was angry with me, I was never afraid because I knew she loved me. In my father's anger, there was no room for me, and there was no room for my feelings. He would be angry for hours before confronting me. During this eternity, I had to remain silent because he was silent. When he finally exploded, I remained silent because he did not expect a dialogue, and by then I was emotionally drained.

At night, I used to lie in my bed and imagine how it would be when my mother came back. I would cry because time seemed too long, but I never asked my father anything about her because I did not want him to be aware of my longing for her. I knew that he grieved for her, because people's sympathy brought tears to his eyes, but his silence became my silence. For months, however, I waited for some signal that never came, some acknowledgment of what I was feeling. This new beginning with my father developed into a lifelong pattern of coldheartedness between us, a kind of rivalry of silence.

Once in a while, my father left to replenish the store with new merchandise. Then I used to stay with Monsieur and Madame Meffre, who owned the cooperative grocery store next to our store. I would occasionally spend the night with them when my father did not return the same day. The Meffres cared for me because their children were already grown up.

As I often went to buy groceries and bread, I speedily reconnected with the village fabric. By then everyone was nice to me again, but I did not care much for that. On my grocery missions, I was stricken to hear people tell their glorious tales of war. During every one of my visits, for instance, Auguste Fage heroically claimed for my benefit that, being in the Resistance, he had owned a submachine gun. "When they came to arrest Madame Levandel," he proudly stated in front of his customers, "I would have gone out and gunned the pigs down, if my family had not held me back." Having one's relatives protecting one's security was a luxury few Jews could afford. Incidentally, all the people who had cheered Pétain during his 1941 visit were claiming now that they had been in the Resistance. Baffled by this change of attitude, I felt as if I had awoken suddenly from a bad dream. My heart still pounding, I was back in familiar surroundings, but the nightmare monsters seemed to exist only for me. How easy it was for crowds to change sides when the wind changed, readily forgetting the anguish and the pain they had inflicted on us. How easy it was for people to "turn their jackets inside out," as the French say.

Of course, the villagers got some help in forgetting the past. In Avignon, as in other places, the summary trials and executions were still going on at the hands of the FFI (Forces Françaises de l'Intérieur), the union of all the groups who had fought the guerilla war against the Nazis. In a ritual of vindictive righteousness, the outer wall of the Avignon cemetery near the main road between Avignon and Le Pontet had been chosen as a public execution place to "teach them a lesson." Although the children were told to stay away, I could see, during a bus trip to Avignon, the wall completely covered with bullet marks. That in itself was enough to rearrange the memory of a Frenchman of good descent.

Although most of the purges had occurred before my return to Le Pontet, the memories were still fresh. FFI Commander Paul Montlahuc and Lieutenant Raoul Davidou established their headquarters at the village hall; from this position of authority they presided over the administration of popular justice. Under the leadership of Davidou, the purge committee recorded its proceedings in collaboration files, which disappeared when the legitimate government took office and remained hidden for forty-eight years. In 1992, I followed a rumor claiming that a loyal *résistant*, disappointed by the apparent immunity granted to many collaborators, had decided to keep the files as a silent testimony.[1] Fortunately, these files reappeared at last in 1993, and are currently in the possession of Serge Klarsfeld, a Parisian lawyer, Nazi hunter, and historian of the Holocaust. The purge files abound with details of villagers' testimonies and include a list of eighty *miliciens* from the area. Among the documents, the signed confession of Victor Cisterni, the deposed mayor of Le Pontet, confirms my memory of him.

Monsieur Cisterni denies . . . having followed Vichy's directives, but admits having indirectly participated in collaboration. Monsieur Cisterni recognizes having posted in the hallway of a Jew a poster bearing his name, Jacques Cohen, but denies having posted the name on the outside. In addition, Monsieur Cisterni declares having posted the names of all the tenants in furnished and unfurnished apartments.

Done at Le Pontet on October 4, 1944
(Signed by Cisterni and witnessed by Davidou)

Frustration and anger, accumulated during the German occupation, burst out into the open, and settling accounts became part and parcel of the joys of liberation. In a letter to the president of the Vaucluse purge committee, Le Pontet's vice-mayor, Marcel Doux, invokes popular furor against a collaborator, Madame Bruno.

September 18, 1944

Monsieur le Président,

As vice-mayor, I am honored to convey to you the expression of popular dissatisfaction about the attitude of Madame Bruno, so far arrested three times and three times released.

Le Pontet's population is astonished, since this person has shown enough proof of her attachment to the German soldiers,

either in her acts or in her words. The entire population is asking for an exemplary punishment. However, nothing of that kind has happened so far. On the contrary, this person has been able to move freely in Le Pontet between arrests and continues to flout the honest people who surround her: prisoners' wives, résistants' wives, all the Gaullists and FFI sympathizers.

If this person, who has been arrested for the fourth time, were to be released once more despite the complaints [against her], we could not be held responsible for the incidents or accidents which might result.

A large number of testimonies focus on the economic benefits of collaboration. For example, Jean Chaleyer, the owner of a large herd of cows, served as the exclusive supplier of meat and dairy products to the German headquarters in Avignon.

The witnesses also declare that Monsieur Chaleyer was the official provider of Hotel Crillon, which was seized by the German operation troops. He provided them with calves, sheep, lambs, pigs, chickens, vegetables, milk, butter, and cheese. (This is not the case now for the provisioning of the FFI, to whom he delivers only rotten potatoes for which he requires immediate cash payment.)

Monsieur Cerutti adds that Monsieur Chaleyer benefited from the privilege of transforming milk into butter and cheese, a privilege granted to him by Monsieur Richard. Monsieur Chaleyer also kept his employees under the menace of denunciation to the Gestapo. Among other things, he threatened to denounce one of his Jewish employees to the Gestapo, to the point that the employee had to resign his job in order to avoid deportation as a Jew.

Cerutti, the witness, was no saint either, since a few weeks later he was caught stealing hay from the FFI. Neighbors were pitted against neighbors, and changing sides added to the confusion. For instance, our neighbor Gros, the restaurant owner who himself had been a host to the Gestapo, testified that he had to fire an employee, Auguste Allegre, for bringing bread stolen from the Germans and selling it on the black market. According to Gros, Allegre, claiming membership in the Parti Populaire Français (PPF), had threatened him with arrest by the Germans.

Since economic collaborators had been able to flourish while their starving countrymen were barely able to subsist on their meager rations, economic collaboration triggered intense hatred among the villagers and was swiftly punished during the purges. Sexual collaborators, on the other hand, were treated with a contempt deeper than that normally reserved for the worst kind of prostitutes. After seventeen-year-old Elise Pascal confessed having had "intimate relationships with a German soldier," her head was shaved and she was publicly paraded, a punishment commensurate with her crime. Lucienne Escudier, the hairdresser, was also the object of public outrage. Investigation proceedings summarize the testimonies against her:

> **Mademoiselle Escudier from Vedène is established as a hairdresser in Le Pontet. She appears to have easy morals, and some say she is pretty naive.**
>
> **She has had numerous relationships with German soldiers (diurnal and nocturnal) and has probably been associated with a number of Gestapo members, since she often threatened her neighbors with denunciation to the Gestapo.**
>
> **For instance, two persons who were seeking counterfeit identity cards were arrested by the Gestapo three days after she became aware of them. . . .**
>
> **I must add that Mademoiselle Escudier was arrested on September 16 [1944]. She remained in jail approximately one month before she was released.**

When I came back to Le Pontet, Lucienne, who had gone into temporary seclusion to wait out the storm, quietly reappeared. At the café, the men proclaimed for the benefit of their delighted audience that she should have named her toddler "Fritz" in a blunt reference to his German father. I felt some secret sympathy for her, however, because of the loaves of German bread she had provided for us one year earlier and because of her banishment by the villagers.

The victory over Germany was the subject of every conversation, and it seemed as if every Frenchman had won that victory personally. People were particularly delighted with the pictures of German cities reduced to rubble that appeared on the front pages of the newspapers. It dawned on me that the German soldiers, who occupied our area in November 1942, had civilian family members left behind in Germany, but I did not care because no one else did. Germany and the German Nazis were one and the same to me and everyone else.

The presence of the American military on French territory was also a reminder of the recent German defeat. The villagers did not like the young Jeep drivers because they drove like crazy and flipped over at the sharp turn of the road toward the village of Montfavet. Nevertheless, the Americans were still very popular. Also, their presence provided a certain amount of comfort to a small group of profiteers and traffickers, and to their chain of customers. I would often see some of my neighbors carrying home army gasoline cans. Since the Americans colored the gasoline pink or green, it was easy to guess who was using stolen fuel. These practices were usually overlooked. Once in a while, though, somebody got caught tapping into the American military pipelines to steal gasoline and sell it on the black market.

My father received a pair of shoes for me from a war prisoners' relief organization. Unfortunately, they were girls' shoes with high heels, and I did not want to keep them; boys don't wear girls' shoes. My father, however, insisted that I wear them because there was no other choice. I so badly needed my father to reassure me that I was a boy like other boys, but apparently this was of no concern to him. I hated his insensitivity, so I staged a little comedy. I acted as if I were incapable of walking in those shoes because of the heels. When I twisted my ankle, my father gave up because he feared doctors and did not want to risk any injury requiring treatment. Fortunately, one of our handy neighbors was manufacturing sandals with soles made of worn-out car tires. He sold these makeshift sandals at a premium because he did not have any competition from the legitimate shoe stores.

Little by little, life returned to normal. Heavy traffic had taken over Route Nationale Numéro Sept, and the newer cars that could drive up to eighty kilometers an hour were the talk of the day. For the first time, rear-light blinkers had replaced the electromagnetic turn signals that used to come up and down on the sides of the cars like little luminous arms.

People were back on the streets and filled the tables of the outdoor cafés, while children played outside on the sidewalks. We often ate lunch at the Café de la Paix, owned by Monsieur Lagriffe, because my father was seldom able to cook. At the lunch table, the men would speak of their wartime feats and miseries with great gestures and intonation, as is customary in Provence. They also talked about the concentration camps and what had happened there, because this was becoming public knowledge. Many of the graphic details about the camps came from the weekly newsreels they had watched at Monsieur Gros's movie theater. They spoke, too, about "poor Monsieur Beccarud who did not come back." They always called him "poor Monsieur Beccarud," because, in Le Pontet, this is the way one refers to someone one knows well who had died. Sometimes I also heard them say "poor Madame Levandel who did not come back," but this was always said behind my back. Stating that my mother did not come back seemed less permanent than calling her "poor."

After lunch, I usually went back to play with my friends, as my father lingered to play belote, a popular card game for two, three, or four players. Sometimes I stayed and watched the game, and once the men took me in as a fourth player because there were only three adults on hand.

One day, I noticed that my father had started going to the Sporting Bar for a cup of coffee after the card game. When I told him that Monsieur Gros, the owner, had been a collaborator, he confronted the man and ceased going there.

At the end of the school year, my father registered me for a summer camp at Digne in the Alps. I did not want to go, but he did not ask me whether I wanted to go or not. My mother would have asked, and I probably would have refused to go. The camp was organized for children of war prisoners, and it was supposed to be a big deal, but I just did not want to meet new kids. Also, I feared moving again. I went anyway because my desires did not matter that much.

In the camp, most of the children were wild, and the counselors acted as if they were doing us a favor. There, I met Jacques Saltzman, the child who, together with me, had defecated on our rug when my mother locked us up in the bedroom. His mother had also been taken by the Germans and had not come back. This gave a special unspoken meaning to our relationship. Many times in my later years, I have experienced the same silent bonding when I met a Jew who lost a parent during the war.

Most of the kids at the camp were Catholics, and we stayed away from them. However, one boy named Jean Schwartz stood out. Jacques and I approached him and suggested that he was Jewish. Fearing a trap, the boy denied it. So we invited him to a penis identification in the boys' bathroom: we would show ours first. We had taken our penises out and he started showing his when we heard the voice of the counselor behind us: "Ah! Ah! We are measuring it, aren't we?" It was an embarrassing moment, but I had finally found a use for the branding of my body. Jean Schwartz was indeed Jewish, and we were now three of a kind. Our circumcisions had become our real "covenant,"[2] a sort of alliance of fates.

Since the discipline at the camp was rigid, we developed tricks to bypass the system and faked illness to avoid unpleasant activities. The kids were cruel to each other, and survival was the rule of the game. One had to keep one's important things hidden or else they would disappear, and the counselors didn't care. We enjoyed eating the candies of the weaker kids. We also experimented with eating some of the brand-new toothpaste that stores had started carrying instead of the usual hard "tooth soap," and we found the taste exceptional.

I felt so unhappy there that I was so elated to leave, and I found the trip back delightful. For the first time, I was eager to see my father again. As a matter of fact, I was becoming used to him, because he was the only adult in my life. Unfortunately, on my return, he told me that he had decided it would be more appropriate for me to stay with the Sourets, a peasant family in the area, because he had to travel often and could not take care of me properly. Our neighbor, Monsieur Meffre, had recommended the Sourets. I had no say in the matter. I would leave just after the High Holidays. The reunion with my father had lasted three months.

Although we did not fast during the High Holidays, my father took me to the Yom Kippur service. He prepared his prayer book and his prayer shawl, and wrapped them up in a brown paper bag so that "the goyim won't notice." The other Jews approaching the synagogue of Avignon also carried their Judaism inside brown paper bags.

When we entered the circular synagogue, we were greeted by the Jews who had preceded us inside. Dressed for the occasion, the seated Jews greeted the newcomers, and the newcomers greeted their greeters, until the synagogue was full, which occurred well before the service began. With everyone engaged in quiet dialogues with their neighbors, it looked like the community was whole again and everyone had returned.

The community became silent as soon as the rabbi began the service. The prayers in Hebrew and the occasional commentaries in French sounded sad, but my mind was focused on earlier times, and I paid no attention. I was remembering how I had played with my toy car near the center stage of the synagogue when my mother was still with me and how she had argued with the caretaker of the synagogue. Like many other encounters I had in those days, this visit to the synagogue etched her memory a little deeper into my consciousness. In the middle of the day of prayers, my father took me under his prayer shawl when the rabbi started reading the list of *les disparus*, those who had disappeared. Like many in the audience, my father was sobbing. I felt violated by his emotion, but my throat tightened to a knot when I heard the rabbi read the name "Sara Lewendel, born Goldstein."

When we left the synagogue, all the Jews greeted each other with the traditional Yiddish greeting "A git yomtef!" (Have a good holiday!). I did not see what was good about Yom Kippur, since the Jews spent their time flagellating themselves. On our way out, I noticed a large marble plate above the entrance to the synagogue. Etched in stone, in alphabetical order, were all the names of *les disparus*, including my mother's name. Ill at ease with the public display of her name, I was happy to leave.

Just before going to the Sourets, I noticed, to my dismay, that my father was again having his coffee at the Sporting Bar. I do not remember Monsieur Gros ever being implicated publicly during the postwar collaboration trials, although, to this day, the village elders will readily tell you that he was working for the Germans "as surely as death and taxes," lowering their voices as their story progresses. If you ask them why he was not indicted, they will claim ignorance, their eloquent facial expressions suggesting they know more than they are ready to say. They will also tell you with an air of mystery that he was not the only collaborator to melt quietly back into the village. In the 1950s, Gros was shot by one of his mistresses. He died at once, taking his secrets with him to his grave.

During the summer of 1945, my father and I were closer than ever, and yet we did not connect. The routine of our life together had made me feel that, with time, we would open up to each other, but by sending me to the Sourets, my father forever closed the door on this glimmer of hope. This was the beginning of a new separation. When I left, however, my sense of relief overcame my disappointment.

16 | The Family Souret

If you differ from me, brother, far from harming me,
you enrich me.

> —Antoine de Saint-Exupéry,
> *Letter to a Hostage*

September 1945–Spring 1946

The Souret family lived four kilometers from Le Pontet. When my father and I arrived early in the afternoon, we were greeted by Madame Souret, a fat lady three to four times the width of my father. The house stank. There were at least a dozen cats and dogs in sight, and Madame Souret informed me where and when each one had been found and adopted. One of the cats was "intelligent" because he could "fetch olives from the jar." I was to stay there, and my father would visit whenever possible. After making the financial arrangements, he left for the store, and I did not miss him. Madame Souret had me sit down in the dining area to help her peel potatoes. She was inquisitive about my past and present, and she seemed like a nice person. Although she was old, she acted as an equal because she talked simply. I helped prepare dinner while the rest of the family was working. When the family members arrived for dinner, all within a few minutes of one another, I realized how quickly the time had passed. They all stank no matter how far away I stood.

The centerpiece of the dinner was a meatless potato stew. Tomatoes, olives, garlic, onion, thyme, and bay leaves created a strong flavor that compensated for the absence of meat. At the dinner table, I learned what I needed to know about the family. There were four children. Paul, twenty-eight, had just returned from a prison camp in Germany. His experiences there had made him irritable. He was in charge of the cows. Julien, twenty-four, took care of cutting the hay for the cows. He was also in charge of the pigs. Renée, twenty, had not passed her *certificat d'étude*, the grammar school final exam, and had been kicked out of school when she turned eighteen. She was in charge of the chickens and geese. Germaine, seventeen, was still in grammar school because she had not yet passed her *certificat d'étude*, which one normally passes at age fourteen. She had to go to a parochial school, La Grangette, because the public school would no longer accept her. She had been warned that she could not stay in parochial school beyond the age of eighteen. She was in charge of feeding the chickens and picking the eggs. Monsieur Souret was skinnier than I was, and his left elbow was stiff because he had broken it many years earlier. He was in charge of collecting food rejects from the military camps and restaurants in the area to feed the pigs. During the cabbage and cauliflower season, he would also pick up rejects and trimmings for the cows. He traveled for miles around with a horse-drawn wagon to bring the fodder back. Madame Souret was in charge of everything, most important being the finances, because, she said, "Monsieur Souret, incapable of standing on his own, declared bankruptcy in 1935 when he was the boss." She obviously ran the family with an iron fist. Everybody was expected to help when needed, and so would I until the start of school.

The Sourets made clear to me that their sympathy did not lie with the Germans. In fact, Monsieur Souret had been a valiant soldier at the battle of Verdun during World War I. He had shot so many times against the Germans that his gun had become too hot for reloading by hand, and he had to use his feet and a rag. Also, I was told in no uncertain terms that during the recent war they had taken advantage of every opportunity to sabotage the German war effort, as Radio Free France had recommended. They used to collect the food rejects from the Hotel Terminus in Avignon, which served as the German headquarters, and would throw metal pieces into the huge food processors there to cause machine breakdowns. This action separated them from the "cowardly collabos." They told me this story many times, in each instance savoring it as if they had never told it before.

At night, Paul and his father slept in the same bed in one bedroom, because Monsieur and Madame Souret had been sleeping apart since the birth of Germaine. Renée and Germaine slept in one bed, and Madame Souret in the other, all in the second bedroom. Julien preferred to sleep in the hay above the cows because it was warmer at night. I would sleep in the same bed as Madame Souret since I was still small. A large bucket with a cover was set in the middle of the bedroom because it was "more convenient than outside" if you needed to use the toilet. The bedroom stank. I did not fall asleep immediately, and soon everybody was snoring. The sound gave me comfort. The next morning, I woke up to the rhythmic sound of a hammer. Everyone was already up. I went to the window to check, and as I passed near the big bucket in the middle of the bedroom, I almost fainted from the smell. This time it was uncovered.

Downstairs Julien was "tapping" the blade of the scythe to sharpen it. He would do that daily before leaving for the field, where he would cut the grass, load it into a horse-drawn cart, and bring it back for the cattle. The yard was messy. A big pile of manure lay in the middle. The chickens were kept in an improvised structure at the edge of the yard. While I was exploring the area, I was suddenly attacked by a bunch of irate geese. Julien came to my rescue with a big stick. Then he showed me how to crack a whip to keep the geese at bay. It was pretty easy.

Breakfast consisted of café au lait and bread. I also got jam since I was "so skinny." During my first days, I went with Germaine to watch the cows in the fields. We were helped by a trained shepherd dog. I was warned not to step into any of the big cow droppings. Renée brought us food for lunch on her bike. In the evening, we had to take the cows back to the farm and pump water for them before herding them into the stable. I was in charge of pumping, which was a hard job.

At night, everyone came to the table at the same time and started eating without prayers. During one of my first dinners, I picked up an old newspaper laying around, and they suddenly realized that I could read fluently. From then on, Madame Souret brought *Le Provençal* for me to read aloud at the dinner table. *Le Provençal* was the only newspaper Madame Souret trusted because it was the one her father used to buy. Since I knew how to read and Madame Souret knew how to recognize flowers, I also cut out and saved the daily flower quiz for the monthly flower contest.

Soon I was asked to check the biweekly payments for the milk; Madame Souret had found out that I was good in math. She was amazed at how I did the calculations in my head. From then on, I was exempted from hard physical work; I was supposed to keep the accounting straight. I did not have to pump water anymore, and I started choosing jobs that I particularly liked. When the time for preparing hay for winter came, Julien let me drive the horse-drawn raking machine and rake the hay after it had dried a few days in the meadow. I raked it up into large mounds so that Renée and Julien could load it into the cart. I was proud of my ability to control the huge horse and the machine. I was also responsible for helping Germaine do her homework when classes started, and I was always called in when supporting data was needed for a financial decision. My words were sacred, and I felt extremely important.

The Sourets were concerned about my health because they found me so skinny. To encourage me to eat, they used to say with a warm smile, "Jacky is eating like a bird, but shitting like a cow!" When I did not respond to their prodding to eat more, Madame Souret used to say, "If you spent eight days on a tree, you would have a better appetite after you come down." Popular wisdom was the backbone of her life, and she used to punctuate each of her comments with an appropriate, and irrefutable, saying. The Sourets never served each other at meals because "one is never served as well as by oneself." I was the only exception to the rule; I was always copiously served because I was "all skin and bones." Madame Souret was not sure that her feeding would work because she used to tell me, "Put stones in your pockets so that the mistral does not blow you away in winter." Their care made me feel wanted, and I let them tame me. Although the house and the bedroom still stank, after a few days I began to fall asleep before everyone else.

With time, I learned more about the family. Madame Souret, born in 1892, had eighteen brothers and sisters. She and two of her sisters had married three brothers of the Souret family. Her sister Fifi (diminutive for Josephine), who lived in Orange, was a widow from World War I. Fifi had one son, Marius, who was thirty-two years old and single. Madame Souret did not get along with the second sister and never talked about her. I heard her name only in a torrent of curses. As for her sixteen other brothers and sisters, she never mentioned their names.

The Sourets did not have many friends. Their saying was: "Fais du bien à Bertrand, il te le rend en chiant!" (If you are good to Bertrand, he returns the favor by shitting [on you]!) Even if someone behaved nicely, he could not be trusted; one needed to "beware of dormant water." The Sourets were strong believers in personal responsibility. If the neighbors had some trouble with their kids, it must be their own fault, since it is said, "As one makes one's bed, so does one sleep!" (Obviously, this was not a reference to the Sourets' own beds, which were never made, except when the sheets fell apart.) The Sourets were loyal to those few they counted among their close friends, and certainly to me, but they felt that a solid dose of suspicion toward anyone else was justified, as my own experience had taught me.

The Sourets barely made ends meet and owed money everywhere. As a result, getting food and supplies on credit was an acrobatic feat, and they had to rob Peter to pay Paul. They changed grocery stores frequently to keep their creditors from catching up with them. The food at their house was simple and ordinary, but sometimes Gruyère cheese or steaks would show up. They ate horse meat because it was cheaper, and they added garlic for better taste. They either bought second-rate produce or stole vegetables at night. Because of their poverty, even a soiled piece of food was never discarded because it was obvious that "one does not fatten pigs with clear water!"

Eating was an obsession, and Madame Souret, referring to her huge body, used to say: "Il vaut mieux faire envie que pitié!" (It is better to draw people's envy than their pity!) She often claimed that no store carried underwear large enough for her.

The family larder was an altar to the Sourets' respect for food. It was a cubicle covered on all sides with a metal screen to keep away the flies and with a padlock on the door to keep out "sticky fingers." Madame Souret used to store cheese, preserves, cans of tuna and sardines—and she always kept the keys. Since I had learned how to unlock the door, Germaine was nice to me, and once in a while I agreed to raid the larder with her. I felt uncomfortable betraying the trust of Madame Souret, but I had to manage all my relationships.

Because of their financial problems, the Sourets always lived on the edge. Once, they got caught "wetting the milk," that is, they had added too much water to the milk before selling it to the cooperative. Adding only a little might have passed unnoticed. After they lost a court hearing on the matter, they moved all their cows to their cousins in Les Agassins (the neighborhood between Le

Pontet and Avignon) because they were afraid of a government seizure.

Initially, I went to school on foot and had to leave early. There was some comfort in returning to the school I had attended during the war. The material was easy, and I was always the top student. Everyone, teachers and students alike, would defer to me because of my knowledge. After walking back to the farm, I would help Germaine with her homework. I was able to do mine while she was writing hers. She was good at drawing and painting, but her talent was never recognized. She showed me a beautiful watercolor collection of regional flowers that she had painted. The Sourets exempted me from work and always made sure that I had enough time to do my homework. Their "Jewish" attitude toward my studies contrasted with the careless behavior of my schoolmates' parents. It certainly departed from their own habits.

One morning, I overslept and was late for school. I rushed getting dressed and slid my right foot into one shoe, then my left foot into the other. Then, I felt a slippery feeling in my left shoe and smelled a foul odor. Since this was my only pair of shoes, I did the best I could to clean up the mess before running to school. I was unable to figure out which of the ten cats had done the deed, and to this day I do not trust cats.

When winter came, wood became critical. The fireplace was used for heating, and in the winter months Madame Souret would also cook in it instead of the stove to save coal. So, without apology, the Sourets would steal wood from anyone who seemed to have more than a minimum, thereby implementing their own form of social justice. When lightning would strike a big tree in the large neighboring estate of Roberty, the men of the family would discreetly retrieve the wood during the night. I was once allowed to participate in the pilfering under the condition that I not talk about the raid in front of my friends, the Manzons, because everyone knew that "their butt could not even hold one glass of water," a reference both to the inability of the Manzons to keep a secret and to the difficulty of holding the water of an enema for too long. I was proud of having been part of this swift, victorious expedition, which became one of many little secrets I shared with the Sourets.

The Sourets stole with a clear conscience, seeing their own deeds as a well-deserved preemptive strike. When one was on the Sourets' side, one never felt any guilt, and I soon found myself becoming one of them.

In winter, the nights came early and everyone was home long before dinner. Helping to prepare the meal was a peaceful routine. Most of the food was simple but flavorful, because Madame Souret used her mother's recipes, heavily loaded with the herbs of Provence found in the neighboring hills. We had to pick them before the end of summer and dry them for preservation. Other spices, like sage, bay leaves, and basil, were grown in the garden outside the house. This is how I acquired my taste for the food of Provence and my cooking experience. The Sourets encouraged me to improvise with the meals, and sometimes I was allowed to bake a marbled chocolate pound cake. I was proud of my contributions to the Sourets' table.

Before going to bed, we would wrap in rags big stones that had been heated in the fireplace and then take them upstairs to bed. What a comfortable feeling it was to slip into the hot bed and cover myself with the thick down blanket! The bedroom, the bed, and Madame Souret still stank, but I no longer paid any attention to it. I just felt good. Madame Souret used to promise with a smile and a wink that "next year, after Easter," she would go to the public baths in Avignon, but she would immediately add, "water was not created for people and cats to wash up." Despite her promise, the stink continued long after Easter. Until they could get to the public baths, the Sourets used to "wash" their faces with cold water after getting up in the morning. I suspect that it was more for waking up than for hygiene. Nevertheless, I adjusted quickly to their way of life.

When our clothes were "really" dirty (as Madame Souret proclaimed, they were standing on their own and they could have gone to wash all by themselves), Renée and Germaine would take them to the rivulet on the other side of the road and wash them with *le savon de Marseille,* a raw all-purpose soap that came in ten-centimeter blocks. This was the only soap Madame Souret trusted, because it was the soap her mother had used. When the laundry was done, it was hung to dry on long parallel ropes near the vegetable garden.

There was no toilet inside or outside the house. During the day, the family would relieve themselves in the little irrigation stream that passed between the neighbor's farm and the end of their garden. The Sourets referred to this as *poser culotte,* or "drop the trousers." Madame Souret would relieve herself standing up because she was huge and could not squat. In her case, however, there were no trousers (or underwear) to drop.

I learned that the neighbors on the other side of the stream, the Perino family, were Italian immigrants who "used to pour wine in their soup." Madame Souret was proud of "showing them [her] butt" because they were Italian and she believed they should have stayed in Italy. When I went to the stream, I made sure to imitate Madame Souret, but my anatomy was not as impressive as hers.

The Sourets did not like foreigners, because being nice to them might send the wrong message. For them, foreigners also included the inhabitants of Vedène, the small village three kilometers away on the other side of the hill, because they did not "grow vines like us." In her anecdotes about the neighboring village of Morrières, Madame Souret characterized its inhabitants as simpletons. She savored retelling how the vicar of Morrières had alerted his parishioners to a miracle. "Our church is growing! Our church is growing!" the vicar shouted as he ran across the village square. Having allowed his farmer neighbor to stack manure against the steeple, the poor vicar did not realize that the manure was settling, leaving against the wall a mark that seemed to rise. Madame Souret did not hold the other inhabitants of Morrières in high esteem either. She remembered well, she said, how the entire village had come to celebrate the launching of a flying donkey invented by a local villager. Its legs tied with ropes and a large cape on its back, the donkey was being inflated through a hollow cane inserted in its butt. All Morrières inhabitants formed a line to blow air into the frightened animal. The mayor was expected to give the last blow before takeoff. As the donkey was becoming large enough to fly, the mayor approached with his lungs ready to burst. Full of mayoral respect, the inventor stopped the mayor. "Mister Mayor cannot blow in the same end of the cane as the rest of us!" said the inventor as he flipped the hollow cane into the donkey's butt. As sure as death and taxes, Madame Souret claimed without blinking that she had indeed seen with her own eyes the mayor of Morrières blow into the other end of the cane, the side which all along had been inside the butt of the donkey.

The Sourets profoundly disliked Italians in general, but they particularly hated the Perinos. When Madame Souret took me with her to her landlady, who lived in rue Paradis in Marseille, I realized why. The rich landlady also owned the property leased to the Perinos, and Madame Souret coveted the Perinos' meadow because her own meadows were too far from her farm. To no avail, she tried to convince the landlady to switch tenants and give her the Perinos' land, but the landlady did not give in, since the Perinos always paid on time.

Like the Sourets, the villagers of Le Pontet disliked Italians, Spaniards, Poles, or anyone different—their hatred was ecumenical. They certainly did not like the Armenians, who, since the end of the war, had established themselves in a colony, the tenement of Barles, halfway between Le Pontet and Avignon. The Armenians were war refugees who for decades had survived the cruelty of the Turks, the Communists, and the Nazis. Barles was also the name of the red tile manufacturing plant that employed them for pennies and provided them with lodging in the dilapidated tenement. Eight Armenian children attended our school. Parents encouraged their children to be hostile to them because the Armenians were "savages." The young Armenians were caught in a catch-22: if they reacted against discrimination and harassment, they were labeled as antisocial; if they did nothing, they invited more of the same abuse.

"We'll show them after school!" was the rallying cry one day at the beginning of spring. In a pressing need for acceptance, I joined the locals who had decided to meet outside school and block the young Armenians on their way home. Our leader, the Spaniard Jean Fernandez, brought homemade spiked rings for us to wear on our fingers as weapons. In a time of crisis, the village children preferred a Spanish commander and a Jewish private to the lowly Armenians. Hiding near the cemetery, we saw them coming, walking around Metaxian, their leader. There were thirty of us against eight of them. As they approached, our bellicose righteousness reached its paroxysm: we would rid the school of the menace! Suddenly, the village municipal guard, who had been tipped off, appeared at the cemetery gate. Ordered to go home, we took delight in imagining what a lesson we would have taught them if the guard had not intervened on their behalf! We were inebriated with victory.

Ironically, I had chosen the comfort of the group over compassion for the victims whose history had been so similar to that of the Jews.[1] As a matter of fact, I do not remember making any choice, and I do not think that the word "compassion" even figured in my thinking. My feelings about the Armenians had become the same as the other students' feelings about me during the war. I was now as insensitive to the Armenians' pain as my schoolmates had been to mine. Living with the Sourets, I was becoming used to the stink and oblivious to other people's pain—a real Frenchman.

On my way home from school I would stop at my father's house. Since he was very busy provisioning our store, I never knew in advance whether he would be at home, but he would leave information on his whereabouts with Monsieur and Madame Meffre, our neighbors. Every time I would get my regular dose of Bible stories, but that was all right because I was able to put an end to the visit when I wanted, since I needed to get back to the Sourets before dinner. This was a manageable arrangement.

My weekend visits, however, were less comfortable. I always felt best visiting my father when I accompanied Madame Souret to collect the monthly payment for my staying with them. The ties to my father felt too burdensome, and I was ready to give them up. In contrast, I found it easy to satisfy the Sourets, and their unconditional love was enough for me. Also, my sense of loss was becoming less acute with each passing day.

In December 1945, Madame Castagnier, the teacher who organized the Christmas celebration, designated me to sing "Stille Nacht" as a sign of respect for my mother's disappearance. When my father heard the news, he had the same reaction as when I was three and I wanted chocolate Easter eggs. He immediately went to the teacher to prevent my singing: he could not accept my singing a song with such Christian significance. The teacher complied with his request, although she did not understand why he would turn down such an honor for his son. I, too, did not understand my father's reaction. I was looking forward to singing in public for Christmas. Singing the carol was an open invitation to become like everyone else.

My father was able to avoid the Christmas carol, but he did not escape the invitation to Madame Souret's Christmas banquet. The Sourets talked about the feast for months in advance because it helped them accept the lean times. For the Christmas banquet, the Sourets "stove in the pantry door" (*défonçèrent la porte du garde-manger*, as they say in French to explain the abundance on the table). Madame Souret marinated wild rabbits in olive oil for three days and used a secret family recipe that included garlic, onions, thyme, wild mushrooms, and thick red wine. After she started browning the chunks of rabbit in hot olive oil, they began releasing the stinking gases, which had been generated during the three-day open-air marinade. At the right moment, she flamed the rabbits with *aigue arden*,[2] a grape brandy, and then simmered the dish for hours, until the meat was so tender that it fell off the bones. As the cooking progressed, the stinking gases gave way to a sublime aroma—a typical Souret paradox. The taste of rabbit that Madame Souret gave me before lunch was delicious. Outside, Julien had set up an improvised roasting pit and was rotating a whole sheep covered with spices and bacon. At lunchtime, the chunks of mutton, the rabbit stew *à la chasseur*,[3] vegetables, salad, cakes, and wines filled the table like a picture from Breughel. The men filled their glasses with wine and drank them dry in one gulp. Challenged to eat an entire mutton leg, Julien attacked it slowly but surely. He lost his bet, though, because he threw up just before finishing. The "little man," as Madame Souret used to call my father, who had arrived around noon, left at six completely exhausted, unable to finish all his food. For the Sourets, the Christmas feast memories lasted for the entire year.

In spite of their Christmas feast, the Sourets were not religious at all. On the contrary, they prided themselves on having never set foot in church. Indeed, Madame Souret claimed that they were Republicans because her father had been a Republican, and that was reason enough never to go to church. She had inherited from her father a ferocious anticlericalism that set her apart from most of her Catholic neighbors. To her, the other villagers who regularly frequented church were *des grenouilles de bénitier*, frogs in the holy water vessel that stands near the entrance of a Catholic church and is used for baptism and blessing. She was proud of having thrown Vicar Souchon out of her house when he urged her to hold a communion for one of her children. I savored Madame Souret's attitude toward the vicar because I did not like the contemptuous way he passed me on his way to the cemetery during the war. Madame Souret was on my side. At the Sourets, I would be able to avoid going to the synagogue without having to go to church.

Though they were not religious, the Sourets were superstitious, like all the peasants in the area. They believed that talking about bad things was enough to make them happen. They made sure that no one turned the bread upside down because that brings bad luck. I was ordered never to spin a knife at the dinner table, because "that may kill the person that the knife designates when it stops spinning."

As time went on, I felt more and more at ease with the Sourets. The grown-ups started accepting me as an equal because of my contributions to the economy of the family. Germaine was somewhat jealous of me, but she slowly accepted me as her little brother. Madame Souret started replacing my mother because she really cared for me. In spite of the tight budget, she bought me a beautiful leather soccer ball that must have cost a fortune. I also got some "special grease" to take care of it. She knitted woolen clothes for me so that I didn't catch a cold, and she provided me with a bike to go to school. The entire family used to go everywhere by bike, and Madame Souret was agile in spite of her heavy build. While riding back home, she would jump off while the bike was still rolling and hit the ground running.

The Sourets were very physical, and touching was part of their way of expressing love. I accepted from them the physical contact that I rejected from strangers, but I remained stiff with my father. The Sourets were not only kind to me; they also made it a point to adopt any stray cat or dog in the area. After the stray animal (which usually had been abandoned by its previous owner) had been fed for the first time, the Sourets then gave it a colorful name that best described their first impression of the pet. Later, they studied its behavior for signs of special talent. The Sourets liked to see at least one redeeming value in every living creature.

Being used to various languages, I picked up their patois very quickly. Like Yiddish, the Provençal dialect is very colorful. *Jus vert*, "green juice," means parsley, and *pommes d'amour*, "apples of love," means tomatoes. *Joues du cul*, "cheeks of the butt," means the buttocks. The Sourets affectionately called me the *caguo-ou-nis*, "the one who shits in the nest," because I was the youngest. I loved belonging to them.

The Sourets had explosive tempers that would flare up every so often. Madame Souret would be at the center of the fights. She would pick on her husband whenever he made a costly mistake, such as forgetting to pick up food rejects from a restaurant. She would nag him about "his" bankruptcy, and he, in response, would threaten to kill her someday with the hunting rifle hanging on the kitchen wall. She used to reply, "When you shoot me, be sure you don't miss, because I will not miss you!"

Madame Souret was continuously upset at her daughter Renée, who could not get out of bed in the morning. She would shout litanies of wake-up calls from the bottom of the stairs leading to the bedroom, but would not go upstairs because of her weight. It was obvious from the tone of her voice that she did not expect immediate results. When Renée finally came down, she was usually greeted with the words, "Lazy! You'll see when I am dead: you will starve!" Renée then used to burst into tears because she was terrified at the idea of having to manage on her own. During one of these arguments, Paul, who was irritable because of the war, threw a tantrum and left home to live with the cousins in Les Agassins who were keeping the Sourets' cows. Several months later, the Sourets asked for the cows back because they felt that they were no longer in danger of being seized by the government, but the cousins refused to return them. They claimed that Paul, who was now living with them, had always taken care of the cattle and deserved to keep them now. On this occasion, I learned that *lou pissaïre*, the bizarre man with the black coat who had terrorized us as young children, was related to Monsieur Souret. He was now living in Les Agassins with these same cousins.

In the fall of 1945, German prisoners of war were encamped in the area and made available to work for French farmers in exchange for lodging. This was a good opportunity for replacing Paul. The Sourets quickly brought a German prisoner home. I was uncomfortable with him, and always made sure to sit opposite him at the table. I did not like the idea of sleeping with him under one roof. In spite of my repulsion, I served as the interpreter between him and the Sourets when there were misunderstandings about work assignments. Fortunately, he did not stay long and was soon repatriated to Germany. During his entire stay, the Sourets insulted him, using French that he did not understand. They also made sure that he did not eat too much, because "*they* took enough from us during the war." Like the Sourets, I felt that he got off easy.

Although she was twenty, Renée was dependent on her mother, because she was epileptic and had frequent seizures. On one occasion she fell on her butt and got an ill-positioned abscess. The poor young woman was in pain and could not sit. She had been moaning for several days. So she stayed in bed until Docteur André, who made house calls, arrived. He went upstairs and gave Renée one of the aspirin pills that he always carried in his briefcase. Because of the power of suggestion, Renée stopped moaning as soon as the aspirin touched her tongue. This was a striking testimony to the magic influence of Docteur André on the villagers.

Docteur André had more than one trick in his bag. He would prescribe cupping glasses or cataplasms for illnesses that looked like the common cold. A cupping glass is a small bell-shaped glass with thick edges. This simple technique consisted of dipping a cotton ball into alcohol, lighting it, tossing it into the cupping glass, and then applying the glass to the back of the patient. The flame from the cotton ball would quickly exhaust the oxygen in the glass and create a vacuum strong enough to keep the glass tightly attached to the skin of the patient for several minutes. Docteur André claimed the cupping glasses had "the power of sucking the illness out of the lungs." The cataplasm was a soft, moist, hot mixture of flour, mustard, flax seeds, and various secret ingredients wrapped in a cloth and also applied on the back of the patient. Twelve cupping glasses would cure a minor cold and twenty-four would take care of a more severe problem. If that did not help, the cataplasm would do the job. Beyond that, you were in God's hands. I was lucky to always get better after twelve cupping glasses.

After Madame Souret had exhausted Docteur André's science and her own bag of tricks, she took me to a *guérisseuse*, a woman healer in Avignon, to cure my skinniness. Inside her colorful den, she gave an irrefutable prophecy and a sure prescription: she claimed that I would grow up to be a commander in the French navy and that I would put some fat on if Madame Souret would feed me Gruyère cheese every morning. Madame Souret walked back to the bus in the company of a future admiral of the fleet and declared that the healer could be trusted. The prophecy for my future has not materialized so far, but the prescription of Gruyère cheese worked quickly.

Medical treatment for the cats was less advanced. If a sick cat did not recover within twenty-four hours, Julien was ordered to apply the "ultimate" technique. He would take the cat outside and cut one centimeter off the cat's tail with an ax, because, they believed, the illness "is concentrated at the tip of the tail." The treatment could be repeated depending on how often the cat became very sick and how long the tail was. That explained why some of the cats had very short tails; it also proved that the method worked. The efficiency of the technique was based on the short-tailed cats that had survived; the ones who died did not count.

It had not taken me very long to become a Souret, dirty and stinking, warm and fun-loving, prejudiced but loyal, dishonest but sincere, simple and giving, just as they were. The Sourets separated friend from foe by love and hate. I liked what they liked, and I hated what they hated. They loved me wholeheartedly, and I responded with my entire soul. By the time summer came, they had given me a second life, a simple way to feel good about myself again. They loved me the way I was, just as my mother had.

My father did not worry about the Sourets' influence on me because, in his mind, the Sourets were fulfilling a simple surrogate role. He had likely had surrogate parents in his native Poland and thus saw nothing wrong with my having them too. The Sourets were providing food and a roof over my head. My father did not appear to attach much importance to the nurturing part of parenting.

17 | In My Mother's Shoes

Occasionally, my father would take me from the Sourets to go home or visit his friends. On one of these occasions, we went to the Schneiders, his friends who had moved from Beaucaire to Avignon. The Schneiders had a son, Jacques, who was older than me. He was the one who smashed my thumb on a visit to my mother's store in 1941. Their real name was Schneiderowicz, but they preferred the shorter version. Years later, they would change their name to Nederovique, which made them almost French, as long as they did not speak. For their Jewish friends who felt ill at ease with this total capitulation, they remained the Schneiders. They relished telling and retelling my past accomplishments: my divine rescue in Buis-les-Baronnies and about the suitcase at the train station. They also told about the visits my mother and I paid them during the war. They were the only people who talked about my mother and me openly. They enjoyed the memories, and I enjoyed their openness, but I did not reciprocate. I was not ready to talk about her to anyone, not even to the Sourets. I was too afraid that someone might shatter my dream that she might some-day come back.

During one of our visits to the Schneiders, I met a tall woman named Ruth, who gave me two Swiss chocolate bars for no apparent reason. Since I did not know her, this gift made me feel obligated. She seemed to have something to say on every topic, and the tone of her voice made it clear that no one else's opinions were wanted. The Schneiders treated her and my father with special interest, and I was surprised when she left with us in our car. My father drove me back to the Sourets and returned home with Ruth. At the time, no one talked to me about Ruth's role. She had appeared out of the blue in the margin of my life.

I soon realized that, every time I passed by my father's house on my way to school from the Sourets, Ruth was still there. If I came too early, she was still in bed, the same bed as my father. With time, she behaved as if she had been part of the household forever.

It was not by accident that Madame Schneider had introduced Ruth to my father. In Avignon, Madame Schneider used to fulfill the traditional role of *shadchen,* the Jewish matchmaker. The story of how she tried (and failed) to match a young couple, Maurice and Paula, sheds some light on her technique. Maurice was thirty years old and not very enterprising. Paula was twenty-nine and still single. Madame Schneider had arranged for the two families to meet "by accident" at an outdoor café near the opera in Avignon. To make it look more natural and to satisfy their curiosity, friends of the family also met "by accident" at the café. Of course, the two young people were assigned seats next to each other. After the usual greetings and comments about the remarkable coincidence, Madame Schneider noticed that Paula and Maurice were not talking to each other. Sensing that the couple was inhibited by the company, Madame Schneider suggested that Maurice go and buy opera tickets for himself and Paula. He readily went, but when he came back he said, "They had only one ticket left and I bought it for myself." Paula went back home with her mother, and Madame Schneider claimed that the young man was a misfit.

With time, I learned bits and pieces about Ruth. Before the war, she had been married to a man named Adolf Seefeld in Karlsruhe, Germany. They were expelled from Germany during the expulsion of the Jews from Baden and the Palatinate on October 22–23, 1940, and tried to immigrate from Marseille to the United States in 1942. The French police picked up Ruth's husband at the American consulate on the day the French suspended Jewish emigration.[1] He was interned at the Les Milles camp near Marseille, then deported to Drancy during the August 1942 roundups. From there he was sent to Auschwitz. Fortunately, Ruth did not rejoin him in Les Milles because of a friendly warning; she was interned in the Gurs camp near Pau. She escaped deportation several times as an employee of the Quakers' charitable mission and was freed from Gurs with the help of a French family. During a roundup, the Gestapo skipped her hotel room by accident. Another time, she left a farm where she worked just before an informer led the police to her hiding place. After the war, she established herself in the southern town of Castres, where Madame Schneider, always on the lookout, discovered her.

Early on, Ruth started tearing apart my mother's house. Every time I visited, something had changed. First, a gas appliance replaced my beautiful stove. Next, she got rid of our manual water pump in favor of a more "appropriate" faucet connected to the new city water supply. The light green dresser that my mother had purchased was replaced by another piece of furniture, to which I had no connection. Ruth redid the storefront and modernized its furniture. It no longer had that familiar appearance and looked more like the stores in Avignon. She even replaced the familiar door chime with a top-of-the-line electrical one, which would keep ringing until the door was closed. Slowly, I was being dispossessed of all my memories, and my father acted as if he did not notice. I was sure, however, that he realized what was going on. How I hated the friends who would visit and marvel at the destruction in progress, giving all the credit to Ruth, who knew "how to keep a household and move with the times." The Sourets understood that I resented Ruth. To show me their support, they started calling her by a nickname in the Provençal dialect, *la gommous*, which means "the lacquered one." This was an obvious reference to Ruth's compulsion for external polish and cleanliness. The Sourets, who could detect a compulsion for cleanliness even in the middle of a moonless night, had maliciously given Ruth the same nickname as their unruly cow.

During one of my visits, I overheard a discussion between Ruth and my father about my mother. She was speaking in German, and he responded in Yiddish. They were debating how to obtain a death certificate. They paid no attention to my presence and did not realize that I understood Yiddish, thanks to the Steltzers. Through Yiddish, I also understood some German. This was the first time that my mother and her death were explicitly connected in my presence. My blood froze in my veins, and I wanted to shout that this was a lie and drown out their voices. Instead, I lowered my head and concealed my emotions. I retreated into the silence I had imposed upon myself since my mother's departure.

Although I did not tell the Sourets about the conversation I had overheard, they intuitively understood my pain and were sensitive to my needs. They knew that I did not have a real home because my ties to my father and Ruth were tenuous. Realizing the importance of having a place of my own, they gave me a little brick cabin adjacent to the farm. Julien helped me install a workbench and shelves, and he gave me a bunch of tools. I became the proud owner of a workshop and laboratory. It felt good to finally have some possessions of my own. There, I did my first electrical and chemical experiments—precursors of my future interest in engineering. Connecting bulbs, electromagnets, and switches, I constructed battery-operated circuits while the Sourets marveled. Once, I almost blasted the whole place apart while producing hydrogen by a method that I had found in an old chemistry book. I used to spend many hours in my laboratory, while my friend and neighbor Jean-Pierre Manzon used to keep me company, watching my experiments and constructions. His family used the French version of their real name, Manzoni, because they knew the villagers did not like Italians.

I spent a lot of time at the Manzons visiting my friend. His parents encouraged my visits, happy that their son should "associate with such a good student." They lived in a small rented farm without electricity and had to use acetylene lamps in the evenings. This is where I learned how to refill such lamps with carbide and water when the flame would go out. The acetylene lamps reminded me of the wartime cars with their gas generators. Since I was very close to my friend, Madame Souret used to say that he and I were "like the butt and the shirt—always together!" This was one more testimony that the Sourets did not believe in underwear. However, when I was not with my friend, Madame Souret reminded me to keep some distance from him because I was much better than he was. "The two of you," she said, "you are not figs from the same basket!"

In early May, the Roberty racetrack reopened for the first time since the war. The bombing damage had been repaired. A few days before the races, the first race crews appeared in the area, causing a feverish curiosity on the part of the villagers. At the same time, the village mothers started paying more attention to the virtues of their nubile daughters, because "the jockeys [were] only after their bodies." Therefore, Madame Souret increased her watch on her daughter Renée. The Sourets, who lived on the Route de Vedène just behind the estate of Roberty, declared that we would go to the races by "jumping the fence" at a secret place where it was lower. From Julien's winks, I understood that he had worked on the fence ahead of time. On the day of the race, I was innocently strolling around the bookmakers' booths where my mother and I had walked two years earlier, while the Sourets cautiously kept away from the ticket checkpoints. Much of the scenery was the same as in 1944, except for the absence of the German officers—and my mother.

Toward summer, tragedy struck the Sourets: Renée became

pregnant by a farmer's son who lived a few kilometers away. Although Madame Souret did not know it, Renée's virtue had already been compromised before the May races. The situation exploded when Madame Souret noticed her daughter's rounded shape, and a yelling contest ensued. This was the story of Claire Steltzer all over again. To add insult to injury, the young man was Italian and not French. A whole series of past incidents suddenly became clear. In early fall of the preceding year, Renée had suddenly decided to take me with her to pick herbs in the hills of the nearby village of Vedène. She was always met by the young man. They would send me to buy ice cream in the village, which gave them plenty of time to make love. They made me an accomplice by asking me to keep the whole thing to myself. When the weather was bad and no one was home, they would make love there. That explained the cigarette butts that Madame Souret had found in the bedroom. She had unjustly accused her son Julien of smoking behind her back. Realizing my role in the catastrophe, I kept my mouth shut and did not mention that I had served as an alibi for Renée. By the time the pregnancy became public knowledge, it was already too late. In late summer, the illegitimate Paulette Souret was born.

At the same time Madame Souret's sister Fifi became ill with cancer. Madame Souret sent her daughter Germaine to Orange to help with the household work, since Fifi's son, Marius, was busy running the farm.

At the end of the school year, my teacher, Madame Gonnet, suggested that I take the entrance examination for the Lycée Mistral, the high school in Avignon. One could go to high school at the age of ten and obtain a high school diploma seven years later, or stay in grammar school until the age of fourteen and obtain a lower-grade diploma, the *certificat d'étude*. I really did not want to go to high school; I preferred to stay in grammar school. I felt comfortable where I was, and it did not matter to me that a grammar school diploma was a dead end. Reluctantly, I took the high school entrance exam, trying to fail by making a few deliberate errors. Unfortunately, I "passed brilliantly," as my teacher said, either because I could not bring myself to make enough mistakes or because the other candidates were miserable.

At the beginning of the summer vacation, on July 14, the people of Le Pontet celebrated their first real Bastille Day since before the war. All the festivities took place in the Place de l'Eglise. The public ball, a key event, was held on a large concrete area in the middle of the square. The municipal band, which had been rehearsing for at least six months, performed on the festively decorated wooden stage, and farmers from the surrounding villages came to town for the occasion. All the girls were chaperoned and ostentatiously waited beside the dance floor, because this was proper. All the eligible bachelors plotted how to make their moves, while the girls giggled nervously. Some older girls, too shy to wait for an invitation, danced among themselves, as did the young children, boys with boys and girls with girls. The married women did not dance because that would not be a good example for their children and that was the way things were supposed to be! So they chaperoned their younger sisters or sisters-in-law. As a reaction to the restraint of the war years, the rhythm of the music was so frantic that you had to watch your back and your sides as well as your feet.

Even the people who were too heavy to dance had much fun commenting on the dancers or on the band. The bandleader had composed a special dance for the occasion, *la danse atomique*, the atomic dance, to celebrate the "lesson" that the Americans had given to the Japanese in Hiroshima and Nagasaki. The connection of the dance to the atom bomb was that the male dancer had to lift his female partner high up in the air. The *danse atomique* was daring entertainment for the conservative village. Java, tango, waltz, rumba, and foxtrot were more acceptable rhythms. One of the older girls took me to the dance floor and taught me the basic steps. I had a lot of fun.

For the occasion, many stands and rides had been set up on the church square. We got free tickets for the bumper cars because they were owned by a rich cousin of the Sourets. Julien took me with him. After many rides, he suggested a visit to a "special" stand. The audience sat inside a closed stand facing an improvised stage. My eyes practically fell out of their sockets when I saw a totally naked young woman parading onstage to the music of a poor recording. It was now Julien's turn to use me as an alibi. Hoping to keep me quiet about the episode, he remarked, "This is educational, isn't it?" I thought to myself, "Educational? My foot!"

In summer, I was sent to a camp organized by the OSE, Oeuvre de Secours aux Enfants (Institution for Relief to Children), an organization that had helped hide Jewish children during the war. The camp was in the mountains above Nice, a tourist town near the Mediterranean Sea. Fearful because of my previous camp experience, I was pleasantly surprised. The atmosphere was friendly and warm because the counselors understood us. They did not try to overwhelm us with excessive rules. They told us beautiful stories and organized games to loosen us up. I wrote a postcard to my father that started with the words "Cher Papa," Dear Daddy. He responded angrily because I had addressed the card only to him and not to Ruth. He suggested I say "Dear All" or "Dear You Two." He had not dared suggest a more personal address that included Ruth. I decided to use the terse "Chers," the plural for "dear." That also saved me from the word "Papa."

When I returned from the OSE camp, I stayed a few weeks with my friend Albert Kurlandczyk in La Couronne, a small village near the Mediterranean Sea. His mother had asked another friend, Lucien Sokolowski, and me to stay at their small rented house. A maid took care of us while Albert's parents were working. Albert, Lucien, and I spent our time wandering near the sea in the hills covered with pine trees. The sky was so blue and clear that one could see the boats sailing in the far distance. As usual, the chirp of the cicadas burst from the heat of summer. All along the hills, as far as I could see, the seashore was lined with abandoned German bunkers. Some of the bunkers were completely hidden underground and contained rooms and corridors, which we explored by going down steel ladders. Other bunkers were guard-posts emerging from the rocks with narrow windows on all sides.

We discovered a camouflaged long-range cannon used against warships. It looked like a real rock from the distance, but as we approached, I could distinguish the concrete structure and the hidden entrance. Inside the bunker, the long cannon had been damaged by sabotage, but it was still pointing at the sea through a narrow horizontal slit. We were able to move the gun left and right with the manual crank, but vertical motion was impossible. The floor was littered with equipment parts and military boxes.

The ground under the pine trees was still covered with live ammunition of every caliber. The Germans had probably blown up entire arsenals before leaving. The hills were a staggering display of military power that I knew only from my uncontrollable fear a year earlier. I finally understood the destination of the German convoys flowing to the south on the Route Nationale Numéro Sept in November 1942.

When I returned from La Couronne, I went to the Sourets for the remainder of summer. My father and Ruth did not object. I came back just in time for the grape harvest. The Sourets had rented a small vineyard on the side of the Vedène hill that was well exposed to the sun. To effectively tackle the job, the whole family went to pick the grapes. When we finished, Julien brought home a borrowed winepress. It was a primitive winepress, because people who owned more advanced ones did not lend them to the lower classes. The grapes were poured into the press, and I was given the honor of inaugurating the winemaking season. I was told to take my shoes off and climb into the press, because the pressing had to be done by trampling on the grapes until there was no more juice. Since I was hesitant to get into the press with my dirty feet, Julien said that it makes the wine taste better, and he joined me in the press straight out of his milking boots. The crushed grapes felt like a moist, slippery pillow, but the grape stems felt like the shaft of a feather that inadvertently stuck out of the pillow. After hundreds of steps, the grape juice started dripping at the bottom of the press and flowed into a huge demijohn.

For several hours, I alternated between the winepress and my old shoes filled with grape skins. At the end of the day, we had produced five huge demijohns of grape juice that was to become "the best wine ever, even better than that of our Italian neighbors." The Sourets, who did not waste anything, rinsed the grape pulp out with water to extract the last drops of juice and made *piquette* from this poor mixture. *Piquette*, a bubbly drink with little alcohol, had to be consumed immediately because it was quick to spoil. Finally, the battered pulp was left to ferment for a few weeks until ready for the distillation of the alcohol. Since moonshining was illegal, everything had to be conducted in the utmost secrecy. This is why the pulp was stored in the back of the yard and the distillation was done at night. We took the open barrels of fermented pulp to a farmer near the village of Vedène who owned distillation equipment. From the resulting "fiery water," Madame Souret prepared an assortment of "healthy" concoctions for every occasion. One bottle with sage leaves was good against indigestion; another one with mint leaves was effective against colds; a third with basil promoted longevity; one plain bottle was reserved for cooking, while another one was set aside, just in case.

Madame Souret gave two bottles of *piquette* to my father, who left them unattended in the kitchen wall closet until they popped their corks and made a mess. The Sourets made fun of my father's naive city behavior. A real peasant would have known better than to cork "live" *piquette.* The Sourets also relished Ruth's dramatic reaction to the mess in the closet. "She is trying to fart higher than her own butt," claimed the Sourets, in reference both to her haughty attitude and her obsession with cleanliness. The whole disaster was a joyous topic of conversation at the Sourets' dinner table.

At the end of August, Fifi died in Orange. Madame Souret did not want to take me to the funeral, because I was "too young for that." When she came back, she was furious because her daughter

Germaine had refused to come back home. She wanted to stay and live with her first cousin Marius. Madame Souret exploded for the benefit of whoever was ready to listen. Living with one's first cousin, she said, was as bad as incest. I thought to myself that I was never going to tell her that my parents were also cousins.

By the end of the summer of 1946, the Sourets' lives were full of tears. My life was not that great either. As a part of Madame Souret's family was falling apart, she held on to me a little tighter. Before Ruth's arrival, I was ready to give up my father in exchange for the Sourets, to let him fade away. I had chosen the Sourets because they allowed me to keep the dream of my mother alive. Now, I intuitively felt that my Souret identity was on a collision course with my father and Ruth, and I feared the encounter.

18 | *A Souret or a Lewendel?*

The Governor's wife wants to recover the child that she had given away to be raised by Grusha, the farmer woman. Her two lawyers plead her case in front of Azdak, the High Court Judge

AZDAK: Plaintiff and defendant! The court has listened to your case and has come to no decision as to who the real mother is; therefore, I, the judge, am obliged to choose a mother for the child. I'll make a test! Shauwa, get a piece of chalk and draw a circle on the floor. (Shauwa does so.) *Now place the child in the middle.* (Shauwa places the child in the circle.) *Stand near the circle, both of you.* (Both women step up to the circle.) *Now each of you take the child by one hand.* (They do so.) *The true mother is she who can pull the child out of the circle.*

FIRST LAWYER: High Court of Justice, I object! The fate of the great Abashwili estates, which are tied to the child, as the heir, should not be made dependent on such a doubtful duel. In addition, my client does not command the strength of this person who is accommodated to physical work.

AZDAK: She looks pretty well fed to me. Pull! (The Governor's wife pulls the child out of the circle on her side; Grusha has let go and stands aghast.) *What is the matter with you? You didn't pull.*

GRUSHA: *I didn't hold onto him.*

SECOND LAWYER: *What did I say! The ties of blood!*

GRUSHA (running to Azdak): *Your Honor, I take back all what I said against you. I ask your forgiveness. But could I keep him till he can speak all the words? He knows a few.*

AZDAK: *Don't influence the court. I bet you only know about twenty words yourself. All right, I'll make the test once more, just to be certain.* (The two women take their positions again.) *Pull!* (Again Grusha lets go of the child.)

GRUSHA (in despair): *I brought him up! Shall I also tear him to bits? I can't!*

AZDAK (rising): *And in this manner the Court has determined the true mother. Grusha, take YOUR child and be off . . .*

—Bertold Brecht, *The Caucasian Chalk Circle*

October 1946–Summer 1949

The summer of 1946 was a turning point in my relationship with my father. Although I had just turned ten, I was conscious of a widening abyss between us. If he had not sent me away to the Sourets a year earlier, an alliance could have developed between us, a kind of huddling that one commonly finds among survivors of the same tragedy, like the closeness that was so obvious between Esther and Rose Margolis when I visited them in Chicago. On the contrary, my father and I were more like the pins in a bowling alley after a good bowl: they often hit one another before scattering away.

At the end of summer, I got a piece of bad news. I knew that I was supposed to go to the Lycée Mistral in October, but I had assumed that I would ride the bus and return every day to the Sourets. However, my father and Ruth had made different plans for me. During the preceding months, they had been trying to sever my ties to the Sourets, to no avail. Now, they had finally found the perfect way to tear me away from them and from their influence: I would be sent to the boarding school at the lycée in Avignon—because it would be good for my future, they said.

Madame Souret was the one who gave me the bad news. I cried openly in public for the first time in two years. I was terrified to lose my only support once again, and I hated my father and Ruth for tearing me away from my source of security. I was ten years old, and since the French lycée covers seven years of studies, including high school, I felt I had been sentenced to life imprisonment. I protested and proposed that Madame Souret hide me in another house, because I had experienced that before. She gently but firmly refused and told me that there was nothing she could do. She was sorry too, but she had given me up. Like Grusha, the farmer woman in Brecht's *Caucasian Chalk Circle*, Madame Souret had stopped pulling and let my blood-father win. Unfortunately, no one contested the outcome, and Azdak, the high court judge, was nowhere to be found. I felt abandoned and kidnapped at the same time. I had felt abandoned when I had to go stay with the Brès family after my mother's arrest. Then, however, I had not felt kidnapped; I felt welcome.

Now, there was only one consolation. It was agreed that Madame Souret would deliver me to the unknown. I had refused to let anybody else do it. This was my first open confrontation with my father. We arrived at the lycée early in the morning, and I was shown my dormitory. It was a long room with three rows of beds, one in the middle and two against opposite walls. There were about sixty beds in all. Each student got a closet without a lock.

The school year did not go well for me. My grades plummeted, my discipline declined, and I blended into the viciousness of the boarding school. There were surveillants everywhere. Most of these proctors were partially accredited teachers who got paid for watching the kids while completing their credentials. They watched us in the yard, they watched us at the study hall, and they watched us in the huge dormitory, where a plywood enclosure had been specially constructed for them. The enclosure did not have a ceiling and had windows with curtains all around. Inside, the light stayed on long after our curfew. This would allow them to work on their upcoming exams while keeping us in sight.

As time passed, I became the target of the surveillants, who hounded me for my lack of discipline. The standard punishment was weekend detention, and I "stayed glued" at school two weekends out of three. The principal even stopped warning my father and Ruth that I would not be coming home for the weekend. They would then visit me on Sunday around noon and generally bring cold roasted chicken for lunch. On Sunday mornings, the detained boys were gathered in a study hall with a surveillant, who certainly would have preferred to be elsewhere. With my flair for getting into trouble, I behaved badly and usually got detained for the following Sunday.

In spite of (or maybe because of) their emotional emptiness, the Sunday detentions were more comfortable for me than going home to my father and Ruth. By staying at the boarding school, I did not have to make the painful choice between them and the Sourets. But I was gradually becoming used to the separation. At the boarding school, it was not so obvious that my family was not like that of the other kids. Since everyone had left their parents at home, we were all equal at school. This gave me some comfort.

When I was not detained, I was to return every weekend to my father's house. I used to take the bus to Le Pontet at noon on Saturday and come back to school on Monday morning. Often, I announced on Sunday morning that I was going to the Sourets and that I would spend the night there. I could sense the tension when I made the announcement, but I acted as if I did not notice it. I was determined to keep my link to the Sourets in spite of the mounting pressure. On Monday morning, I would walk back to the bus loaded with food that Madame Souret had prepared especially for me.

At the beginning of the school year, I had been required, like everyone else, to bring a huge food chest, or canteen. At four o'clock, the canteen room was opened, and we rushed in for our daily snack. Every boy leaned over his own padlock so that no one else could see the combination. This was our best defense against the skilled food pirates. My food chest with its four o'clock delicacies—Camembert cheese, salami from Arles, chocolate, and special dishes from Madame Souret—became my fragile and difficult connection to the Sourets. This is when I started disliking Mondays.

People around me behaved as if my mother were dead and gone forever. I neither accepted this nor believed them, because I still badly wanted her back. Unable to talk to anyone about her, I used to fantasize. Maybe my mother was still held by the Germans? Maybe she was ill in some remote hospital? Maybe her memory was gone? At some point, I even thought that she had been deported to a remote place in Russia, because I had heard that my father was trying to reunite us with his nephew who had been deported to Uzbekistan. Every so often, I would make up a new story just for myself.

A nagging emotion began to infiltrate my longing for my mother. I became angry with her. I was angry with her for not hiding in time, angry for abandoning me, angry for subjecting me to the boarding school cruelty, angry for making me face my father and Ruth. And, above all, angry for not responding to my prayers.

One weekend in the spring of 1947 after returning from school to my father's house, when I announced that I was going to the Sourets for the weekend, I was surprised not to feel the usual tension as I announced my intent. I did not feel guilty when I left for the Sourets either. After returning to school on Monday, we had our customary agitated canteen lunch. After we were served, we had to talk quietly, because one surveillant was always watching. Georges Friedman, a Jewish friend, asked me point-blank why I did not attend the wedding of my father and Ruth on Sunday. My fork fell into my lentils. My father had killed my secret hope of ever seeing my mother again, and he had done it behind my back. I was angry and embarrassed in front of everyone. Even my friend Georges seemed to be more important to my father than me, because he had been invited. My father never mentioned his wedding, and I never discussed it with him. But this event and my father's insensitivity to my feelings sent me into a whirlpool of anger and resentment. I started building a glass rampart between him and me.

During these stormy years, my ties with the Sourets slowly loosened, even though I resisted the best I could the attempts of my father and Ruth to exorcise the Souret in me. My high school years remain for me the history of my undercover resistance to this design. Above all, I remember my inability to verbalize this conflict. It was as if my father, Ruth, and I, three victims of the same tragedy, had spent these few years face to face in the arena without ever really locking horns. Our circumstances had placed my father in a situation he was ill-equipped to handle.

During one of my visits at home, my father decided that it was time for me to start my musical education. He and Ruth asked me whether I wanted to play an instrument. I said that I did, and was given a "choice" between the violin and another instrument. I felt that the violin was a sad instrument because my melancholy cousin Leon Laufbaum, who had arrived from Uzbekistan with his wife, Leonora, and his baby daughter, Amalia, used to play the violin. During gatherings of friends, Leon would play between stories about the war, merchandise problems, and digestive-tract difficulties. He vibrated his fingers on the strings to squeeze a whining sound out of his violin and a concerto of silent sighs out of our Jewish friends. That assembly reminds me today of *Fiddler on the Roof*. In contrast, the accordion seemed to me an abundant source of happiness, because the village parties were always bursting with accordion music and hearty laughs. The accordionists looked far happier than our violinist. So, when my father asked me what instrument I wanted to play, my response was, "The accordion!" Without any hesitation, I had chosen the instrument of the Sourets. My father and Ruth stared at each other; their expressions proclaimed that I had gone Gentile. Sensing my mistake, I quickly switched my choice to the piano, but my father and Ruth insisted on the violin. After all, they explained, a person could easily take a violin wherever he went. Obviously, relocation is always on the mind of a Jew!

I ended up taking violin lessons with my high school music teacher, Limouze, "scratching the strings" as my schoolmates used to say. Once a week, I dedicated my entire lunch period to Limouze and Paganini. While I was studying violin, though, I secretly played the harmonica. It reminded me of the accordion.

In the years immediately following the war, anti-Semitism had receded, and the Jews were even treated with some sympathy. But prejudice was not long in returning once the nation had exorcised its guilt about French collaboration. In a history class, the teacher, Paul Jaffrès, maliciously emphasized the role of "Jewish bankers" during the economic difficulties that afflicted royalist France during the Mazarin years. His lengthy pause after mentioning the bankers was accompanied by a large smile in my direction. His pause seemed to last longer than the Hundred Years' War. After the teacher resumed his monologue, some of my classmates began whispering toward me, "les juifs! les juifs!" (the Jews! the Jews!), loud enough to be heard by the entire class and the teacher. Jaffrès did not react, even when I punched my neighbor in the face during the lesson. My bouts with racism did not improve my lot.

I did not find much comfort in the other Jewish children. Though being Jewish among Catholics was no easy thing, I had let

Maxime Tardieu, a good friend of mine, know that I was not a Christian, and it did not affect our friendship. One day, an older Jewish boy, René Malel, told everyone that he had missed school because of his sister's wedding, but I knew that he was celebrating his own bar mitzvah. I told the truth to my friend Maxime, who immediately spread the news around. When Malel heard what I had done, he was furious and knocked a baby tooth out of my mouth. One of my peers had just taught me that one does not trifle with someone eles's Jewishness.

The adults around me were no more at ease with their Judaism. I approached Pierre Liebschutz, my German teacher, whom I suspected to be a Jew, but he steadfastly denied it. Ironically, forty-six years later I found out that his assets had been taken over by an Aryan administrator in 1943.[1]

Having lost my connection to the Sourets, I was slowly turning back into a Jew. My Jewishness, however, was becoming a burden: I felt pressed to carry it in a brown paper bag as my father did on his way to the synagogue. Being Jewish was one more thing I would have to keep to myself. This is why it had been easier to be a Souret at the grammar school than to become a Lewendel at the high school.

Naturally, I was not very enthusiastic when I was enrolled in the bar mitzvah class held by Rabbi Sal at the Avignon synagogue. Every Wednesday I was allowed to leave the boarding school for a few hours to attend religious classes from five to seven in the evening. The Orthodox, bearded rabbi conducted lively classes, and I was the main objector to his religious stands. In a memorable argument, I claimed that prophets never existed but were invented to impress gullible followers. My reasoning was that some prophets should surely manifest themselves today if prophecy were possible. Since none can be seen today, there is no reason to believe that they ever existed. He replied that they probably exist today, but we are unable to recognize them without the distance of history. The entire year was laced with controversies

between the rabbi and myself, and although I did not dare directly question the existence of God, this was the real question hidden
behind my multitude of disagreements with the rabbi. If God really existed, how could he have let my mother go? Whether Rabbi
Sal understood my struggle or was just openminded, he nevertheless treated me with respect. The way he let me (and sometimes helped me) develop my arguments made me feel good. He
enjoyed the challenge, and I felt like his equal.

One evening, he invited me for dinner at his home. His wife
served the same bland food I used to have at home. While his wife
was in the kitchen, the rabbi whispered in my ear, "Is nonkosher
food tasty?" I replied, "Yes! But peasant food is tastier!" At the
end of the year, I learned my prayers and my lines, and I had my
bar mitzvah under protest. Since my bar mitzvah made me an
adult according to Jewish law, Rabbi Sal brought to Le Pontet my
personal set of phylacteries, two small cases with leather straps
that a pious Jewish male must wear during daily prayers, one on
his forehead, the other on his right arm. Years later, I learned that
Rabbi Sal had left religion for a more secular business, used-car
dismantling. This probably explains his tolerance of my questioning. He certainly did not need my opinion on nonkosher food anymore!

In spite of my denials, Rabbi Sal had brought to me the human
side of Judaism by engaging me as an equal. He made me accept
my Jewishness by allowing me to question it, and he provided a
timely connection to the world of my parents, a world I would
have readily rejected because it promised so much pain. At the
center of their world, I saw a deep conviction that Jews were not
put on this earth to have fun. On the contrary, God had intended
them to win a place in heaven by relentlessly going through hell
first. The experience of generations had prepared the Jews well
for this godly design.

19 | It's Hard to Be a Jew

The Lord will scatter you among all the people from one end of the earth to the other, and there you shall serve other gods, wood and stone, whom neither you nor your ancestors have experienced. Yet even among these nations you shall find no peace, nor shall your foot find a place to rest. The Lord will give you there an anguished heart and eyes that pine and a despondent spirit. The life you face shall be precarious; you shall be in terror night and day, with no assurance of survival. In the morning you shall say, "If only it were evening!" and in the evening you shall say, "If only it were morning!" because of what your heart shall dread and your eyes shall see.

—Deuteronomy 28

Telling a story was my father's favorite way of making a point. Although a well-reasoned argument may be more elegant, the punchline of a good story will forever remain etched in one's memory. Instead of tersely stating, "A Jew is always a Jew," he would tell the story of the *yeshiva bucher*, a young Orthodox theology student, whose ungodly young neighbor regularly urged him to have a good time. "Go to the Christian side and visit the fun house with the jolly girls," said the impious friend. "They will make you forget the hardships of life." The theology student would gently smile with embarrassment. One day, after months of enticement, the secular young man met his friend on Friday, neatly dressed in his Orthodox costume, carrying under his arm a package wrapped in brown paper. "Where are you going?" he asks. "To the house with the girls you told me about so many times," says the theology student. "What are you carrying under your arm?" asks the friend. "Oh! This is my tallis [prayer shawl]. If I like it there, I will stay until the end of the Sabbath."

Scattered by the Lord among all the people, our parents, too, were going through secular life with prayer shawls nicely wrapped under their arms. They regularly met at the synagogue of Avignon not only to worship, but also to commiserate. The synagogue was a place of questioning—questioning the Lord, questioning oneself, questioning one's peers. "Did you hear that the city of Carpentras has increased the fees for merchant stalls on market days?" asked one Jew. "Did you read about the anti-Semitic statements of Poujade?" asked a second Jew. (Pierre Poujade, the leader of the Union of Small Merchants, in his bid for election to the French assembly, tried to channel the traditional mistrust of the lower middle class toward the "domination of the rich." He used anti-Semitic slogans in a racist appeal to voters.) "Will the government again raise taxes on small businesses?" asked a third Jew. "What can a Jew do?" was the response. Although it seemed like a question, it was in fact an answer, because it was always followed by a long sigh and a pause. Then the Jews would return to their prayers, at least for a while.

Inside the synagogue of Avignon, they did not need to hide their Jewishness, and they agreed and disagreed with an unequaled passion. With the diversity of their origins came different religious practices. Once, an angry disagreement about the right way to proceed even interrupted the Yom Kippur service. I was amazed by the emotion of the dispute, given the subdued behavior of the Jews outside the synagogue.

Since the synagogue did not allow for longer dialogues, our parents regularly attended the salons of Madame Kurlandczyk, ironically named after the salons of Madame de Maintenon, the second wife of King Louis XIV. Madame Kurlandczyk would reign over ten conversations at once without missing a beat, meanwhile serving tea and cookies. In one corner, she was starting a conversation about Israel; then, in the back of the room, she was feeding another lingering discussion about inflation and the cost of merchandise. She would find the time to push the kids into the sunroom, serve more tea, and talk about the Glicks, who were absent. But Jewish hardships were the favorite topic.

Since most of the Jews pursued glamourless professions, Madame Kurlandczyk made sure no one forgot that she came from Warsaw and therefore had a better education than the rest of the guests. This is why the Numerus Clausus in Poland was her favorite subject of conversation, since it allowed her to mention that she had been evicted from Warsaw University because she was Jewish. She owned a little store in Avignon and had been reduced to selling garments in outdoor markets like the rest of the guests. Resentful of her air of superiority, my father sarcastically called her "the former student" behind her back.

As for Monsieur Kurlandczyk, he used to sit quietly in a corner and smile around the room. He was a kind man, and he enjoyed telling slightly self-deprecating anecdotes. Countless times I heard how he took the night train from Avignon to Paris and unexpectedly found himself back in Avignon in the early morning: he had left the train in Lyon to buy a drink and reboarded the wrong train. He was so embarrassed that he took the next train to Paris without mentioning the incident to his wife for months. She regularly addressed him as Zalman, but no one else did. "Zalman," she would say, "tell how you escaped from the czar's army." Then he would tell the story that everyone already knew by heart; afterward, he would return to his smiling silence. If not addressed, he would remain silent, and when left unprompted by his wife for too long, he would quietly disappear into his bedroom for a well-deserved nap. I could not imagine this gentle Jew riding away on a horse, pursued by a band of Cossacks.

Storytelling was the main purpose of our parents' gatherings: mostly sad stories and some happy stories, but almost always stories with morals. Storytelling was a team activity. While the "story leader" owned the main story theme, always a personal experience, the audience would add details that the teller had mentioned in the past but had omitted this time. When the story was well developed, another member of the audience would contribute his own anecdote on a related theme. At this point, he would smoothly become the "story leader." The movement of the story from one congregant to the next affirmed real connections between different and seemingly unrelated facets of life. This ritual resembled the prayers in the synagogue. Although I did not identify with the generation of our parents, I got my taste for storytelling at those colorful gatherings. This is also where I was taught to always look for hidden connections under the surface of things.

The stories also served as a way of teaching the children the "dos and don'ts," and as a continuous reminder of the boundary between Jewish and Gentile "conditions." One could not argue with the punchline of a good fable. In the salons of Madame Kurlandczyk, our oral history was transmitted to the younger generations. These stories perpetuated my link to my parents' ancestry in spite of my rift with my father and the absence of my mother.

At the salons, I was continuously reminded that it is not easy to be a Jew. Our parents often punctuated a good story of suffering with a Yiddish saying: "Es ist schweier tsi zein a Yid!" (It is hard to be a Jew!) As it was, they were convinced they were carrying the world on their backs. For them, life was never as simple as it looked, and I must confess that I often sympathized with their viewpoint. I have always been amazed by the ease with which the Gentile world periodically writes some of the darkest pages of my people's history and still remains at peace with itself.

As a Jew, I am astonished by how comfortable the anti-Semites are with their own prejudices. My early schoolmates' racism did not seem to affect their innocence in any visible way, and, frankly, that often made me jealous.

The persecutions of the Jews at the beginning of this century in Central Europe were a constant subject of conversation, because every guest had come from that part of the world. In Madame Kurlandczyk's salons, we, the children, were exposed to tales of Jewish miseries recounted by the victims themselves. From these stories, I had concluded that a Jew must always be ready to run away (*entloyfen*, as they said in Yiddish), in order to avoid being killed (*gehargent*). The salons were an island of Jewishness, *Yiddishkeit* as they say in Yiddish, amid an ocean of Gentility. Besides the synagogue, this was the only place our parents could be openly Jewish. From the pulpit of Madame Kurlandczyk, the message came loud and clear: "Being Jewish in the wilderness was not meant to be easy."

Through endless stories about "drunken Poles" who sought entertainment by beating the Jews right under the noses of the bored police who looked the other way, our parents were trying to distinguish Jews from Gentiles through the palate. "Unlike the Gentiles, Jews don't drink," they relentlessly drilled in our souls. Our parents' sobriety and the pain of the beatings created a moral barrier against the villainy of these Polish anti-Semites. For the parents, sobriety and hardship had become cardinal virtues. As they say in a famous joke, "Jews don't drink because it interferes with their suffering."

In the salons, our parents traded the names of their medicines, their doctors, and even their healers. At times, they even seemed to share their illnesses, real or imaginary. From these conversations about their bodily difficulties and their best remedies, I acquired the certitude that hypochondria must be highly contagious.

The only subject that did not reinforce the traditional theme of passive suffering was the emergence of the Jewish state of Israel out of the land of Palestine. Proof in hand, Madame Kurlandczyk proudly declared the independence of Israel. She had just received a letter from her Tel Aviv relatives with a new Israeli stamp instead of the customary Palestinian denominations. It is quite amazing that, in spite of this event, the creation of Israel passed high above my head, as if it had occurred on another planet. Even more surprisingly, I did not notice the earlier stream of Holocaust survivors who were heading to "clandestine" holding places in our area to await their departure for Palestine from La Ciotat near Marseille. Perhaps, many of us who had recently known bondage did not feel worthy of the Promised Land.

Because their entire lives had been a long struggle for survival, food was a prime preoccupation of our parents, second only to safety. In postwar France, restoring food quantity and quality to their prewar levels was the first priority, and the French definitely measured up to the task. Abundance returned to the stores, and, with it, pilgrimages to fancy country restaurants became a Sunday ritual. In a subtle contradiction to their deep desire to remain different, our Jewish parents were hoping tacitly that the status of the notable Gentile patrons of the restaurants would "rub off." Reservations had to be made weeks in advance to avoid being reduced to a "second-choice" restaurant. Several families would sit together at a huge table in the middle of the restaurant. Menu selections took an inordinate amount of time and stretched the waiter's patience like the skin of the roasted duck. The poor waiter would get lost several times in the confusion of changing menu selections around the table, and often he ended up bringing the wrong dish because he had missed the last change of mind. Contrary to the uninhibited palate of their Gentile table neighbors, our parents' choices were more in line with their "kosher tastebuds."

After the selection brouhaha had died down, we prepared for a long wait, since service was traditionally slow, leaving ample time for tumultuous conversations. Typically, one would critique the restaurant of the previous Sunday and plan for the upcoming weekends. A good culinary performance and the appropriate display of respect by the owner would qualify the place for future "raids." Conversely, some intangible dissatisfaction resulted in a fatal and irrevocable verdict, a kind of death sentence for the restaurant's fame and menu.

As soon as the dishes were served, many activities started in parallel. First, an assessment of one's choice was essential. Second, an exchange of impressions across the table was required. Third, a jury verdict about dish selection was rendered. A winning restaurant needed to receive at least one "exquisite" verdict for each course. Since I could not stomach so much food, I always finished last, which was interpreted as an "inedible" verdict, and I had to explain what was wrong with the food. After three hours of gluttony, I would leave the table with a profound disgust for food that would last several days. Monsieur Estryn, who had the largest paunch, generally concluded the meal by saying, "I am digging my grave with my own fork."

Years later, during a visit to France in 1989, Elsa and I were treated to one of these gargantuan lunches. Most of the guests were now in their eighties, but they still handled their forks with great dexterity. To their disbelief, Elsa and I shared one four-course meal instead of each ordering one five-course meal.

We, the Jewish children of Provence, were not proud of our parents because they were a living reminder that we were different. Although they tried hard to be like the natives, they were not successful, since they did not look or behave like them, whether they spoke or kept silent. Comedy was our weapon against the discomfort our parents' distinctiveness caused us; imitating them was our response. Their involuntary puns, a result of their misuse of French near-homonyms, provided much of our colorful material, and the heavy Yiddish accent of their French added to our entertainment.

Even in silence, their blend of Semitic and Slavic facial features separated them from their neighbors. No matter how hard they tried, they could not hide their real identity. Since most of them were textile merchants, their slightest gesture would betray this traditional Jewish occupation. When meeting an acquaintance neatly dressed for an occasion, a Jew would first feel the quality of the fabric between his thumb and fingers, declaring, "Good material!" The Jewish men wore excessively elegant hats, while the French were content with the usual beret. Our parents shied away from the elaborate spicy food of Provence, preferring simpler concoctions more reminiscent of the kosher food of the ghetto. The way most of them drank tea was another distinctive behavior: instead of mixing the sugar with the tea, they insisted on putting a sugar cube between their teeth and sucking their hot tea through the sugar. They had developed this habit in their countries of origin, where bulky chunks of unrefined sugar were much cheaper, although more difficult to dissolve. The gurgling noise was terribly embarrassing for me when I was sitting with them in a coffeeshop.

The more "integrated" Jews drank coffee, but they could not bring themselves to have a glass of wine in the coffeeshop like the French men did—except Estryn, whom they called a *bauer*, a derogatory Yiddish term meaning "peasant." For them, Estryn was too much like the French Gentiles, perhaps too much like the Poles they had left behind, "thanks to the Lord."

In front of Gentile friends, we were embarrassed by our Jewishness and that of our parents. In public, the adult Jews made a point never to mention any Jewish topic, never to read a Jewish magazine, and always to mention a Jewish holiday only in a murmur or by an oblique reference. Nevertheless, we who knew them intimately believed their Jewishness was written all over them. My Jewish friends and I could not stand the thought of acting out our victimization as our parents did through the endless stories of their miseries. Surprisingly, we, the children who had been uniquely touched by the war just two or three years earlier, suspected our parents of paranoia. By laughing at their involuntary puns and imitating their accents, we were affirming our Frenchness and distancing ourselves from our parents' generation. But we faced a dilemma: could we separate ourselves enough from our parents and still remain Jewish, or did we have to go all the way and melt into the Gentile world? As far as I was concerned, I was ready to travel halfway around the globe to escape the choking grip of their brand of Judaism.

When I look back, I miss the Yiddish music of our parents' gatherings. They refused to deny their indelible differences, a symbol of their fury to live. Most of them are gone now, having taken with them forever their parabolic wisdom and their colorful accent; parody is their only legacy. While growing up and away from them, I carried with me the memory of that legacy, in spite (and maybe because) of my earlier resistance to Rabbi Sal, long after he and I had drifted away from religion.

In the Meantime . . .

In the meantime, a lot of things will happen. There will be a tormented adolescence and even the temptation of delinquency. There will also be a problematic high school graduation in 1953, and the preparation for engineering school. Finally, in the east of France, there will be the School of Mining and Metallurgy, from which I will drop out to engage in a left-wing Zionism that will bring me to Israel in 1957. At a crossroads and threatened by a Soviet anti-Semitism so flagrant and so familiar, I will thus avoid the profound temptation of Communism. My determination to fully integrate myself into Israeli society will lead me to choose a new Hebrew first name, Haim, my fifth identity.

I will leave France with little baggage in my hand but with a treasure in my heart. I will carry with me a little of all those who granted me their limitless support when I was little—my mother, the Steltzers, the Brès, and so many others, whose nobility sprang from their very ordinariness. I will keep in my heart a particular place for the Sourets, who, by remaining on my side even when I was sliding toward the edge, taught me never to take the moral high ground.

Upon my arrival in Israel, I will enroll in the parachute corps, defying the powerlessness I felt as a hunted child. Then, in 1960, I

will join Kibbutz Beit-Kama, a small collective agricultural commu-
nity of 180 souls in the southern Negev desert. There, spared the need
to face my fear of having a family life. I will try myself at almost
every job—agriculture, fixing farming machinery, welding, and
chicken farming. For five years I will put my soul into the education
of children born in abuse and violence, children traumatized by alco-
holism, poverty, prostitution, and crime. Touched by their abandon-
ment, so similar to mine, it is the Souret in me who will come to their
aid. In 1965, I will be sent to Morocco by the Israeli government to
organize the clandestine emigration of a Jewish population con-
fronted by the threat of Pan-Arabism, a precursor of Islamic funda-
mentalism. As one might have expected, my clandestine life in
Morocco will enable me to develop my sixth and seventh identities, a
necessity to which I will adapt easily. My interest in the fate of dis-
tressed children as well as endangered Jews will testify to the pro-
found imprinting left by my war years.

In 1967, I will dare marry Elsa, a woman of comfortable
Christian origin. Our wedding will provoke a general commotion in
her family as well as in mine. Back in Israel, we will settle in
Beersheba, where I will restart my studies, this time in computers.
Two wars—one in 1967, the other in 1973—and two mobilizations
will revive my nightmare of the bombardments of 1944, and every-
thing else.

Although the admiralty of the French fleet will not be at the end
of my rainbow, as Madame Souret's healer had foretold in 1946, the
study toward a Ph.D. in computer engineering at the University of
Southern California will bring Elsa and me, together with our two
children, to the United States, where we will settle. In Avignon, the
news of my academic coronation in 1976 will bring radiant smiles to
the faces of our Jewish friends. "Ikh hob ihr gezugt!" they will tri-
umphantly declare. "A richtige yiddishe kop!" ("I told you so! A real
Jewish mind!") Our third child, born in Illinois in 1980, will be eli-
gible to run for the presidency of this country. As for me, at a loss for
new identities, this is where I will wind down and finally stop my
waltz of names.

In spite of my departure from Israel, my stay there will have blessed the Jew in me with the opportunity of finally coming out of hiding and proudly affirming his identity. From now on, I will be a real Jewish Jew and proclaim my Judaism in the open. Much later, in 1992, Elsa will uncover a continuous lineage of women linking her all the way back to a German great-grandmother of Jewish origin. Her feminine ascendance will make her—what an irony—a full Jew in her own right, even in the eyes of the most Orthodox of us.

With time, my family will have provided me, by its constant support, with a safe bridge over the turbulence of my memories, and I will finally muster the courage to embark on my search for lost time, echoing Proust's title A la recherche du temps perdu. *After having relied, for decades, exclusively on dead heroes to teach me history, I will, at long last, be ready to visit my own past.*

20 | Do Not Turn Around

But Lot's wife looked back, and she thereupon turned into a pillar of salt.

—Genesis 19:26

For many years, I have avoided every opportunity to reopen the past that was so vividly present in me. The pain would not go away, but I kept it locked inside. For one thing, sharing my feelings was like asking for undeserved sympathy. I had, after all, survived. The real heroes, dead or alive, were those who had had to endure the concentration camps, not someone like me who had stayed behind and was lucky enough to find a safe haven. During my seventeen years in Israel, had I not been engulfed by the cult of the dead hero, this individual bigger than life who had fought in Warsaw, Vilna, and Treblinka without a thought for his own salvation? Ashamed of grieving for the loss of my mother, I took refuge in a long silence.

When I was twenty, my father broke his silence about my mother and proposed that I take advantage of the German financial reparation process. He even provided the name of a psychiatrist who would readily testify that I had sustained irreversible psychological damage, as he had done for Jacques Schneider. I angrily refused, stating that I did not need *their* money. In truth, I could not accept anything in exchange for the loss of my mother. I would not betray her again as I had in Carpentras when I accepted the *osselets* after her arrest. This was the first and last time my father and I talked about my mother.

I stayed away from the people who had helped me. When I was young, my father and Ruth deliberately kept a distance from the people who had been close to me. They never talked about my helpers. It was as if they deeply resented my bond with people like the Steltzers, the Brès, and the Sourets. They certainly did not open their arms to my rescuers as my rescuers had done to me. Perhaps they feared that my helpers would try to redeem the debt and pressure them for favors, or perhaps they were jealous of my attachment to them. Or maybe it was the determination to forget.

When I grew older, I myself could not go back to those who had helped me. When visiting Avignon, I would often drive near familiar places where I had been during the war, but I never got out of the car. The longer I waited, the more difficult it became to break my long "vow of silence." While in Paris in 1967, for example, I ran into the Gold family, who had been in Carpentras during the war. They mentioned that the Steltzers would be delighted to see me again after so many years. I made an appointment to see the Steltzers, who were then living in a suburb of Paris. But at the last minute I backed out, because I was afraid of facing the past. By the same token, my inability to express my gratitude to them made me feel guilty.

The Steltzers, the Brès, and the Sourets had given me a second life, but along with intense gratitude I also felt an unbearable debt. Like many around me, I was thinking in terms of quid pro quo: I saw no way I could possibly repay them. I felt like the eighty-seven-year-old Polish woman who told Nechama Tec, "Gratitude is something few of us can afford."[1] With regard to my rescuers, I was in for a surprise.

In 1989, after forty-five years, I finally dared to stop in Sarrians and ask about the Brès family. No one knew their whereabouts. After crisscrossing the area, I found the familiar road and the farm hidden behind rows of cypresses. I recognized the fields, the building, and the gravel yard where Monsieur Steltzer had left me. The farm was now occupied by people who had no idea about the wartime tenants. Every time I went to Le Pontet, I became increasingly frustrated in my search. Then I finally got a clue. A farmer whose fields were adjacent to the Brès farm was able to provide their new address. He had been a few years old during the war, but he remembered his parents talking about the Brès. "They had the bad habit of taking in other kids in spite of their dependency on welfare," he said, remembering his parents' stories. "You always came to eat with us since the Brès did not have enough," he added scornfully, carrying on his face his parents' contempt of 1944.

I was apprehensive before seeing Mireille and Michel Brès, who now live together in a poor little shanty between Sarrians and Carpentras. I imagined that they would make me feel how much I owed them and how angry they were about my long silence. Their reaction was completely the opposite. Their faces lit up with joy when they recognized me at the metal gate of their yard. They arranged for Magali, who is married, to come the next day and surprised her with my visit. She was in shock and over-joyed to see "the little Jacky now grown up after so many years." She was still grateful to me for "saving her life" when she accompanied me on my first day of school in Sarrians and I had to make up a story to satisfy the principal's curiosity.

In the meantime, Fernand, the *sourcier*, and Madame and Monsieur Brès had passed away. Magali told me that, until his death, Fernand frequently talked about me and my "talents." My wife and I left their house laden with cherries and a homemade medicinal concoction that was "good against any illness or injury with guaranteed success." I also received a few old pictures, taken of me when I was eight years old. Elsa and I were showered with hugs and gifts as if they owed me something, while I was the one who had never thanked them. In fact, during a recent visit, Magali was deeply disappointed that we had brought her a box of pralines, because she had brought one for us too. Since we were even, she felt it were as though she did not give us anything. The Brès do not barter their goodness.

After my visit, Magali wrote me a letter without any mention of their crucial role in saving my life. On the contrary, she wrote only about the joy of meeting me again and of her admiration for me and whoever is connected to me. Even my two older children, whom she does not know, she thinks must be wonderful. She did not feel betrayed by my long silence, but instead was in awe at my ability to find them again. At the end of the letter, she added: "I do not forget you. We often talk about the past when you, Jacky, were a little boy whom my family and I deeply loved. Mireille and Michel also embrace you."

The Brès family is special. By saving me, they knowingly endangered their own lives, yet they did so without acknowledging their own heroism. Their behavior was not constrained by the prevailing sentiment since they did not conform to their surroundings, and, being independent, they sympathized with me as a victim. For them, things have always been simple; they acted *comme ça, sans trop y penser* (like that, without thinking too much about it). They are convinced that *I am the hero* since, they affirm, I am the one who saved *their* lives when I lied to the school principal.

In a later letter, Magali explains further:

> Indeed we were taking risks, but, if we acted without hesitation, it was because your life was in greater danger. We would have done anything so that nothing happened to you. We succeeded. We were all elated. My poor parents, my poor brother loved you very much. For Mireille and for me, you were our little brother and

we adored you. Alas, it was your departure [after the Liberation] that was hard. It took me a long time to recover.

The Brès were not alone in their simple goodness. Recently, I attended in New York a conference of children hidden during the Holocaust. Some rescuers were brought from Europe and honored at the plenary session. One rescuer, a white-haired Dutch woman who saved scores of Jewish children, took the microphone and said to the attendees, "I do not understand all the fuss about what we did. We did it because this is the way we were."

The other side of the coin is precisely that these "good souls" had little effect on the collective crime being perpetrated, since they were only a small minority. There were not enough of them for all of the victims—and could it have been otherwise? Although I rejoice at my own survival, I cry for my lost people. I cry for my lost Polish relatives. I cry for my own mother.

After my visit to the Brès, I started reopening the past and freeing myself from my long silence. Meeting the Brès triggered an avalanche I was no longer willing to contain. In the past few years, I have become obsessed with that part of my life, always searching for more information.

While considering the work of the "professional historians," I am struck by the arrogance that some of them display, particularly those who have declared themselves the guardians of objectivity, meanwhile engaging in endless academic debates to avoid succumbing to the temptation of memory, in order to preserve the virginity of their judgment. On the opposite side of the spectrum is the recent flood of "fresh" memories, this "excess" of memory belonging to Jews of the 1990s, which Annette Wieviorka explains as "a fear of the future and the absence of project."[2] As for me, the bearer of a personal truth, I recognize myself neither in the undertaking of these professional historians nor in the excess of memory of the Jews of the 1990s: the former often lack memory and the latter do not have any past. This is why I decided to continue until I could explain everything. At the time, little did I realize that I was about to clash with the common establishment belief that, as a son of a deportee, I had no right to find out who had contributed to the arrest of my mother, that I had no right to know who had sealed the fate of hundreds of Jews and other undesirables of Vaucluse.

21 | *"Political" Deportee Number 23925*

History is far too serious to be left for historians.

—Pierre Vidal-Naquet[1]

After the end of the war, no one had been willing to talk to me openly about my mother and what had happened to her after her arrest. At times there had been intimations of the worst, but I rejected them and retreated into fantasy. I clung to odd bits of information that I had picked up by accident and used them to build explanations for her absence. One day, for instance, I overheard Madame Kurlandczyk mention that my mother had become meshugga because of her brutal separation from me. In Yiddish, this word can mean "tormented by anguish," but it literally means "crazy." I took her literally, and came to believe that my mother had been taken to a French asylum for the insane and had possibly lived there for years. I further imagined that my father and Ruth were conspiring to keep her whereabouts secret so that their marriage would remain valid. Since my late teens, this fantasy had taken on the feel of reality in my mind because of the persistent memory of a dream. In the dream, Madame Souret was taking me to visit my mother in the asylum of Mondevergue, where she was locked up. We bicycled there, bringing her a light blue sweater that Madame Souret had knitted for her. Upon my return, however, my father and Ruth expressed their profound displeasure at our trip, and I responded by accusing Ruth of hiding the truth from me.

That dream, and the fantasy that my mother had survived the war in an asylum, came to mind in 1989 when I read a newspaper article about Serge Klarsfeld, a Parisian lawyer who had documented the fate of the Jews in France. I contacted him and asked for his help in tracing my mother's fate after her arrest. Based on what I had told him about my memory of the asylum, he first advised me to check the admission records of mental hospitals in the Avignon area. A few hours later, however, he called me back with starker news. He had found my mother's record. She had not been admitted to a mental institution. Instead, on June 30, 1944, she had been sent by convoy 76 from the French camp of Drancy near Paris to Auschwitz, and she had not survived.

Klarsfeld subsequently sent me a copy of his book, *Memorial to the Jews Deported from France*, which contains the names of all the Jews of France who were deported to the death camps by the Nazis. The book contains 664 pages of statistics and endless lists of names, convoy by convoy. Among the last convoys to leave the transit camp of Drancy was convoy 76. It included

approximately 600 males and 550 females, including at least 162 children under 18. Amongst the families were: Ernest Touitou (44), his wife Sara (40), and their eleven children: Marcel (18), Henri (17), Joseph (16), Isaac (14), Haim (14), Jean (13), Simon (10), Fernand (8), Josette (7), Louis (5), and Gilbert (3); . . .

Upon their arrival in Auschwitz, 398 men were selected and received numbers A16537 through A16934; 223 women were given the numbers A8508 through A8730. The rest were

"POLITICAL" DEPORTEE NUMBER 23925

immediately gassed. In 1945 there were 182 survivors. One hundred and fifty of them were women.[2]

In the middle of Klarsfeld's list of more than 1,100 deportees in convoy 76, most of them murdered in Auschwitz, one line stood out:

LEWENDEL, SARA BORN MARCH 1, 1904 IN LIPSKO

Here, finally, was evidence strong enough to dispel any of my doubts about my mother's fate. Her name did not appear on the small list of survivors. After her arrest, she ended up first at Drancy. Then she was shipped to Auschwitz and murdered. Oddly enough, even after the shock had worn off and I had accepted the reality of her death, the old fantasy about the asylum still remained. Halfway between dream and reality, I still harbor the fuzzy memory of visiting the asylum with Madame Souret and of the argument with Ruth that ensued. The dream (or was it the dream of a dream?) is still present, but it does not serve the same purpose it once did. In the past, the dream kept me from looking for my mother among the dead. Today, the dream is the only remnant of the fantasies that sustained me for so many years.

After I found my mother's name on Klarsfeld's list of convoy 76 deportees, I found myself reading through the hundreds of names of those who had died with her. Oddly enough, the youngest child listed was: "BENYACAR, Sylvain, born February 15, 1944, in Le Pontet."

He was only four and a half months old and had been born in my village. He was deported along with his mother, Lisette Benyacar, twenty-two, and his father, Moise Benyacar, twenty-four. Only Moise returned. In 1944 I had not been aware that the Benyacars lived in our village because they had arrived only shortly before being arrested and deported. However, the daughter of Guendon, the village street sweeper, whom I met recently, remembered them well. She had been their neighbor and Sylvain's babysitter.

It was now painfully obvious that my mother had survived her arrest by only a few weeks. My confrontation with the stark facts in Klarsfeld's book triggered a memory that I had apparently repressed for many years, preferring to keep my hope alive. I should have known better, because shortly after my father brought me back from Carpentras, Beracha had indeed mentioned the deportation of my mother. He had even told us that she could not bring herself to jump from the moving train and described her familiar large handbag.

Shortly thereafter, I returned to Paris, hoping to learn more about convoy 76. While I was there, I was able to locate Georges Wellers. Before the war, he had been a brilliant biologist in Paris. Sent to Auschwitz in convoy 76, he was one of the few to survive. After his return, he dedicated his life to the history of the Holocaust. When I told him that my mother had been in the same convoy, he offered to give me his book, *The Yellow Star during the Vichy Regime: From Drancy to Auschwitz*,[3] covered with a multitude of annotations. We went to his apartment, where many rows of books occupied entire walls of shelves. Although Wellers was an old man, he spoke energetically about his experiences during the war and about his subsequent battles with those historical "revisionists" who would deny the Holocaust.[4]

Later that day, I read Wellers's account of June 30, 1944, the day he was shipped from Drancy in the same cattle cars as my mother. I was surprised to read that he mentioned the day the train departed but did not state when it arrived at the death camp. It was as if time had lost its importance upon reaching Auschwitz. Without knowing that arrival date, however, I was unable to determine the exact day my mother had arrived there, only to be immediately gassed and have her body consigned to the flames of the crematorium. During those days of early July 1944, I had been sitting in a French class in Sarrians, burying inside me the hope of her return.

I became determined to find out exactly what had happened

to my mother between the time of her arrest and the day she died. By searching telephone books in the area of Le Pontet, I was soon able to locate Gaston Vernet, the neighbor who had taught me card tricks and mathematical riddles when I was seven. Over the phone, he told me that he had witnessed my mother's arrest on June 6, 1944. Around noon that day, he said, a front-wheel-drive Citroën limousine had stopped in front, and two Frenchmen had entered the store to arrest my mother. In panic, she ran out the back door, straight into the house where Gaston Vernet lived with his parents. Only Gaston and his mother were at home. The two Frenchmen followed my mother into their house, and she begged them in vain to let her go. "You have no heart," she said. "Yes, we do," one of them replied, "but it is made out of steel." At that point, my mother seized a kitchen knife and cut her wrist. Then she was brutally dragged back to our house. That was the last time Gaston Vernet saw her, bleeding and desperate. He added that, a few hours later, French militiamen had come with a truck and emptied our house and the store of merchandise and valuables. The rest was left for the looters.

Some of Gaston's information about my mother's arrest was later corroborated by an unexpected source. Walking down the street in Avignon in January 1992, I happened to run into my old schoolmate Robert Fage. For an instant, all I could think of were the anti-Semitic slogans he had written on our back door in 1944, but I kept the memory to myself, and we chatted. The first thing he wanted to talk about was my mother.

"I will never forget my last sight of your mother," he said. "The news of her arrest spread through the village at lightning speed, and my father took me by the hand to the sidewalk of your storefront. A black limousine was parked near the sidewalk. Through the glass storefront, I could see your mother lying on the floor between two men who were beating her up with all their might to force her out."

When I talked to Gaston Vernet on the phone, he also remembered Madame D., whom he described as "a young woman of small virtue who had survived Auschwitz and was fooling around with other men although she was married." He said that Madame D. had been an eyewitness to my mother's fate at Auschwitz. On her return to Le Pontet, Madame D. had said that my mother, sick and indifferent, had been gassed immediately upon her arrival at Auschwitz. This confirmed Klarsfeld's information.

Gaston Vernet's testimony provided me with the beginning and the end of my mother's final weeks, but it was not until after I had hung up that another crucial point struck me. Gaston had reiterated several times that my mother had been arrested by *two Frenchmen!* They had spoken perfect French with the southern accent of Marseille, and had worn leather jackets and fancy felt hats, just like those frightening visitors to Monsieur Gros, the owner of the Sporting Bar. This was a shock because, for all these years, I had believed that my mother's arrest was the work of the Germans, thanks in part to Claire Steltzer's bitter words to her mother after our return to Carpentras: "There is nothing you can do. The Germans did it."

The fact that my mother had been brutally arrested by two Frenchmen reminded me of something I had long tried to forget: traditional French bigotry and the antipathy of many French Christians toward the Jews during the dark years of World War II. Interestingly enough, the Germans were always blamed for the "unfortunate events" of 1939–44, while the French portrayed themselves as innocent victims. In reality, however, the Germans became a convenient excuse for French racism and anti-Semitism. At times, growing up in Le Pontet, I had experienced an impenetrable wall of contempt and isolation. My mother had apparently suffered an even more virulent form of French hatred, arrested by the French and somehow turned over to the Nazis.

On the advice of Klarsfeld, I contacted the office of French war veterans, where the deportation archives were stored, and requested a search to trace my mother's whereabouts. After two unanswered letters and several phone calls, I finally got a response. It read:

"POLITICAL" DEPORTEE NUMBER 23925

Sir,

You have solicited my services for information about the deportation and the death of your mother, Madame Sara LEWENDEL nee GOLDSTEIN, on March 1, 1904, in Lipsko (Poland).

I am honored to inform you that the research we have undertaken in the name lists and archives in my possession allow me to establish that Madame Sara GOLDSTEIN, LEWENDEL's spouse, born on March 1, 1904, in Lipsko (Poland), was arrested on June 6, 1944, in the <u>département</u> of Vaucluse. Interned in Marseille, she was transferred to the camp of Drancy on June 13, 1944 (number 23925), from which she was deported to the concentration camp of Auschwitz on June 30, 1944.

An act of disappearance was established by my services on March 29, 1947.[5] In addition, the title of political deportee was granted to her on May 10, 1963, for the period from June 6 to June 30, 1944.[6]

Please, accept the expression of my best consideration.

In the Name of the Secretary of State:
The Director of Pensions,
Social Rehabilitation and Statutes
Flavien ERRERA

I could not help but notice how the letter euphemistically referred to my mother as a "political deportee" instead of accurately describing her as an "innocent victim of murderous hatred and bigotry." My mother's only political act was to attempt suicide when she was captured. This letter also made me brutally aware that the French government had no interest in taking any responsibility for the actions that led to the death of my mother. Indeed, the government carefully restricted its responsibility to the period of her arrest and incarceration from June 6 to June 30, 1944, when she was deported to Auschwitz. The letter makes my mother's delivery to her murderers sound like a casual trip abroad.

After the war, a public perception was created that the far right was responsible for the anti-Semitic excesses in France. This perception partially arose from the militancy of the far right during the war, but Zeev Sternhell has shown in his book *Ni Droite, Ni Gauche* (*Neither Right nor Left*) that French anti-Semitism has traditionally transcended political affiliation and can be found anywhere along the French political spectrum.[7] Bernard-Henri Levy goes much further, claiming that all French people share an ideology close to Fascism.[8] Levy's position may be excessive, but my own feelings of isolation prior to going into hiding in 1944 point toward a broader hostility than Sternhell wants to admit. Blaming the far right for the anti-Semitic horrors in France during the war was a convenient fiction, which all too many Frenchmen found it comfortable to hide behind.

Of course, rewriting history to reduce one's guilt is not just the prerogative of the revisionists of Holocaust history. In June 1988, for instance, I was driving through Germany when I arrived by accident in the small town of Dachau, nine miles outside of Munich. I was surprised by how close this small town, site of a notorious concentration camp, was to Munich. The camp itself has been preserved as a memorial to its victims, and when I visited it, I was even more astonished to discover that it actually lay within the Dachau city limits. In front of the former administrative building stands a simple monument with the dedication: "To all who perished because of their opposition to the Nazi regime." Although the camp was used beginning in 1942 for the transit of Jews toward the death camps, and beginning in 1944 for their evacuation from these camps, there is little reference to the role of Dachau in the persecution of those people whose only "political" crime consisted of being Jewish. How much easier it is to categorize the death and concentration camps as unfortunate extensions of political disagreement than to brand them as the hellish engines of racism and hatred that they were.

In 1991, searching in the archives of Avignon provided me with an unexpected eyewitness account of the days immediately following my mother's arrest. The archivist told me about the testimony of a woman, Estrea Asseo, who had been arrested on the same day as my mother. When I telephoned Estrea, she remembered "the woman from Le Pontet who had left a little boy and was crying without respite." Estrea had been incarcerated with my mother during the twenty-four days preceding their deportation to Auschwitz. "In Birkenau, your mother was immediately selected for the gas chamber, and I was sent to work because I was younger and looked healthier." She added, "I had also left my son, who was three and a half years old."

A few months later, I visited Estrea in Avignon. A frail but sparkling eighty-seven-year-old woman opened the door. She talked to me for hours, until darkness filled her living room. She often tied stories of her own life to current events, evoking for me a powerful image of Jewish continuity.

During the roundup of Jews a few months before Estrea's arrest, the Gestapo visited her home in search of her husband. She writes in her 1974 memoir:

> All the Jews of the rue de la Carreterie were being driven away. . . . Tonight things were different, and cars were continuously passing by. . . . One car stops and somebody noisily knocks on the door downstairs. It is our turn. . . . We arrange the bed and my husband disappears into the closet armed with a bat just in case. . . . I act as if I was alone and wear a bathrobe and put lipstick on. . . .[9]

Estrea's identity card was not stamped with the word "Juif," but her husband, fearful of the consequences of not registering, had registered the family. According to Law No. 2333 of June 2, 1941, the declaration is done by the husband for the wife. She tried to convince the police that her husband was being held in the camp of Le Vernet by showing them a letter in which he was ordered to present himself at the camp. Still suspicious, they combed the house without discovering her husband. Fortunately, the children remained asleep. Estrea claimed that the children were Christians and that the vicar had the certificates of baptism, which she would produce the next day. "Next to the soldiers, the closet is ajar, and, behind the clothes, my husband, hidden, tries not to breathe; extremely tense, he was ready to attack the men with his bat. . . . We had decided to fight to the end if they touched the children."

Still unconvinced, the men renewed their search for Estrea's husband without success. They finally left, promising to come back the next day to check the children's certificates of baptism. Estrea and her husband did not wait for them to return. They fled with the children immediately.

Unfortunately, a few months later, on June 6, 1944, Estrea was arrested on the street while seeking food for her family. Lucien Blanc, one of the men who arrested her, knew her and her husband, since he had worked with him as a salesman at the Bouchara fabric store in Avignon. Blanc, who had been fired from the fabric store because of low sales, had joined the Nazis. Having avoided the census of 1941 and the *JUIF* stamp on her identity card, Estrea claimed again that she was not Jewish, but Blanc confronted her with the city census record, where she was faced with the tragic fact: her name was indeed on the list. Left alone with Blanc for a few minutes, Estrea personally appealed to him to let her go, offering to pay him whatever he wanted. When he contemptuously said that she did not have enough money for him, she responded with a warning. "I will make sure," she said, "that you pay for your actions."

In her book, Estrea provides details about the twenty-four days from June 6 to June 30. She, my mother, and other arrestees were first placed in the Seventh Engineering Corps jail, where they spent a desperate night. Estrea recorded my mother's painful premonition: "'I have left my son behind. . . . I do not know where he is. . . . I will never see him again.'"

In the middle of the second night in jail, they were taken by groups of four in a private limousine and driven at high speed across the city. Estrea vividly describes the terror that engulfed them:

> We were preparing ourselves to spend a second night in
> the jail when, suddenly, the door opened and three indi-
> viduals from the Militia, well perfumed and smiling
> ironically, told us to prepare to leave this place. Indeed,
> a car was waiting, and others were certainly following.
> Four by four, we were driven to the Sainte-Anne
> prison. We traversed Avignon: lost in a daze, I had
> already mentally left this world. I was sure that we
> were being led to our execution. Across town, the car
> was driving at high speed, taking away four women
> drained of any life. One of us had passed out.

Beside that last sentence, Estrea had made a handwritten note in
my copy of her book: "Your mother, Madame Levandel."

The women spent two more days at the Sainte-Anne prison
near the Popes' Palace in Avignon. The night of the second day,
they were driven to a train track some distance from the train station, to keep the operation away from the public. There, they were
loaded into a cattle car that had arrived from Marseille and
already contained deportees from other towns. Estrea repeatedly
mentions the active role of the French militiamen in the secretive
loading of the prisoners into the cattle car. Even while the prisoners were being loaded, the militiamen continued pressing them for
information about family members still at large. The militiamen's
license plate code, A 13, indicated that they came from Marseille,
sixty miles away.

All the secretive handling by the French militiamen was done
at high speed in the middle of the night, when criminals do not
need scruples. In Avignon, a typical French provincial town, midnight inaugurates the kingdom of boozers, prostitutes, and shady
characters; it's a time when respectability retires to a well-
deserved tranquillity. At midnight, the legitimate hotels are kept
under lock and key so that they cannot be mistaken for brothels.
At midnight, there is no guilt on the sidewalks.

The journey to the transit camp of Drancy took several days.
There was no food or water in the sealed cattle car, which was

hooked to a regular passenger train. While on that train, Estrea managed to smuggle a letter to her husband with the help of a friendly train employee. The letter included food coupons for the children and the name of the collaborator, Lucien Blanc. During the trip, Estrea witnessed the same escape that Beracha had described to my father and me in 1945. According to Estrea, Beracha and another man had been able to flee through a man-sized hole in the cattle car with the complicity of the train engineer, who slowed the train between two tunnels. However, neither my mother nor Estrea was able to jump. When the cattle car arrived at Drancy, Estrea says that the functionaries counted eighty-five Jews instead of the expected eighty-seven. However, Serge Klarsfeld has located the Drancy arrival list of June 13, 1944, which counts just sixty-six Jews "arrived from Marseille."[10] In Drancy, the deportees were immediately processed in three parallel lines and registered with an astonishing simplicity, as their files had each been reduced to three-by-five-inch cards, containing all that the Nazis needed to know. My mother's card reads:

23925	
CC	**B**
Name:	**June 30, 1944**
	LEWENDEL
	née Goldstein
First Name:	**Sara**
Date of Birth:	**3–1–04**
Place:	**Lipsko**
Nationality:	**Polish**
Profession:	**Saleswoman**
Home Address:	**Pontet**
	Rte Nationale
ID Valid Until:	**Marseille**
	6–13–44

"POLITICAL" DEPORTEE NUMBER 23925

I first became aware of this card[11] in July 1991, when a friendly employee in the French Veterans Affairs archives conceded to me in a private telephone conversation that both the card catalogue of the Drancy transit camp and the census of the Paris Jews were held in the archives. It is by pure coincidence—and because of my ignorance—that I made this discovery. A few months earlier, I had the opportunity to find in the YIVO archives in New York a copy of the Census of the Jews in the occupied zone. Assuming by mistake that I had found the original, and having noticed that the Paris segment was missing, I called the French Veterans Affairs archives, where the employee admitted the existence of the Paris census. On the same occasion, the employee indicated that the lists had been kept secret, "because this was racist material, which was not supposed to remain in the government's hands." Of course, I immediately told the story to Serge Klarsfeld, who had tried unsuccessfully to obtain these files since 1981. Based on my lead, in September 1991 Klarsfeld triggered the famous legal action to release the census.[12] Had I known that the YIVO files were only copies, I probably would not have pursued my investigation in the direction of the Veterans Affairs archives. I did not know either that the lists held by Veterans Affairs were not originals. They were apparently copies used by the Vichy police in its action against the Jews.[13]

It is therefore by sheer ignorance that I triggered, in France, a public debate and, at the Veterans Affairs archives, a commotion, which deeply interfered with my own research. After my accidental discovery, it took seven months of futile conversations before I was able to obtain a copy of my mother's card. The Veterans Affairs archives invoked Klarsfeld's judicial proceedings to justify the delays. Trying to help me, the archive employee finally took it upon herself, in January 1992, to send me the long-awaited document inside an anonymous envelope, without letterhead, as if it were pornographic material.

The date at the bottom of the card (6–13–44) is the date my

mother arrived in Drancy. She was given the registration number 23925; she had become "Victim Number 23925" on the list of the camp commander, Aloïs Brunner. Next in line, Estrea was given the number 23926. From his appointment on June 18, 1943, to the end of his Drancy tenure on August 18, 1944, Brunner's total would reach 26,418 victims. The designation CC at the top of the card stands for classification code; my mother was given the code B according to Aloïs Brunner's efficient coding system:

A: **Aryans, spouses of Aryans, and half-Jews.**
   Nondeportable and eligible for work in the West.
B: **Complete Jews without nationality or with a deportable nationality. Deportable.**
C1: **Interned people employed in the camp. Nondeportable or deportable later.**
C2: **Jews from enemy nations. Temporarily spared.**
C3: **Wives or mothers of war prisoners. To be sent to "hosting camps" (in fact, deported later).**
C4: **Interned awaiting other family members (used as bait and ultimately deported).**
C5: **Candidates for liberation. Awaiting material proof of eligibility.**[14]

Those assigned code B, signifying a "complete Jew" (*Volljude*), were subject to immediate deportation. The date casually stamped next to the name (June 30, 1944) indicates the deportation date. Theoretically, my mother could have claimed that my father was a war prisoner and obtained the classification code C3. That could have provided a delay, but she received instead the fatal code B. Possessed by a pathological hatred toward the Jews, Brunner was frantically trying to round up as many as possible. Earlier, he had maliciously granted some Jews the code C4, hoping that these internees would draw their loved ones into his net. To meet deportation quotas in spite of the German collapse in June 1944, and sensing that this was his last opportunity, he arbitrarily changed the more lenient classification codes to B. For instance, Georges Wellers, who had been working in the camp and had the code C1, was also deported on June 6, 1944, after his code was changed to B.

After registration, the prisoners were ordered by the French police to surrender their money and jewelry in exchange for a receipt. In the grand scheme of the French accomplices of the Nazis, the money and valuables pirated from the prisoners were used to finance the prisoners' own deportation and pay the train bills. The residual assets—money, jewelry, bank titles, artworks, and personal effects, robbed in Drancy from tens of thousands of Jewish detainees—were transferred by the French police to the national Caisse de Dépôts et Consignation (Deposit Fund). The assets were then liquidated to feed the French treasury. To date, the French government has no itemized list of dispossessed individuals or their assets.[15] How convenient it is to single out Switzerland for having profited from the Jewish tragedy![16]

My mother's receipt reads:[17]

CAMP OF DRANCY	
23925	
Received from	**Mme Lewendel**
	Sara
	Le Pontet
	(Vaucluse)
The Amount of	**Four hundred seventy francs plus**
	one gold wristband watch "Tissot"
Drancy June 13, 1944	
The Chief of the Camp Police	

The receipt lay together with thousands of similar receipts in the archives of the Center of Contemporary Jewish Documentation, until it was brought to my attention by a kind trustee of the center, Vidar Jacobsen. My hands were shaking when he handed me three books of receipts surrounding the date June 13, 1944. I found my mother's receipt in the third book. Hidden for so long among its silent companions, this receipt finally began to speak. It told me something about my mother's powerlessness when she faced the French Nazi bureaucrat on the other side of the reception table. I remembered the scene in 1941 when my mother received the watch with the gold wristband from my father by registered mail. How proudly she displayed it to her friends! On June 13, 1944, she had no choice but to surrender it. Just behind my mother's receipt was the receipt of Estrea Asseo. The number assigned to her was 23926, confirming her memory that she stood behind my mother when they arrived at Drancy.

Their deportation from Drancy to Auschwitz started on June 30, 1944. For five days they were packed in sealed cattle cars with no space to move and without any food or water. On their arrival in Auschwitz, a few were "spared" and sent to work, Estrea among them. All the others were gassed, including Sara Lewendel. The date was July 4, 1944, four weeks to the day after she was arrested. The numerous "dead-on-arrival" were the only ones who escaped selection at Auschwitz.

The moving testimony of an Auschwitz survivor, Lucie Politi of Avignon, confirms the date as July 4, 1944:

> **I undersigned, Lucie Politi, declare that I saw for the last time Sara Lewendel born Golsztein on July 4, 1944, after leaving the train at Birkenau in High Silesia, where, after a selection, Madame Lewendel, who was ill, left in the direction of the crematoria with other deportees of the same convoy who never came back.**
>
>

Avignon, November 12, 1946
Signed: Lucie Politi[18]

>

At least my mother was spared the degrading disintegration of body and soul that became the predicament of those "spared" at the first selection.

Sadly, Lucie Politi, who had returned from Auschwitz barely

alive enough to write her statement, died a few years later, unable to drag herself back from the dead. According to Estrea, Politi had been subjected to the barbaric sterilization experiments conducted on female inmates in the infamous Bloc 10 at Auschwitz.[19]

In an absurd respect for the witness's privacy, the archive employee who provided a copy of Lucie Politi's declaration erased the first reference to her name. Fortunately, the archivist forgot to erase the signature.

Lucien Blanc, the French Nazi who had arrested Estrea and rejected her pleas to let her go, had followed the Germans in their retreat. He came back to Avignon pretending that he had been a war prisoner. Using the letter that Estrea had smuggled out of the deportation train, her husband led the police to Blanc, and he was arrested. His postwar trial, like those of other war criminals, was held in Nimes, a small town in the *département* of Gard. Estrea returned to France in May 1945, just in time to testify at Blanc's trial. He was convicted and sentenced to death by firing squad. Estrea's curse on Lucien Blanc the day of her arrest had materialized. A few months after Blanc's execution, Estrea chanced upon his widow in an Avignon street. The woman jibed at her: "Salope!" (Slut!) Estrea, victorious, remained silent.

The arrest of my mother, Estrea, and others was a part of a late, well-planned roundup in the district of Avignon to collect a few more Jews. By this time there was no longer any distinction between French and foreign Jews. Those arrested included residents still living in their homes as well as some nonresident Jews who had been gathered at camps for foreign workers. Some fifteen foreign Jews had been held at Camp No. 148 in Le Pontet.[20] By June 6, they were gone, sent on their way to Auschwitz.

That same day, the Commander of Camp No. 148 wrote to the director of the UGIF, the Jewish organization that the Nazis and their French collaborators had turned into an instrument for keeping track of the Jews and facilitating their deportation. It brings the operation of June 6, 1944, to a "professional" conclusion:

> Monsieur le Directeur de l'UGIF
> 9 Rue de l'Hôtel de Ville
> LYON
>
> In response to your letter dated June 22, I am honored to inform you that since June 6, 1944, there are no Jewish foreign workers on the rolls of our Group.
> In addition, those who were on the rolls before [June 6, 1944] were not needy.
> Please, accept, Monsieur le Directeur, the assurance of my best feelings.
> Le Pontet, June 28, 1944
>
> (Unreadable signature)[21]

In the midst of the brutal final roundup of Jews in France, the camp commander, as had been his habit in earlier correspondence with the UGIF, pays his cordial respects to its director, a Jew. The information he reports is in line with the official Vichy masquerade. There are no longer any "Jewish foreign workers" at the camp. To hear him tell it, the Jews have disappeared, perhaps wandered off, and he is mildly puzzled at their absence. There is no mention of the roundup, which emptied the camp of foreign Jews who had recently been assembled there, and there is certainly no reference to their final destination! The commander's subsequent reference to the Jews on the camp rolls prior to June 6, 1944, who "were not needy" is even more insidious, because it contributes to the fiction that the Vichy government had set up the UGIF to serve Jews in need. "This Union is aimed at representing the Jews in front of the public authorities, specifically for assistance, prevention, and social reclassification."[22]

In the context of the arrest of the Jews outside the camp, the letter of the commander of Camp No. 148 underlines the conspiratorial and premeditated nature of the action of June 6, 1944. This operation surprisingly coincides with two events. The previous day, June 5, 1944, the Vichy government had published its last decree related to the Jews, increasing the salary of the General

Commissioner for Jewish Affairs to 180,000 francs and that of his deputy to 150,000 francs. The raises were to be retroactive to July 1, 1943![23] And on June 6, when the arrests were in full swing and the commander of Camp No. 148 was penning his polite piece of misinformation, the Allies landed in Normandy. The liberation of Europe had begun, but the Nazis, supported by their French collaborators, stepped up their efforts to destroy a few more Jews. The last arrests of Jews in the area of Avignon occurred on July 30, 1944.

22 | *Close Calls*

In January 1944, Gilbert Michlin was arrested together with his mother, Rywka, by two armed men in Paris. He was eighteen years old. After the arrest, as he was being escorted through the street by a French policeman, he rehearsed in his mind an escape scenario. Since he had been able to compete in regional running championships until recently, he still exercised regularly and had remained physically fit. It would be easy to lose the middle-aged policeman in the maze of the neighborhood streets he knew so well. At the last minute, on the edge of darting forward, Michlin decided to stay with his mother and gave up his escape. Deported to Auschwitz on February 10, 1944, with 1,500 other Jews, Michlin was one of fifty-nine survivors. His mother did not return. "I am glad I was able to accompany my mother all the way," he states. "Otherwise, I would never have been convinced there was nothing I could have done to protect her."[1]

On the one hand, I wish I had made Michlin's choice instead of letting my mother leave the cherry farm without me. But, after reflection, I must face facts. Not only would I have been sentenced to death because of my young age, but, on top of that, far from rescuing her, I would have dragged her with me. However, I often contemplate the close call that separated her destiny from mine.

And this gives me the same feeling I felt years ago in the Israeli desert, when I was scaling a cliff and realized that a small error might result in fatal consequences. On that cliff, the thought of slipping into the abyss filled me with terror. Similarly, I realize how close I came to going back to our house with my mother on that summer day in 1944, and, thus, of sharing her fate. When I close my eyes, the abyss looms before me again. I know that the only way I could ever have experienced what she felt would have been for me to have stayed with her all along. Something in me says that I should have been there.

I have often wondered how it happened that I was not with her during her destruction, since they came to arrest her the day after our visit to the cherry farm. If she had waited just a day before taking me there, I would have been with her. But she did not wait. If, as expected, I had refused to stay at the cherry farm and had gone back with her to Le Pontet, we would have been together in that train to Auschwitz and in the gas chamber. But I did not refuse to stay at the cherry farm. What if I had insisted on accompanying her to our home in Le Pontet? Would she have resisted and left alone, or would she have surrendered easily and taken me with her? But I did not insist. In the end, she could have avoided all of the terror and anguish if only she had left for hiding a few days earlier or had not gone back on the fifth of June. But she did go back. She may have gone back to pick up valuables or finish things she had forgotten. Or maybe she was still hoping my father would come back and wanted to leave a message so that he would find us easily.

And, if she had believed after her arrest, as Jews were led to believe, that she was only being deported to live somewhere else, she would have wanted above all to be reunited with me, and she would have given the name and address of the Steltzers. After all, many Jewish people had unwittingly dragged their dearest relatives to their deaths in the belief that all could be reunited at their next destination. But she did not seek the reunion because she knew better.

Obviously, our store, her sole source of independence, was a major reason for delaying our departure until the last possible moment. However, a statement given after the war by Marius Meffre, the grocery store owner next door, suggests still another reason for the noose to tighten around her: "I knew well Madame Lewendel, born Goldstein Sara, and I declare that she was arrested on June 6, 1944, by the German Gestapo. In spite of my wife's repeated advice, she had refused to flee because she was unwilling to separate from her son."[2]

She was unwilling to separate from her son. But her very fear of that separation may have forced her to wait too long to flee, resulting in the precise result she feared so much. Ironically, it was my unusual and unexpected separation from her on that June day that allowed me to live.

During the war, all Jews no doubt had great fear of being separated from loved ones and familiar surroundings. They tended to react to this fear in two very different ways: those who had personally experienced pogroms and violent anti-Semitism were likely to detect the earliest signs of danger and seek refuge in time; others, less wary of Gentile motives, misjudged events and were unprepared when the worst came to pass.

It is no accident, for instance, that my mother was repeatedly warned by Jews like Madame Sokolowski, those who had lived in precarious conditions and experienced anti-Semitic hostility in their native lands. Claire Sokolowski, Madame Sokolowski's older daughter, described her mother to me as "not very sophisticated and without any schooling." Madame Sokolowski had been orphaned very young during a Russian pogrom. She soon developed a strong survival instinct, coupled with a healthy mistrust of Gentiles. Her husband was more educated and initially believed that "here, in civilized France, there will be no danger for us." Madame Sokolowski often took unusual precautions: she made sure never to sleep in her own home, for instance. After her husband developed a secret contact within the prefecture who would provide both counterfeit documents and information about roundups, she took full advantage of the opportunity to escape her current situation.

After finding a hiding place for Ida Tieder, a child who had lost her parents in the roundups of August 26, 1942, Madame Sokolowski made arrangements to hide her own family when the time came. Her husband and two children would go to Spain; her son, Lucien, who was my age, would go to a remote village in the mountains of Provence; she and her daughter Claire would hide in the Avignon countryside, where they would be able to visit their home frequently. Being a caring woman, Sonja Sokolowski had probably suggested to my mother earlier in 1944 that she send me away, as she had arranged for her own son, but my mother angrily rejected her advice because of her reluctance to be separated from me. Today I can appreciate Madame Sokolowski's sharp intuition in sensing the danger and urging my mother to flee Le Pontet. However, if my father, who had been subjected in his youth to anti-Semitic hostility, had been around, it is likely that Madame Sokolowski's warnings would not have fallen on deaf ears.

Others shared Madame Sokolowski's premonition. The OSE saw the danger clearly and sent Jewish children into hiding in many different locations to render them less vulnerable.[3] As the Nazi grip became firmer, the OSE set up several clandestine networks aimed at saving Jewish children from deportation. My mother could have sent me to a hidden OSE children's home, for instance, which would have made it easier to find a haven for herself. Finding a place was more difficult for adults with children because it was more dangerous for the rescuers.

Contacting one of the Christian networks operating in the area could have been another alternative. A friend of mine, Jean Muller, was hidden by nuns in a convent near Paris from the time of the Vélodrome d'Hiver roundup in July 1942 until the end of the war. Jean's mother had been deported, and his father entrusted his three sons and his daughter to nuns, who kept them in scattered hiding places. After the war, Jean wanted to convert to Catholicism and become a priest. Although Jean's father had feared that exposure to the nuns might lead to his children's conversion, their survival was well worth that risk.

Unfortunately, Jews who, like my mother, had been more sheltered tended to be less suspicious and more willing to wait until things would get better. Having had little personal experience of persecution, they were unable to imagine what was about to happen to them. My mother's family, for instance, had been financially comfortable and enjoyed the safety net of the large prewar Jewish community of Przemyśl. A similar relative sense of security born of privilege induced some Jewish leaders in Europe to grossly underestimate the Nazi threat, a misjudgment that was to have disastrous consequences. In France, for instance, several key Jewish personalities helped set up the UGIF, which was used by the Nazis to inventory the French Jews and trap them until it was too late.[4] In sharp contrast with the OSE's combative attitude, the UGIF became a tool in the hands of the Nazis in their Machiavellian scheme to eliminate the Jews.

Did my mother feel secure enough to take no drastic action? Or did she indeed sense the danger but hang her fate on fragile hopes? The decree of August 5, 1942, which had threatened so many foreign Jews with immediate deportation, had a comforting side: it applied only to those who had entered France after January 1, 1936. The French Jews and those who had come earlier would be safe. Indeed, there were few new arrests of Avignon Jews until the end of 1943. In addition, my French nationality, reaffirmed by Judge Chambon in August 1942, provided some safety, and although mine was a tenuous citizenship, there was hope that we could escape the fate of the foreign Jews. In addition to the support of the judge, my mother had even managed to get, at least on paper, the sympathy of the mayor, since my father had volunteered to defend the country. His mobilization would be an additional shield over my mother's and my head. Finally, the facts were on her side. For instance, hadn't she been able to keep the store open and procure decent food? In the middle of madness, hadn't we even found some peace at the horse races?

As long as there was hope, my mother could escape dealing with her painful dilemma, her fear of losing me if she sent me into hiding alone. It is therefore not surprising that she did not take steps to leave. Only when her hopes had almost vanished was she ready to take action. The arrests of French and foreign Jews in April 1944 made the danger painfully clear, and convinced her that no one would be spared. It is only then that my mother decided to leave. We would have made it just under the wire had it not been for her fatal trip back to Le Pontet on June 5, 1944. She thought it would be safe to leave the cherry farm and return to the store one last time. Unfortunately, it was one time too many. Having exhausted all other options, her only choice now was to become a hero. Her attempted suicide on the day of her arrest was her first acknowledgment of the reality of what was happening to her—her last and only act of revolt. Her attempted suicide signified the end of her shrinking hopes and demonstrated that she understood, as did everyone else, the fatal predicament of the Jews. Her deep awareness underscores the absurd necessity of a posthumous debate over who knew what.[5]

The relatively large number of Avignon deportees who were arrested in the spring 1944 roundups indicates that my mother was not alone in her misplaced optimism. The Jews were contemplating shrinking hopes, as had been their lot throughout the centuries. Slowly, their options were disappearing but never seemed to go away completely. As long as they could perceive a small glimmer of hope, imagination kept them looking toward the future. Every time things got worse, they truly believed they had just reached the bottom; from then on, things could only get better—until the next shrinkage. As Jean-François Steiner writes in his book *Treblinka*, the Nazis knew very well how to feed and exploit this human weakness.[6]

If I could go back in time, it is clear that I would be faced with a decision impossible for an eight-year-old. I would have to choose between two equally terrifying alternatives: accompanying my mother to the gas chamber or losing her forever by staying at the cherry farm. It is, of course, her misjudgment that would thrust me into my inextricable dilemma: no way could I make the choice. But after many years of anger and resentment, I have become able to understand her side of the tragedy. Learning the details of her fate has been a great relief.

Many times I have read and reread the passage of Georges Wellers's book that describes the cattle-car journey across Europe from Drancy to Auschwitz. Many times I have imagined what it must have been like for my mother in that sealed car. I have imagined the fear that consumed her during the last miserable days of her short life. She was forty years old, and the last arrests of Jews were only a few weeks away. I can vividly feel her anguish and pain when she was brutally taken away from me. With every cycle of the steam engine, she was torn away a little more: torn away from her family, torn away from happiness, torn away from a full life. In her misery, knowing that I was safe must have been a ray of sunshine. When she was herded to the "shower," she knew that death would descend from the ceiling. What did she feel when she reached the end of the road? As to me, my decision to stay in Venasques still often feels like an unpardonable choice.

23 | *The Train of Memory*

The hangman kills always twice, the second time by oblivion.

—Elie Wiesel

April 5, 1992–April 7, 1992

Forty-eight years after convoy 76 left Drancy, the Train of Memory departs from Paris-East to Auschwitz, the German name for the small Polish village of Oświęcim. Organized by the Sons and Daughters of Jewish Deportees of France, the trip commemorates the fiftieth anniversary of the first convoy of Jews from Paris to Auschwitz on April 5, 1942. This is my first visit to the death camp, although I made the journey innumerable times in my mind. A few times in the past, I had even thought of going there while visiting Europe. But, as the date approached, I always found a reason to postpone the trip. "The visas are not ready" or "We cannot stay away from home for so long" were the usual excuses. This time, however, it is different. This inescapable journey had already started the moment I wrote the first line of my story.

Fortunately, the 750 other passengers provide a safety net for this unavoidable confrontation. Together, it will be easier to reconnect with the past at the end of the rails.

The smooth technicalities of the trip are reassuring. This is a round-trip journey, and we will be back in two days. We are kindly directed to our seats by the unusually gentle conductor, who himself had lost brothers, sisters, and parents to the Nazis. There are only six of us in the compartment, and, at night, we will deploy six beds. We have brought with us plenty of food from home, and we unexpectedly found under our seats a case of oranges and twelve bottles of mineral water, as if food and comfort would securely keep the past outside the windows of the train.

At first, there is silence and solitude inside our compartment. Then, when we speak, we do not talk about the past, although we know it is awaiting us "there," at the end of the track. We want to delay the encounter. Instead, we discuss the schedule, we speak about the arrangements, we talk about the geography from here to "there." After a few hours, we let the past get a little closer. Slowly and carefully, the probing starts with a few dark jokes, a sure sign of what we are all thinking about, and soon my old friendly sarcasm is back. Nobody in the compartment objects to a good dose of dark humor, and we carefully stay within limits. Solitude, and yet everybody is so kind.

Solitude outside the window. Slowly, the train devours the distance, moving past silent woods, faceless towns and villages. Occasionally, we stop at a train station—West German, East German, or Polish—to get out of the way of a regularly scheduled train. On the ramp, passengers look at our train without seeing it. It must have been the same detachment that greeted convoy 76 when it passed along these tracks forty-eight years ago. Now, at least, I can look straight into the eyes of indifference, since we are not sealed in a cattle car. But I notice that indifference does not stare back.

Then the fear begins: fear of being unable to finish the trip still in one piece, fear of my encounter with what lies at the end of our journey, fear of my thoughts—it could have been me on these tracks forty-eight years ago. Once again, the feeling of vertigo in front of the abyss.

As we get closer to Auschwitz, I recognize the familiar countryside of my father's stories: forests and meadows, sparse shacks and little gardens, mud paths and marshes. It seems as if I had been here before. It rains continuously in a thin drizzle. A solitary Polish peasant walks across the muddy landscape. Is he afraid of falling into the hands of hooligans like my father was?

The train slows down. Railroad crossings and narrow roads. "Katowice 12 km" reads a bleak road sign beyond the railroad gate. The town of Katowice was the site of one of the numerous annexes of Auschwitz, feeding the main camp with victims or absorbing its overflows. The history of my people was written by the Nazis all over this Polish countryside, and each of these road signs serves as a memorial.

When the train finally stops at Oświęcim, buses take us to the Auschwitz II annex of Birkenau, next to the little village of Brzezinka. The old deportation tracks now extend right into the belly of madness.[1]

Past the infamous red brick arch, the tracks squeeze for hundreds of yards between a dirt road and the unloading ramp level with the tracks. Electrified fences and watchtowers stand along both sides. Here, on the yellow gravel, convoy 76 regurgitated its resigned load. When the cattle-car doors opened, the victims, ordered to leave their belongings behind, rushed out of the train. For many of them—the old, the sick, and the young—the cattle-car floor was too high above the ramp, and in the panic of the early morning of July 4, 1944, they were pushed out of the cars and trampled upon by the abler prisoners. Only those already dead in the car were spared this orgy of horrors.[2]

I am standing on the exact spot where my mother, sick and soulless, was thrown out onto the ramp. For the first time, I can see what she saw on that early morning: death and fear all around. There was nowhere to hide. The camps and their electrified fences surround the tracks on both sides. The impeccable rows of concrete fence poles are like a thousand silent witnesses lurching in pain over the electrified wires. Between the sky and me looms the higher row of menacing watchtowers. At the end of the track, two gas chambers and two crematoria. Here, Lucie Politi saw my mother alive for the last time. I walk as fast as I can along her last mile toward the gas chambers and the crematoria. Time passes very slowly, and I feel that I will never reach the end. Her anguish is my anguish. It is like a dream: no matter how fast I walk, I do not seem to move. Time stands still where one doesn't want to be. The minutes of agony it took to die in the gas chamber at the end of the ramp must have felt like an eternity.

As if still ready to inhale her soul, the wet clouds reach down to the chimneys of the collapsed crematoria. I seem to stand forever on top of the menacing rubble.[3] It would have been here that a sentenced prisoner of the Sonderkommando, rehearsing his own suspended destiny, would have burned her body into anonymity.[4] Then I see the houses. Literally a stone's throw beyond the electrified fence, the first houses of the village of Brzezinka seem a hallucination. Did the villagers watch what happened here? Did they smell the smell of death? What about the odor of charred flesh in their nostrils, day in and day out? How could they not know?

For the first time in my life, my lively memories of my mother are overwhelmed by the graphic images of her deterioration. By the time she had tumbled down from the cattle car to the gravel ramp, she had been turned into a human wreck, without compass or direction. Near the end in the gas chamber, she fought for her last breath, her body locked against the others. Then, the crematorium attendants extricated her body from the collapsed human mass. After that, nothing but flames and dust.

This is not the way I remember her. She used to be my support; she allayed my fears. Even our last photographs radiate care and hope, not despair. I cannot bear the destruction of my memories.

It is still raining, as I am told it often does here. I do not have to hide my tears, since the constant drizzle is washing my face. My body feels drained. I am relieved to go back to the buses along the same gravel ramp and out through the entrance arch. I pay no attention to the other members of our group. At the arched gate, I look back for the last time. The place is so vast and so overwhelming. The visitors are absorbed into the ground like the daily convoys of deportees once were.

I have been told that the Nazis used to ship the human ashes from Auschwitz to Germany to use as fertilizer. This knowledge unexpectedly allows me to think of my return journey from Birkenau to Germany as the funeral that my mother never got, a procession that covered hundreds of miles. Now I know that she lies in peace in Germany, scattered somewhere alongside the track.

Back on the Train of Memory, waves of emotions. Relief at having somehow performed my long-dreaded duty and given my mother a burial of words in lieu of a grave, thoughts instead of flowers. Anguish and guilt, because it could have been me scattered across the German countryside. In fact, I know it should have been me, because children were never spared. Joy at seeing so many young people who had been my companions on this trip connect with my past, becoming its new trustees. Comfort that memories will remain until they are no longer needed.

Frustration. In the aisle of our car, a few people too young to know ask questions about my past. They want to know what it was like, what I now feel. I want to tell them and serve as their memory. But if they knew the terror of that death that has been my passenger and companion for all these years, they would surely run away and ask no more. This is why I tell them the obvious and hold back the essential, leaving a gap of memories. Could they really understand?

Finally, hope. Hope that our tragedy, the losses we share on the Train of Memory, will not become banal, will not be turned into yet another remote Purim story with little significance—and then only for Jews. Hope that our moral outrage will not dwindle to the prayers of a few pious descendants sitting in a synagogue, shaking their noisemakers at the name of Hitler as we do today during Purim when the name of Haman, the Jew-killer, is read from the Book of Esther.

At Passover the year after my return from Auschwitz, our family held the usual seder. But I was unable to read the Haggadah aloud and retell, as I usually do, the story of the exodus from Egypt. As I silently read the text, I measured the distance separating me from the Jews in Egypt and realized how abstract my own story would sound to the distant generations to come.

24 | *"The Germans Did It!"*

The entire operation in the southern French territory was much more dependent on the French police than in the formerly occupied territory. The German strike force there could only exercise a weak supervision over the operation.

—Heinz Röthke, July 1943[1]

After the arrest of my mother on June 6, 1944, Claire Steltzer told her mother, "The Germans did it!" Little did she know that two Frenchmen had actually made the arrest. Her mistake is quite understandable. In her mind as well as that of many others, the Germans were clearly the enemy—and had to be responsible. The overwhelming German presence overshadowed everything, drawing attention away from the active (and well-known at the time) role the French played in their collaboration with the Nazis.

Once the war ended, the history of French culpability was quickly revised. Perhaps it was because we French were so grateful to those few Frenchmen who had played a role in the Resistance and the Liberation that we were ready to exonerate all the rest without much further thought. Perhaps we had been impressed—and disgusted—by the apparently swift retribution of the *épuration*, the "spontaneous" cleanup of collaborators after the Liberation. There may also have been the realization that the purges could in no way rid France of all the people—large and small—who had played embarrassing roles during the war. Or maybe it was the desire to restore order and put the war behind us. The government was certainly eager to reestablish control over the country and choke the independence of popular vigilantism. Whatever the cause, the initially uncontrollable thirst for justice was soon replaced by the general perception that justice had been served, and people were happy to focus their attention once again on bread and butter instead of blood and vengeance. This is not to say that the war had been forgotten. In fact, the unbridled purges were replaced by a few orderly trials of war criminals, creating the impression that justice was in good hands.

Little by little, the disturbing side of the war receded into memory as movies and newsreels extolled the heroism of the French. The German demise became proof of their wickedness, and, as in a medieval judgment of God, the winners were declared righteous.

Even children's games reflected the changing mood of the nation. Cops and robbers, an age-old game, was replaced by a new version: Germans and *résistants*. Unlike the old game, where either side could win, in the new game the Germans always lost. We would arrange the outcome by designating a few of the clumsiest kids to be the Germans, while the large majority of us played *résistants*. It was not always easy to find candidates willing to play such wicked parts, and sometimes even the leaders had to play Germans to keep the game going. Even then, though, the Germans were expected to lose, and that was good.

As the small number of collaboration trials[2] ended after the war, very few new trials were initiated. To accelerate national healing, the events of the war years were now sealed under a heavy lid of secrecy in the name of national security. All information relating to this "dark" period, if not already destroyed, was now classified "intelligence" and locked away for 120 years. This reclassification included the files on French collaboration.[3] Now justice had a new trustee. The dozing French bureaucracy had sprawled atop the past with all its weight, making access to the truth impossible. French memory was becoming shorter. More recently, by focusing mostly on Paris and its surroundings, even the renewed surge of French Holocaust literature reinforces the false impression that the French had little or no significant role in the deportation of Jews from the south of France—both before and during its occupation by the Germans.

Unexpectedly, in 1991, I was able to get a glimpse into the organizational structure of the Nazi forces and the nature of French collaboration in the southeast of France during 1943 and 1944. Serge Klarsfeld furnished me with a large sample of the indictment files against 149 German members of the SD, the Sicherheitsdienst, or Security Services, which reported to Marseille and operated in the southeast of France.[4] These files document various ways in which French people actively supported the Nazis. There are, for instance, many personal statements of people who attest to being arrested, as my mother was, by Frenchmen. Here is an example:

> **On January 5, 1944, I was arrested at my home by six men who probably came from Marseille. Among them, there were two men in civilian clothes who spoke French fluently and a third one with a strong German accent . . .**
>
> **Deyns Fanny, born Poutchof**
> **April 29, 1946**

In many of the cases described in such statements, witnesses were able to identify some or all of the arresting officers as French, but could not identify the individuals by name. As a result, the SD files cannot help us identify the French collaborators, except—as we shall see later—in the case of some of their leaders.

Another document from the indictment files spells out French collaboration in much clearer detail. On September 23, 1943, the Marseille command post of the SD had expanded to cover seven French *départements*—Gard, Vaucluse, Hautes-Alpes, Alpes-Maritimes, Var, and Bouches-du-Rhône. Several "antennas" reporting to Marseille were created to facilitate the coverage and control of the area—in Nimes, Avignon, Toulon, Digne, Nice, Draguignan, Brignoles, Cannes, Monte-Carlo, Aix-en-Provence, Orange, Hyères, and Briançon. Antennas (in German, *Antennen*) were SD outposts scattered in the area and charged with supervising intelligence gathering and operations against the Resistance and the Jews. The antenna of Avignon was led by SS Lieutenant Wilhelm Müller. In 1947, indictments were sought against Müller and nine other members of the Avignon SD, among them a French secretary, Frida Magey, who had received German nationality because of her services to the SD. In the indictment compiled by Judge Cruciani in Marseille against Jacob Trumpfehler and Heinrich Krabbe, two German SD agents in Avignon, the investigator, Commissaire Léon Castellan, writes:

> **In summary, none of the people contacted, although they had been victims of the German police and of the SD in particular, recognized, at least during their interrogation, Krabbe or Trumpfehler as having participated in their arrest, in their interrogation, or having mistreated them.**
>
> **On this subject, we must mention that most of the witnesses cited [in the case against the German members of the SD] told us they were arrested by the French Militia, the Waffen SS, or the German army.**
>
> **It is quite possible that after deciding about the operation . . . the SD agents used supplementary forces that they were only directing. Anyway, neither Trumpfehler, a driver, nor Krabbe, a police inspector, is recognized as an author of misbehavior or brutality against the French people they or their services arrested.**

> The names of Feroldi, chief of the Avignon Militia, his
> aide, Terrier, and the names of several other [French]
> Militiamen or members of the 8th Waffen SS, already arrest-
> ed or executed (Recordet, Danflou, Bourgue, . . .), recur often,
> and are accused of extortion and brutality.[5]

At their trial, Krabbe and Trumpfehler were acquitted because
"belonging to the SD was not a sufficient charge."[6]

This indictment is remarkable in several respects. First, it
suggests the small size of the Avignon SD force that supervised
the entire *département* of Vaucluse. Second, it summarizes the
point so often made elsewhere in the SD files: that the arrest of
Jews was not carried out exclusively by Germans, but also by a
significant number of Frenchmen. Third, and even more remarkably, the indictment specifies some of the different branches to
which French collaborators belonged: the Militia, the Waffen SS,
or the German army. The indictment is uncertain about the actual extent to which the SD itself participated in the arrests it
ordered, but various Frenchmen—Militiamen or members of the
Waffen SS—are specifically named and accused of "extortion and
brutality."

For instance, Bourgue, one of the collaborators mentioned in
the investigation report, was a French Militiaman who operated in
the small village of Menerbes but reported to the Avignon antenna. Among others, he was responsible for the arrest of Klebert
Guendon, a Menerbes villager and the brother of our streetsweep-
er in Le Pontet. Klebert Guendon was taken from Menerbes to
the Saint-Anne prison in Avignon. According to his niece, who
showed me a newspaper clipping many years later, he was shot
there in 1943. For several months, his relatives kept bringing
clothes and packages to the prison, not having been told that he
had already been shot. Obviously, the packages were "put to good
use."

But how did Frenchmen like Bourgue become so actively
involved with the SD? One reason, apparently, was that the SD

was understaffed and needed to use a much larger number of supplementary forces to carry out the work. The available forces included, among others, volunteers from the French Militia along with French members of the Waffen SS, or even of the Gestapo. In a sense, the SD functioned like the conductor of an orchestra. The French police provided sheets of music in the form of lists or censuses of the Jews, and a large supporting cast—both German and French—played the instruments of arrest and brutality.

It is important to stress that, despite the use of many French persons in carrying out Nazi plans, some of the Germans still actively participated in brutalities whenever possible. The indictment files abound with gruesome details about the techniques used to extract information from prisoners: beatings, toxic injections, electric shocks, the infamous "bathtub" sessions, and bodily mutilation. There is also much evidence of gratuitous, sadistic brutality.

Sadly, some of the French collaborators did not lag behind their Nazi masters in their cruelty. Consider, for example, this report:

> **On the day of my arrest, April 29, 1944, four people in civilian clothes arrived at my house around 15:00 in a black car. They showed me a card saying: "German Police." There were one German and three French men, one of them short with brown hair, around thirty years old. . . . My father, who did not want to follow the police, jumped through the window of the second floor and broke a leg or the knee. . . . The French man with the brown hair asked: "What do we do with the old man? It is better to finish him." He himself shot my father in the head with his submachine gun. . . . It is the French man, short with brown hair, who is the cause of my father's death, because the German and the two other French men were not as eager to hurt . . .**
>
> **Karczmar Nadia, born Slobodzianska**
> **March 1, 1950**[7]

It should be noted that there were several forms of French collaboration in addition to enrollment in the Waffen SS, the German police, or the French Militia. For example, the SD indictment files document the existence of a semi-autonomous French group, the Palmièri group, which operated in the southeast of France under the direction of Charles Palmièri. Originally called Le Bureau Merle (the Merle Office), this group had been set up by Paul Kompe, the SD chief in Marseille, to monitor political and social activity in the southeast. In March 1944, the Palmièri group redirected its attention exclusively to the repression of Jews in five *départements:* Bouches-du-Rhône, Vaucluse, Var, Alpes-Maritimes, and Basses-Alpes.[8] Palmièri himself was sighted by witnesses in many of these areas, including Avignon.

There was even a branch of the French Vichy government, the PQJ, or Police aux Questions Juives (Police for Jewish Affairs), which was in charge of opening cases against Jews and then turning them over for action to the various groups supporting the Nazi anti-Jewish operations. Later renamed SEC, Section d'Enquête et de Contrôle (Department for Investigation and Control), it reported directly to the minister of internal affairs and served as an official organ of collaboration.

Unfortunately, the diverse forms of French collaboration made it difficult for witnesses to establish to which official organization a French arresting officer in plain clothes belonged. This is why people preferred to use the term *milicien* to refer to a French collaborator.

By relying on the assistance of French forces, the Nazis were able to execute their plans against the Jews in a cost-effective way. Using the French also helped them to bridge the language gap. While the Germans found plenty of willing accomplices, their progress was hampered both by the scattering of the Jews and by the awkwardness of their complex organization. Fortunately, the resistance—both active and passive—of other French people made the Nazis' job even more difficult and less effective.

SS Hauptsturmführer Aloïs Brunner was appointed as the commander of the transit camp at Drancy on June 23, 1943, after the Germans had deposed the previous commander, Guibert, in response to a drastic slowdown in the flow of Jews eastward. By then, the deportation convoys had practically stopped.[9] Once appointed, Brunner took it upon himself to reinvigorate the "cleanup" operations against the Jews in France. To relieve himself of the details of running Drancy, he set up a form of self-administration under German control. Then he traveled personally to areas such as the southeast of France, and in particular the Italian-occupied zone, where pockets of Jews were living in relative safety. He showed up, for instance, in Nice, Marseille, and several neighboring localities. He soon succeeded in restarting the deportation process and, possessed by his personal hatred toward the Jews, actively participated in interrogations and arrests. A series of eyewitness accounts documents his trail of merciless operations.

Fanny Deyns, for one, had been arrested during the war in the small town of Pertuis, near Avignon. On March 26, 1945, Judge Cruciani issued Information Request No. 1035 against Rolf Muhler, chief of the Marseille Gestapo, and members of the Avignon Gestapo for crimes committed in the jurisdiction of the Avignon SD: "voluntary manslaughter, sequestration, deportation, and theft."[10] On April 29, 1946, Deyns testified in the presence of two French policemen, Louis Mouret and Marcel Richaud:

> **I was taken with my sister directly to the Gestapo center, 425 rue Paradis in Marseille, where we were interrogated by other Gestapo agents, in particular by a man named Brunner. I was threatened with guns to make me talk. . . . At the camp of Drancy, I was again interrogated by Brunner and brutalized by a man named Bruckler. . . . The five men who arrested us stole from me 80,000 francs and jewelry worth around 100,000 francs.[11] In addition, they took jewelry from my sister.[12]**

Although Brunner succeeded in accelerating the pace of deportation, his French operation remained sluggish compared to the near-total destruction of many Central European Jewish communities. Even after Brunner's appointment, the Nazis' French operation was to remain a continuing source of disappointment.

After the successful Allied landing in France, Brunner followed the retreating German army and continued his hunt for the Jews in the region of Bratislava, Czechoslovakia. Taking advantage of the similarity of his name to that of Anton Brunner, another German Nazi who was hanged in Vienna in May 1946, Aloïs Brunner was able to flee and escape prosecution after the end of the war. In a second statement given on June 7, 1946, Fanny Deyns said:

> I learned from other detainees that Brunner was Austrian . . . Brunner was the commander of Drancy. Every time [anti-] Jewish operations were held in various French towns, he would travel there to decide about the fate of the Jews and direct them to Drancy. I am providing you with an article from the newspaper "SOIR-EXPRESS" No. 552, dated May 27, 1946, in which it is stated that Brunner was executed in Vienna.[13]

Deyns's testimony is echoed by a personal statement of the two recording policemen, Mouret and Richaud:

> The article mentioned in the witness's declaration has the following title:
>
> BRUNNER EXECUTED: The war criminal Brunner responsible of the deportation and death of several thousands of Jews, sentenced to death a few days ago by the Court of Vienna, was executed today in his prison.

Unfortunately, no one realized that the article referred to Anton Brunner, not to Aloïs Brunner. This confusion resulted from Lieutenant Colonel Pétré's response to Judge Cruciani. This probably led the judge not to name Aloïs Brunner as a co-defendant in the trial of the members of the Avignon SD.

Aloïs Brunner finally reemerged in Damascus, Syria, where

he has lived for thirty years under the protection of the Syrian government. Unrepentant and still devoured by his "irreducible hatred" (to use an expression coined by Didier Epelbaum),[14] Brunner stated in 1987 that the Jews "have all deserved to die because they are the agents of the devil and human waste products."[15] Repeated attempts by Beate and Serge Klarsfeld to have him extradited and judged have so far failed due to the complicity of the Syrian government and the complacency of the French, German, and American governments. When he dies of old age, his 26,418 Drancy victims, 23,885 of whom were deported to the death camps, will remain "unrecognized errant souls."[16] Among them was my mother, political deportee number 23925.

Personalizing evil by attributing to small and big monsters makes it easier for us to cope with it—and to distance ourselves from it. Just as in classic Chinese theater where an army is symbolized by a general with numerous flags on his back to represent its size, we tend to attribute the tragedy of the Jews of France to people like Brunner because of the 26,000 Jews "he" deported. Once the "Brunners"—symbols of hatred, evil, and cruelty—are identified, people think, they can be tracked down, and their just punishment will exorcise the guilt from the rest of us. In reality, however, personifying evil in people like Brunner and his ilk simplifies and distorts the truth. What happened to the Jews of France cannot be explained by the heinous crimes of a Brunner alone. Instead, the tragedy grew largely from the compounding of innumerable small evils, seemingly ordinary acts that are far closer to us than we may wish.

For example, the deportation list of August 26, 1942, was prepared by an Avignon bureaucrat who had been preparing lists of all kinds since the beginning of his civil service. These foreign Jews were an administrative nightmare. Why not pass them along to another authority? No one would ask questions anyway. They were, after all, foreigners.

Similarly, members of the French police, each in his own village, arrested the few foreign Jews living there in 1942 because they had occasionally arrested undesirable people since the beginning of their police careers. Plus, these foreign Jews were under the jurisdiction of the prefect, and no one would ask questions anyway, because the Jews did not fit in and the villagers had learned long ago to dislike them.

Even the village clerk of Le Pontet, who came in 1941 to register my family as Jews, and Mayor Delorme, who sent him, set the stage for my mother's arrest. And when the police registered us on May 13, 1944,[17] together with other Jews, the list served a few weeks later as the master plan prepared by several French bureaucrats for the operation against the Jews on June 6, 1944. The plan, and these French bureaucrats who prepared it, are directly responsible for the manhunt that claimed my mother. It is not true that her selection for the gas chamber occurred only at the hands of a German Nazi when she was unloaded onto the Auschwitz ramp in early July 1944. Her selection really started on July 1, 1941, when the village clerk of Le Pontet registered her, and it continued when every French bureaucrat, every French policeman, and every French Militiaman chose in turn to tighten the noose a little more instead of helping her. This is why I have no interest in the monsters of Nazism. I am much more concerned with the "little people" who did the job in their shadows.

Some critics, like Asher Cohen, will argue that France, where approximately 25 percent of the Jews were deported, exhibited a lower level of anti-Semitism and greater support for the Jews than a country like Poland, where more than 90 percent of the Jews perished.[18] To bring things closer to home, I will likely be reminded that I am living proof of that French compassion, a fact I will never deny. However, one could look at the statistics differently and ask a different question: among all the Jews who perished, how many cases involved an action by the local authorities—French or Polish? It is clear that many Jews were deported from France as a result of the repeated censuses by the French administration, their arrest by the French police, the stamping of their identity cards, the mandatory wearing of the yellow star, or a denunciation by their neighbors—factors that particularly affected the fate of the foreign Jews.

The Germans' reliance on the French was essential because, in France, the Jews were difficult to identify, whereas in Poland this collaboration was less necessary since the Jews were more differentiated and segregated. In short, although the rescue of Jews by part of the population and the relative protection the French government offered the Jews cannot be denied, the higher survival rate of Jews in France may also be due to the Germans' difficulty in singling them out. Until the relative importance of these factors is understood, no one can convincingly claim that the higher survival rate indeed reflects the attitude of the French.

I have often reflected on my emotions toward the "steel-hearted" Frenchmen who arrested my mother, wondering what my reaction would be if I could meet them face to face. Although I am tempted by the thought of making them go through the hell my mother went through, one part of me is relieved that it is unlikely I will ever face them, since by now they are probably dead. I wonder whether they died at the hands of the vengeful, bloodthirsty crowd after the war or simply of old age as respected French citizens, possibly even decorated for services rendered to their country. If they escaped the rudimentary popular justice of the early postwar days, as many did, perhaps they moved away from Marseille and Avignon, where they were too well known. They may even have obtained jobs with the French police because of their war experience. They probably married and had families. I can imagine the photographs of their "resistance" days on top of the cabinet in the living room. I can hear their children laugh at the dinner table. Perhaps they went to church regularly and lived devout lives. They probably kept silent about their war experiences for almost half a century, exactly as I did. I am now able to unlock my past, but, unlike me, they will have to remain silent forever, dead or alive. If I met them today, I would have nothing to say to them.

My two "steel-hearted" Frenchmen are not the only ghosts of World War II French history. Many murderers who did not have the notoriety of Aloïs Brunner were able to melt back into society unnoticed. A few spectacular trials singled out some of the "big sharks," but these were no more than a handful of scapegoats made to pay for the crimes of the many. Most of the functionaries of death in France have never been disturbed. These smaller fish could seemingly rest in peace because their crimes have been forgiven—or at least forgotten. It was as if the Holocaust had become a perpetratorless crime.

By the end of 1991, I already had accumulated enough knowledge to begin to understand the depth of French responsibility for what had happened to its Jews. My research pointed increasingly to those who had served as bureaucrats for the Vichy regime.

Before the Nazis strengthened their grip on the "free" zone, the French Vichy government orchestrated the roundup of thousands of defenseless foreign Jews, who went straight to a sure death with the active complicity of the French civil servants, the support of some of the population, and the indifference of most. The fifty-seven Avignon deportees of August 1942 provide a vivid testimony about the real disposition of the Vichy government. These Jews were arrested and sent to their deaths by the Vichy police, under the orders of the Vichy government, and according to a decree enacted by the Vichy government.[19] The Avignon police bureaucrats who sealed the fate of those fifty-seven Jews in the summer of 1942 and the gendarmes who arrested them are directly responsible for their death in Auschwitz. This actively anti-Semitic attitude smoothed the transition to a direct French collaboration when the Germans later occupied the "free" zone on November 11, 1942. The German inherited from the Vichy government a well-tuned mechanism of repression complete with files, a methodology, and a willing staff.

The role of the French bureaucrats during the German occupation after November 1942 is masked by the German presence in 1943 and 1944. However, by 1991, I had found strong indications that the French administration had played a larger role in the subsequent roundups of Avignon Jews than had ever been admitted publicly. I now wanted to establish the exact division of responsibilities between the German occupiers and the French collaborating regime in southeastern France. I wanted to find at least some of those who had furtively slipped back among us after the war's end, after they realized they had made the wrong choice and kept their past hidden ever since. In order to do so, I needed to gain access to the Avignon police archives, which were still kept locked, over forty-five years after the end of the war, by today's French administration. Armed with the courage of the ignorant, I engaged in what was to become a yearlong joust against the windmills of bureaucracy. I already knew part of the truth, but I could not imagine how deep into the fabric of my native countryside the tentacles of hate would reach.

25 | The "Papon" of Avignon

It is necessary to activate large police forces in order to: first, cope with the arrests in Bordeaux and the départe-ment; second, to watch the train stations and the large communication arteries, because of a possible exodus as soon as the Jews learn about the first arrests.

—Note from Maurice Papon[1] to his boss, Prefect Sabatier, in reference to the arrests of Jews planned for July 6, 1942, in the *département* of Gironde[2]

December 1992

In spite of the bullet speed of the train, the landscape outside the window is moving too slowly for me. Every passing minute is bringing me closer to the collaboration files no one wanted me to see. I wish I were already there, holding the truth in my bare hands, finally able to understand the incomprehensible. To kill time, I reflect on the patience and numerous interventions it took to gain permission to view the sealed archives.

A year has passed since I first walked into the police archives in Avignon, hoping to get access to the war files. I was politely told that I could not see the material without the proper exemption, "which, by the way, is normally granted only to accredited historians." The archive curator went on to say that "the W Series is particularly sensitive and is labeled *Intelligence*. If you really want to apply for an exemption, you will have to provide the specific references to the documents you need." To further discourage me, she added, "And we cannot identify the specific files from the topics you mentioned." I was also told that the inventory was not for public usage. Acting resigned, I left her office and returned to the reading hall, where I bluntly asked a low-level employee for the "W Series inventory." The employee hastened to satisfy my wishes, since he had seen me come out of his boss's office and my assertiveness dissipated any of his doubts. Feverishly taking notes, I copied all of the references I could get. The section headings sent chills up my spine:

7W15	**Census of the Jews**
7W16	**Measures against the Jews**
7W17	**Individual Files of the Jews**
8W4	**Collaboration Groups**
6W37	**Lists of Arrests**
22W15	**Individual Files of Collaboration Suspects: A–C**
22W16	**Individual Files of Collaboration Suspects: D–M**
22W17	**Individual Files of Collaboration Suspects: N–V**

I was inching a little closer, but I still had a long way to go.

Immediately after my first visit, I made a phone call to the director of the archives. He was startled when I asked him about the exemption procedure and suggested that I use Aimé Autrand's book instead of the actual archive material.[3] He added, "Autrand's book includes all you need to know, since he worked in the Avignon Archives from 1945 until his retirement in 1965." Even after I pointed out that the fifty-seven Jews arrested before the German occupation on August 26, 1942, are omitted from

Autrand's book and that his official total count of eighty-three Jewish deportees of Vaucluse for the duration of the war is surprisingly low, the director still recommended that I not seek a special exemption because of the "possible media effect." His resistance increased my resolve, so I sent him a request, along with a copy to his superior, the Vaucluse prefect of police, who was next in the approval chain.

My application was never officially acknowledged and remained unanswered for many months. Phone calls and further inquiries received vague responses or none at all. The administration was stonewalling, and I was going nowhere.

Since the prefectorate of Vaucluse came under the jurisdiction of the regional prefect of Marseille, I made a separate request for authorization to examine the regional archives. The answer came promptly:

> **I regret to inform you that we are in no position to provide you with the information for which you asked. The files likely to contain the information you requested are not yet inventoried in a way detailed enough to permit an easy search. However, be assured that we will not fail to communicate to you any material of interest if and when our current work uncovers this information.**

At a loss for a solution, I told my story to a good friend in the city of Toulouse, who connected me through an acquaintance of his to Guy Penne, a French senator. It was only after the intervention of the latter that a tentative agreement was reached with the prefect of police in September 1992. As a compromise, I agreed to accept reasonable limitations and "not use the information to damage the honor of individuals." But I was not given an official exemption, just a promise.

To capitalize on the help of Senator Penne, the next day I visited the director of the archives without an appointment. I was accompanied by Peter Hellmann, an American journalist. Being the subject of so much attention overwhelmed the poor civil servant. When he saw me, he withdrew his arms into his jacket like a startled turtle. He went on to confide, "Do you think that it is pleasant to have so much influence on my back?" Without looking me in the eyes, he added, "Your request is very delicate . . . very delicate . . . very delicate." Echoing three times the fear of his own thoughts, he made clear that he knew the contents of the files. "You will see names of people you knew," he explained. His caution clearly indicated that he was concerned with my personal involvement, but he immediately stressed that he had already approved my request much earlier. Eager to make me understand that we were all at the mercy of the wheels of bureaucracy, he also indicated that the matter was now in the hands of his boss, the prefect of Vaucluse, and that he had nothing to do with the delay. To make me appreciate his views on bureaucratic care, he read to me an administrative instruction, dated July 1992, urging him to increase his vigilance when responding to a request for access to the war files and to verify the legitimacy of the applicant. This official circular was read in the presence of Peter Hellmann. It appeared to be the official reaction to the "media effects" that followed the unusual access Kurt Schaechter gained to the regional archives of Toulouse in May 1992, and the publication of his findings. Schaechter smuggled out archive material pertaining to French collaboration. This information was published in several newspapers (*Le Point*, *L'Evènement du Jeudi*). In the wake of the "Schaechter affair," this directive reminded the heads of the regional archives that they would be held responsible for any further blunders. The author of the circular had justifiably expected that the archive heads, often self-effacing accomplices, would need no additional incentive to execute faithfully the instructions that the administration had written between the lines. Then, abruptly leaving an embarrassing topic, the director drew a parallel between World War II and the French revolution of 1789. "Both the revolution of 1789 and World War II," he said, "were like vast machines crammed with gears. In both cases, people were uncontrollably drawn into the gears, leading to all the excesses that we well know." His sudden desire to educate me about the war gave me a clue that I was getting closer to an approval.

The approval did not come immediately, however. After two more reminders, followed by an inquiry from the Ministry of Culture (undertaken on my behalf at the direct request of Yves Gaudeul, the French consul in Chicago), I flew to Paris with only a vague promise in hand. Upon landing, I was preparing to take my case to the French newspapers when I decided to make one more phone call. To my surprise, I was granted a verbal authorization.

Now, as I ride the train on this sunny morning of December 1992, the other passengers are reading the daily newspapers or napping in their seats. I am thinking about the search, which is about to begin when the train reaches Avignon, and I am rehearsing my reconnection with the past, as I have often done during this past year. My mind is flooded with childhood memories.

The census of 1941 comes back to me. I remember my mother's reaction of terror, and I relive my own feeling of powerlessness as if it were yesterday. I can still see the man who registered us, a small-town French bureaucrat with a thick mustache and the usual beret on his head. He wore his customary gray smock over his regular clothes, a clear sign of the official nature of his visit. Will I find his name? Will I discover who ordered the census—and who executed it? Who kept updating the lists and singled us out as Jews, thus turning us into easy targets?

I remember the *JUIF* stamp on our documents and our embarrassment when we had to hand them over in public, fearful of people's reactions. Who was the French government official who did the stamping, exposing me to my schoolmates' harassment?

I remember the Jews who visited our store in 1942. Today, some of them are real to me, like the Margolis sisters and the Tieders, people whom I was able to locate later and interview.

Others, though, were deported to Auschwitz and remain only names on a fifty-year-old list, with only a few, like me, to serve as witnesses to their memory. Will I find the name of the French bureaucrat who orchestrated their deportation? Will I see irrefutable evidence?

Did the Germans really act alone—and what was the role of the French? I remember the black front-wheel-drive Citroën loaded with the menacing members of the German police who frequently visited Monsieur Gros, the owner of the restaurant next door. Was he ever prosecuted for collaboration?

As much as these memories pound in my head with an ever-increasing persistence, they are still the memories of a child. Floating in the past, they have remained unconnected for fifty years. Only when I am able to actually trace them back to the perpetrators will these memories become a reality, for everyone to see.

I receive my first file of documents, "Measures against the Jews."[4] Now, finally, I am holding the past in my hands. I am told that I will get a second file only when I return the first one. Upon entering the archives, I am so eager to see the material that I do not remember what document I signed or what promise I made before I was given my first file. I just remember the small entrance door at the base of the huge facade of the Popes' Palace, where the archives are located.

I untie the rope, which had imprisoned this pack of documents for decades, not only holding them together but, by cutting into the documents themselves, risking their destruction before they can reveal their contents to history. Hundreds of pages of yellowed documents, lists, letters, and drafts lie in the folders of the file. Some drafts are corrected and redone three times, until the bureaucrat was finally happy, and the successive versions, handwritten and partially typed, are still preserved in the file. Strangely, all the drafts are written on the back of discarded documents and pamphlets. It appears that paper shortages nearly shut down the entire bureaucratic machine. In the middle of the file, I recognize the familiar list of the 111 Jews of 1942. It is identical to the one I had received in 1991 from a friendly source. The original list was attached to a letter sent by Prefect Henri Piton on August 24, 1942, two days before the massive action against the Jews in the "free" zone (Henri Piton had been appointed on December 1, 1941, to replace Louis Vallin).

Prefectorate
of Vaucluse
1st Division
2nd Bureau
No. 1704

Avignon, August 24, 1942

SECRET AND URGENT

The Prefect of Vaucluse
to the Gendarme Unit Commander
Avignon

In accordance with your conversation with the competent Division Chief of my prefectorate and the General-secretary, I am honored to ask you to arrest this Wednesday, August 26, 1942, at dawn, all the foreign Jews on the attached list.

These individuals will then be assembled in the closest brigades and driven under guard to the camp of Les Milles near Aix-en-Provence using two buses which I am providing to that effect, and which will be made available on that day at 7 o'clock in front of Avignon city hall. . . .

You are expected to acknowledge these instructions and report to me the results of the various prescribed operations.

The Prefect

The letter cryptically mentions "the competent Division Chief" as an important figure in preparing for the arrest of the Jews that was to take place on August 26, 1942. One more important clue can be found in the letterhead. Although tersely signed by the prefect, this letter was issued on the stationery of the First

Division, Second Bureau (D1 B2), apparently the division headed by the "competent Division Chief." In every prefectorate across Vichy France, the same D1 B2 unit was in charge of anti-Jewish repression. Thus, behind the prefect's name, there was the division chief of D1 B2 who actually prepared and dispatched the order for the arrests, along with making the necessary arrangements for the buses to take the Jews from the Avignon city hall to the Les Milles camp.

Following his conversation with the "competent Division Chief" on Monday morning, August 24, 1942, the commander of the Gendarmerie of Vaucluse delegated the job of arresting the Jews to his contingents stationed in different towns and villages. At the end of the day on August 26, dozens of police reports were sent from the field to the prefect, apprising him of the arrest results. As Captain Ferrier, commander of the section of Orange, relates in one of the reports, things did not go totally as planned.

National Gendarmerie
15th Legion
Vaucluse Company
Section of Orange
No. 7714
SECRET

Orange, August 26, 1942

REPORT

of Captain Ferrier, Section Chief in Orange
about: roundup of the foreign Jews
Reference: note of the prefect of Vaucluse date 8/24/1942
No. 1704

> The roundup operations of foreign Jews listed in the attachment to the prefect note No. 1704 dated August 24, 1942, started on August 26, 1942, at dawn and took place without notable incident.
>
> In ORANGE—Only Salomon JERUCHEMSON, living in CAMARET, could not be arrested. Information provided by

the other members of the family indicates that he is already in the camp of Les Milles.

In VALREAS—Ludovic STERN could not be located.

In BOLLENE—The head of the GOLDBERG family, taking advantage of a moment of inattention, tried to flee by jumping through a window of the third floor. He fell first on a trellis, and then to the ground without any harm. One of the children was missing, and the parents stated that he had gone to AVIGNON the previous evening. However, further search located him in a hay barn.

In that house only 9 people could be arrested instead of the 14 targeted.

Joseph SAPIR, Esthera and Rose MARGOLIS were absent. Search did not bring them out, and it is probable that they were traveling. Joseph SAPIR was in possession of a travel permit to MARSEILLE.

The military police who went to the home of Esthera MARGOLIS found her in bed after surgery. She could not be moved.

Szayne SAPIR went into shock at the sight of the police, and we had to contact a doctor, who declared her untransportable.

In BEAUMES—The police who arrived at 4:15 at the home of the TIEDER family in SABLET did not get any answer. At 5:15, the mayor of the village was called, and he had to bring in a locksmith to open the door. In vain, the bedrooms and the attic were searched. They finally discovered the husband hidden behind the basement door and the wife, Brucha TIEDER, hidden in a corner of the basement, completely covered with garbage.

The daughters: Sarah TIEDER is in a scout camp in BUSSIERE-VIEILLE (Creuse) and Ida TIEDER went to AVIGNON yesterday and is expected back in SABLET tonight.

The son, Martin TIEDER, is in a preventorium in MAVERJOLS (Lozère).

In VAISON—Only Robert JOKL and his wife, née Madeleine BLUMENSTEIN, could be arrested.

The FREUNDLICH family, the husband, the wife, and

two children, who live in LE CRESTET, could not be found, having left for AVIGNON.

Madame FREUNDLICH, who had come to LE CRESTET last night, left for AVIGNON this morning by the 6:00 bus to rejoin her family, who has moved to a hotel there.

The commander of the AVIGNON brigade was alerted by telephone so that he can arrest her at her descent from the bus and find the whereabouts of the other members of the family.

No other incident took place and the population of these villages made no commentaries about this operation.

Captain Ferrier's comment at the end of his report is surprising. Apparently, the police, who were hunting the Jews like pestiferous mice, were still concerned about public opinion.

Since most local villagers remained silent and did nothing to help those running for their lives, the kindness of a few was invaluable. Three medical certificates signed by Doctors Descalopoulos, Madon, and Basch for Szayne Sapir and three for Esther Margolis are attached to the police report. Both patients are said to suffer from so many illnesses that they should not have lasted more than a few hours if the illnesses had been real. As the Margolis sisters recently confirmed, these illnesses were fabricated by the three doctors. One of the doctors, Mariane Basch, who now lives in Paris, had made it a habit to help people in need contrary to the wishes of her peers, who complained to the police about her selection as chief doctor of the Bollène district. This is confirmed in a complaint letter, dated May 10, 1943, and sent by one of her colleagues to the general commissioner for Jewish Affairs. The colleague complained that he himself should have been selected as chief doctor because he was "the candidate of the French Combatant Legion," whereas "the prefect administration has designated . . . Dr. Basch, daughter-in-law of Victor Basch,[5] a Hungarian Jew who has lost French citizenship, herself also known as Mariane Moutet, daughter of Marius Moutet, past socialist assembly representative, a Freemason."[6] Finally, Doctor Basch, who had everything going against her—her Jewish husband, a Freemason father, and her own compassion—had to run for her life and left the area.

All of the Gendarmerie's field reports about the roundups were consolidated in a final summary, which was sent in early September 1942 to the chief of the government, Pierre Laval, who also served as minister of internal affairs, and to the general secretary of the National Police, René Bousquet. The final report was issued by the Section of Foreigners of the Prefectorate of Vaucluse, as was the arrest order of August 24, 1942. A list of arrested Jews was provided, as well as a list of fugitives.

This summary reports 76 arrests and engages in a complicated accounting to demonstrate the competence of the chief of operations. However, a closer analysis of the final report and its attached lists indicates a more chaotic reality. For instance, 12 persons whose names were on the original list of 111 names but were omitted from the final report were arrested on August 26, 1942, and deported to Auschwitz. The "competent Division Chief" had apparently "lost" 12 arrested Jews due to an accounting error. He had, in fact, arrested 88 Jews—not 76, as he thought.

A second discrepancy, however, had grimmer consequences. Fourteen Jews were reported arrested in camps for foreign workers, even though these 14 did not appear on the original list of 111 names. Had he wished, the division chief could have let these foreign workers go free, since their names did not appear on the original list, but he did not seize this opportunity, and all 14 perished. It is difficult to avoid the conclusion that the division chief willingly allowed these unanticipated victims to die in order to increase the numbers netted in the operation and to quietly cover up the escape of so many Jews from the original list. The not-so-competent division chief was unwilling to pass up such a convenient opportunity to enhance his image in the eyes of his superiors. But at what cost?

The division chief must have realized that his operation against the Jews did not look like a resounding success despite his "padding" of the arrest results. So, in the final report, he assured René Bousquet that he had done his best:

> **I have ordered active searches to find the tracks of all the foreign Jews that eluded the regrouping measures aimed at them or who had recently moved.**
>
> **In AVIGNON, specifically, where some fugitive could have found a refuge more easily than in smaller towns, I have ordered roundups and identity checks in all places where Jews could be found. . . .**
>
> **Although these operations allowed us to verify the situation of many individuals, they did not lead us to the discovery of any fugitive.**

Accounting for every name in the final report brought up a third discrepancy. Among the Jews arrested and transferred to the camp at Les Milles, 17 escaped back into hiding and were never deported. Several of them were sighted in the area during the remainder of the war. This last adjustment lowers the total from 88 to 71 Jews who were delivered to the Germans by the division chief and murdered at Auschwitz.

On the evening of August 26 and on August 28, 1942, the Vichy administration summarized the entire operation in the "free" zone.[7] According to its count, the administration expected to find 12,608 Jews but succeeded in deporting only 6,584 of them by the end of the first day. Six suicide attempts and four successful suicides occurred on that same day.[8] Interestingly, the underestimate of the division chief made its way into Vichy's final count, where the *département* of Vaucluse accounted for 55 deportations instead of 71, which is closer to the truth.

While sifting through the archive file, I noticed a small letter written on half a page. It was a reminder for a bill sent by the Rapides du Sud-Est, a well-known bus company based in Avignon, the same company that operated the buses I used to ride in my school days.

Les Rapides du Sud-Est
32, Boulevard St. Roch
Avignon, Tél 11-75

Avignon, December 8, 1942

Monsieur Autran [sic]
Prefectorate of Avignon

Monsieur,

We are honored to remind you of our note concerning the transport of August 26, 1942, to the camp of LES MILLES for the amount of 2866.50 francs.

Hoping for your prompt answer, accept, Monsieur, our special greetings.

The Director

So here is the truth at last. Aimé Autrand, who omitted the Jews of 1942 in his 1965 book, also had a significant role in organizing their roundup. This explains the archive director's reluctance to let me see the documents, and his September 1992 comment about the system of gears that sucked people in against their will.

I review all of the pages again. In my haste, I had overlooked the initials A.A. on almost all the drafts of outgoing letters. Does A.A. stand for Aimé Autrand? Then, one more piece of evidence stares at me from the middle of the documents scattered on the table. It is a letter from the Aryan administrator assigned to P.M.F., a seized Jewish leather manufacturing company belonging to Joseph Filipovics and two other associates.[9]

P.M.F.
Manufacture of Luxury Leather Goods
6, Rue Sainte-Garde
AVIGNON

October 7, 1942

Monsieur Autrand
Chief of Division
Bureau of Foreigners
Prefectorate of Vaucluse
AVIGNON

Monsieur,

Following our visit to you, we are honored to indicate to you a list of Jews that we consider indispensable:

1. David KREIKMAN—32
2. Gustave BAUMEL—45
3. Jacques BAUMEL—20
4. Avram BLEYER—35
5. Joseph SYZLOWITZ—28
6. Nicolas SCHACHTER—21

In leather manufacturing, it is impossible to find qualified French Aryan personnel. Our only resort is to educate young men and women, but a very long apprenticeship is necessary.

The departure of these 6 specialists would force us to close the factory that occupies 30 employees and has orders that would guarantee full production until next spring.

If these Jews were to be deported, which is what some expect, we would be very grateful to you for leaving those who are indispensable. . . .

This letter provides the ultimate clue. Autrand was the chief of division, head of the Section of Foreigners and Jews. He was the "competent Division Chief" mentioned in the order, dated August 24, 1942, to arrest the 111 Jews two days later. Being the leader of the D1 B2 anti-Jewish repression machine, he was also the man who wrote the final report to René Bousquet, chief of the national police, a few weeks after the operation.[10]

Did Autrand know the consequence of the roundup of the foreign Jews that he organized in 1942? A staggering document from the same file provides an answer. This is a police report dated September 12, 1942, which documents the interception of a letter sent by a certain Monsieur Léon to Bommeyer, an official of the OSE in Montpellier.[11]

Office of Foreigners
and Police Affairs
O.E. No. 2263/OE

Date of Interception: 9/12/42
Date on intercepted letter:
No date—unreadable post stamp

Sender
LEON 70 Rue Joseph Vernet
AVIGNON (Vaucluse)

Recipient
BOMMEYER at the UNION O.S.E.
12b Rue Jules Ferry
MONTPELLIER (Herault)

Summary: Request for intervention on behalf of two children
interned in the camp of Les Milles

Extract:

To the Union O.S.E.

It is in the name of a desperate mother, whose husband
just died, that I am appealing to you. It is about saving the
lives of two children, ages 5½ and 7½; as well as the life of their
mother, Madame Regine BOBRYKER, all interned in the
camp of Les Milles. I beg you to intervene urgently; because
these are human beings and <u>particularly children</u> [my empha-
sis]. I am sending you my last desperate appeal. Be merciful to
the cry of a dying mother. Save the two children and respond
in utmost urgency.

I thank you in advance while awaiting a speedy solution.

Signed: LEON
70 Rue Joseph Vernet, AVIGNON

Names of the children:
Rachel BOBRYKER, 7½; Norbert BOBRYKER, 5½
Save them immediately. Have mercy for the lives of these
children.

The address given—70, rue Joseph Vernet—was where my mother and I used to visit the Jewish shoemaker Léon Rosenthal. Although the author of the letter could not have known the exact fate of the victims, he makes no bones about the critical situation of the Jews who were being deported into the hands of the Nazis in the occupied zone. Since the Bobryker children do not appear on any list of deportation from France to the death camps, they likely survived the war, but it is unclear whether they were saved by the police or by private individuals. However, their mother, age forty, was deported to her death at Auschwitz by convoy 33, which left Drancy on September 16, 1942, with 993 Jews. The letter also explains why the father, Joseph Bobryker, age forty-four, was not deported, although he was part of the 111 targeted Jews. According to the interception report, he had just died.

A recent inquiry into the OSE archives in Paris brought up more information about the Bobryker children, who ended up with the OSE at the end of the war.[12] On September 16, 1942, the Red Cross rescued them from the camp of Rivesaltes, where they had moved after the "departure of their mother from Les Milles to the occupied zone." On October 15, 1942, there was an attempt to send them to Elias Cohn, their uncle in Brooklyn. However, their visa request of October 15, 1942, was turned down by the U.S. representative on October 31, 1942, despite the sponsorship of their uncle, because they were deemed "too young." Apparently, the Bobryker children did not seem as worthy of interest as the "free" zone endangered artists and scientists, who were offered asylum in the United States by the Rescue Committee[13] and its head, Varian Fry, until June 2, 1942.[14]

In the OSE files, a receipt attests that money was smuggled out of the camp of Les Milles by a helper named Roger Sicard at the request of Regine Bobryker, the mother. Surprisingly, the money was delivered on February 14, 1943, to none other than Joseph Bobryker, the father of the children, who was in fact still alive. His address on the receipt was listed as "70, rue Joseph

Vernet, Avignon," the same address as Monsieur Léon, the author of the desperate plea for the life of the mother and the children. Rachel and Norbert Bobryker carry not only the memory of evil but also information about the people who helped them. I wish I could hear their story. The desperation that led Joseph Bobryker to fake his own death, as is indicated in the letter intercepted by the police on September 12, 1942, and Regine, his wife, to entrust her children into the hands of strangers proclaims their profound awareness of the Jewish condition in the summer of 1942. How could the police not share that awareness?

With the discovery of Aimé Autrand's role, the roundups of the Jews of 1942 became real to me, and through the documents I was able to share the anguish of their disappearance. Following closely the directions of his boss, Prefect Henri Piton, Autrand ordered the arrests in utmost secrecy, requested the French military police to hunt their prey at dawn, ordered them to deliver their human bounty in front of Avignon city hall, and shipped them by bus to the camp of Les Milles. From there, together with hundreds of other Jews, Autrand's victims were herded to Drancy and on to Auschwitz during the few weeks that followed.

On the evening of my first day at the archives, my first archive file had, like a time capsule, plunged me back into wartime Avignon. On my way out, I find myself at 70, rue Joseph Vernet, in front of the house where Rosenthal the shoemaker used to live. The past mixes with the present, the memory of leather smell with the aroma of neighboring restaurants. A few purposeful passersby are returning home, satisfied by a full day's work at the office or at the store, while the terrified memory of Joseph Bobryker walks in the shadows along the darker side of the street. Bobryker's mind is tortured by the thought of his wife and children at the camp of Les Milles. His fear of being caught before he can do anything for them wrestles in his heart with the anguish of their imminent deportation. On their way home, the passersby are planning their next vacation or anticipating what is awaiting them on the dinner table.

I swap my first file for the Census of the Jews.[15] Two large notebooks dominate the material, one for the French Jews and the other for the foreign Jews. Strangely enough, although I find my mother in the listing, there is no trace of my own name. Just behind the notebooks, there are many lists from different dates, typed on sheets of various textures and formats. A letter stands out.

Prefectorate of Vaucluse

First Division—Second Bureau
SECRET AND URGENT

THE PREFECT OF VAUCLUSE
To the mayors of the Department
(Copy to the subprefects)

OBJECT: Census of the Jews ordered by the Law of June 2, 1941

The Law of June 2, 1941, published in the <u>Journal Officiel</u>[16] on June 14, ordered a census of the Jews residing in France.

In order to allow the control of future declarations I am asking you to prepare <u>secretly</u> [my emphasis] a preliminary list of all the Jews, French or foreign, or reputed Jews.

I am honored to ask you urgently to establish this document and to send it under double envelope, <u>with the notation "secret"</u> [my emphasis] on the inside envelope, to the Prefectorate. . . .

Avignon, June 25, 1941

The Prefect
For the Prefect of Vaucluse
By delegation
The Chief of Division
A. Autrand

The line containing Autrand's name was proudly written in green, following four lines stamped in red. One must notice that, so early in the war, few people had significant doubts with respect to the future of Vichy. Once again, the role of Aimé Autrand is unambiguous: he was in charge of identifying us Jews secretly so that we were not tempted to elude his grip. The mayor of Le Pontet responded ten days later, on July 4, 1941, by listing my father and my mother. My father is mentioned, although he had been absent for more than a year, and once again I am not listed. Similar letters were sent from all the towns and villages of Vaucluse, listing many of our family friends and acquaintances, and subjecting them to the same procedure. An additional list of forty foreign Jews practicing "forbidden" professions includes my mother as "merchant." It is dated June 1941, and singles out engineers, chemists, manufacturers, store owners, teachers, a professional dancer, and so on. My memory as a five-year-old has been vindicated. The material brings back the frightening image of the city administrator with the prominent mustache who had visited our house, a beret on his head, a pair of round glasses with a black frame, wearing the gray smock of his profession, a face without a name. Who was he?

A document originating from Le Pontet, dated October 2, 1943, gave me a revealing clue about that man. By then, he had ten Jews listed in Le Pontet, among them Sarah Lewendel. The list was written in the handwriting of a librarian and with the familiar purple ink of those days. He even gave full attention to the proper rendering of his own name at the bottom of the page. I could imagine him signing his name with bureaucratic pride: Bérard. According to Régis Déroudilhe, Bérard had been duly elected vice-mayor of Le Pontet on May 12, 1935, and remained on the job under the Vichy administration.[17] He also served as village hall manager. Like many others, Bérard represented French continuity.

The label D1 B2 on the upper left corner of the October 2, 1943, list clearly links Bérard to Autrand's anti-Jewish operation. By that time, they were both working for the Germans, who had occupied the area a little less than a year earlier. Among the ten names, the address of two Russian Jewish refugees, Benjamin and Fanny Nemirowsky, was recorded as "Monsieur Gros," our collaborating neighbor and owner of the Sporting Bar. Was there a human side to Gros, or was he simply interested in their rent money?

Since the master lists of the Jews of Vaucluse were officially updated three times (July 1, 1941; August 27, 1943; and May 14, 1944), the update by Bérard dated October 2, 1943, was part of an ongoing process of the Vichy administration, carried out in the Vaucluse by Division D1 B2 and led by Aimé Autrand.

On February 15, 1943, Aimé Autrand received a written request to provide the list of Jews from the German SD, newly arrived in Avignon after the occupation of the "free" zone in November 1942. The man who had deported the Jews from the "free" zone into the hands of the Germans a few months earlier was now having second thoughts, and he politely pointed the finger elsewhere in his response, dated February 17, 1943: "I must inform you that the regional prefects are the only ones who have the authority to provide such information."

Clearly, Autrand could not have taken this delaying stand without the agreement of his boss, Prefect Henri Piton. A few months later, a request from the SEC regional representative in Marseille to the prefectorate of Vaucluse reads:

> **For a reason of opportunity, and because of the current circumstances, it is indispensable that I receive the list of foreign Jews of the district under your control.**
>
> **Consequently, I am honored to ask you to send me this list related to your district with the shortest possible delay.**

A few weeks later, the list was shipped to the SEC regional representative in Marseille to satisfy the "opportunity" mentioned in his request. Among the names was Sara Goldstein from Le Pontet. It had taken six months for the police of Vaucluse to heed the German request for the list of Jews, because this list was undoubtedly used as a bargaining chip with the German authorities. The foreign Jews were disposable.

Abruptly, I stop my search and stare at the evidence on the table in front of me. Once again, fifty years later, I am branded by the lists of my people. A saraband of forgotten words parades in front of my eyes: Jew, Foreign Jew, French Jew, list, control, stamp, secret, forbidden. I am drifting back in time. If Autrand had not ordered the census of my mother—if Bérard had not provided it—would her fate have been different?

Every new page I turn increases my vertigo. Tens of lists from every village and town remind me that each community had its own Bérard who recorded "his" Jews and transferred the list to Aimé Autrand. Hundreds of names march in front of me.

Suddenly, a small list dated February 1, 1943, catches my attention: Sarah Lewendel-Goldstein is said to have visited the Avignon Gendarmerie on January 13, 1943, "to have her identity card stamped with the word *JUIF* as requested by the letter of the prefect No. D1 B2 dated January 27, 1943." Apparently, my mother's stampers were ahead of the official notification by two weeks. Again, this D1 B2 reference is one more fingerprint in the trail left by Aimé Autrand on the correspondence of his anti-Jewish division. Had he not ordered my mother's card to be stamped, would my schoolmates have singled me out? Had her card not been stamped, could she have passed for a non-Jew—and could she have survived?

By the end of my search in the census files, a striking pattern had emerged: my name was omitted from all the lists I had seen. Was this the act of a compassionate helper? Did my mother arrange for my omission? This omission pointed to my mother's efforts to protect me within the system and may be linked to my unlikely naturalization on August 11, 1942. At my request, the archive clerk readily provides the files of all civil cases in 1942 and 1943. Unfortunately, the documents for the month of August were missing, and I could not assess the reaction of the police to Judge Chambon's bold decision on my behalf when he agreed to declare me French. However, I found a similar case in the neighboring town of Orange, where Justice of the Peace Burgède decided on July 28, 1943, to renaturalize the members of the Gak-Gorny family, who had been denaturalized on March 5, 1941, together with

7,000 other Jews.[18] In "the Gak-Gorny case against the State," the judge sided with the plaintiff, invoking the law of August 10, 1927, which was still on the books. However, he charged each side with half of the court fees, namely 36.15 francs. After the judge's verdict, M. Lebon,[19] the Avignon representative of the Vichy SEC, asked Autrand to "investigate the political connections of the Gak-Gorny family and assess whether they had influenced the judge's decision." In the police investigation that followed, no attempt was made to check the motives of the courageous judge. Apparently, Autrand was careful not to challenge a member of the establishment directly, no matter how far he may have crossed the line. However, Autrand listed the Gak-Gorny family as stateless in his census list of August 27, 1943, thus ignoring the lawful decision of Judge Burgède and making the family more vulnerable.

A few weeks later, the census list of 250 foreign Jews made its way into the hands of the Nazis. This list obviously served as a plan of arrest, since 67 of them—men, women and children— were arrested during the following months (first half of 1944); they were deported and died as a consequence. Since they were war refugees, the 67 foreign Jews of 1944, as well as the 71 foreign Jews of 1942, are not mentioned by Autrand in his list of 83 deportees of Vaucluse, which contains only French or foreign Jews who had been residents of Vaucluse before the war. These 138 phantom Jews of Vaucluse were considered lowlier than the lowliest local Jews, since their capture and their death were not even worthy of mention by the man who had prepared their deportation. Hushing up their arrest in Vaucluse may have helped Autrand to sanitize his tenure in the Vichy administration. Together with the 83 official deportees of Vaucluse, however, the evidence of deportation of these 138 people brings the number of Vaucluse's victims—a total of 221 Jews—closer to reality. As to Autrand, his silence about these phantom Jews definitely helped him minimize his own role as a servant of Vichy.

26 | *The Victim and the*
Hangman All in One

I am the dagger and the wound!
I am the slap and the face!
I am the wheel and the limbs,
Both the victim and the hangman!

　　　　—Charles Baudelaire,
　　　　The Flowers of Evil, 1853–57

December 1992

The organization chart of the prefectorate positions Aimé Autrand at the head of the Cabinet Division until the beginning of the war, and, beginning in November 1940, just after the enactment of the Statute of the Jews, at the head of the Division of Police Affairs, with responsibility for the control of foreigners and Jews. This official organization chart lists him as chief of the third division after the Liberation, clearly demonstrating the complicity of silence that surrounded Autrand's past. While Autrand man-

272

aged the first division from November 1940 until September 1943, four prefects—Louis Vallin, Henri Piton, Georges Darbou, and Jean Benedetti—rapidly followed one another as his boss, making him the most stable element of Vichy anti-Jewish repression in the district. Of course, since he was not eager to elaborate about his own role, he understated what he had done during his wartime years in his 1965 book.

> Aimé Autrand was chief of division in the prefect's cabinet in 1940, when "cleansing" measures were taken by the Vichy government. He became a victim of these measures, with three or four other colleagues, under the pretext that "he had too loyally served the Republican regime [before the war]." He was not fired (as the new leaders required) because the new prefect, Air Force General Vallin, a high-ranking official of a rare honesty, deemed it sufficient to move him away from the prefect's cabinet. He charged him with heading police affairs, including control of foreigners and Jews, and weapons.
>
> Of course, these were particularly thankless administrative duties, but the new nominee did not complain, because he would now have the opportunity (and the possibility) to defend the cause of a few of the people who were being singled out by the government of Vichy, more precisely the political refugees, the Israelites, and the *résistants*.[1]

Although Autrand alludes to his own duties, he strongly suggests that his boss, Louis Vallin, took away his responsibilities. In fact, he continued to author countless documents as division chief long after Vallin himself had moved on. In his postwar self-description, he portrays himself, in a strange identification with his own victims, as the man who protected the people targeted by the Vichy government, when in fact he had been charged with organizing their repression.

In addition to misrepresenting his precise role, Autrand presents in his book a misleading picture of the operations against the Jews. For example, another segment of his account is at best incorrect.

> Thanks to the benevolence and "complicity" of the competent service of the prefectorate, numerous Israelites worthy of interest were able to escape for a few months the searches performed by the zealots of the Commissariat for Jewish Affairs of Vichy, but this was to change in 1943, when numerous militiamen or members of the Parti Populaire Française [PPF] were able to obtain their addresses.[2]

It is now clear, however, that Autrand's generic reference to "the competent service of the prefectorate" is a euphemism referring to himself. Contrary to his testimony, the roundups of 1942 could not have been performed by the "zealots of the Commissariat for Jewish Affairs of Vichy," because the Commissariat for Jewish Affairs had no jurisdiction over the French police; its role was limited to investigations. In fact, the decision was made in the Vichy cabinet meeting of July 3, 1942, and carried out by the chief of the French police, René Bousquet, who discharged his mission with the help of the "competent services" of the prefectorates of the "free" zone, including those of Aimé Autrand.

In addition, Autrand reassures us that he helped numerous Jews "worthy of interest" to avoid deportation. Does this imply that the seventy-one Jews of August 1942 who were deported to Auschwitz were not "worthy of interest"? How can the protection of a few Jews, if indeed Autrand did as he claimed, compensate for the deportation of the rest of them? This reasoning, which seems acceptable when Jews are concerned, is inconsistent with both the laws of the land and its ethics. If Autrand had been in charge of deporting French *résistants* instead of Jews, he would not have been exonerated for having saved a few of them. He would have been executed as a traitor to the nation. Are Jews cheaper than "pure" Frenchmen?

Finally, he suggests that the arrests of 1943 and 1944 were made possible by the PPF and the Militia, which had deviously obtained the addresses of the Jews. The truth is that Autrand himself directed and managed the Census of the Jews. The master lists were forwarded to the SD only at the end of 1943, and various updates were made available to the German police by the collaborating administrations of some municipalities. Estrea Asseo testified that she was confronted after her arrest on June 6, 1944, with the census list at Avignon city hall by services cooperating with the Nazis. Didn't Autrand, an experienced civil servant, understand that once the lists of Jews were prepared, they were bound to be used?

Without looking at the social and political climate at the time, one cannot understand how a man like Autrand, who even had left Republican sympathies before the war, could stay on and serve the Vichy regime. How could he participate in determining the fate of hundreds of Jews who had put their trust in the French government? The answer lies in the attitude of his peers inside and outside the administration, and in his own character. In the minds of many members of the Vichy government, France had lost its honor in 1940, and it was essential to exercise every shred of autonomy that could be recovered from the Germans. The heavy fine of 500 million francs a day imposed by the Germans exceeded by far the French treasury's revenue and was a stinging reminder of French powerlessness. The French cause could be advanced by giving away a certain number of Jews, an act that pleased the Germans and was acceptable to the French population because "these Jews did not belong to us." This explains why staying on the job was in line with the national interest as perceived by the Vichy administration, especially as long as Nazi Europe looked like it was here to stay. In addition, Autrand, a fifty-year-old civil servant, would have needed extraordinary force of character and strong motives to revolt against a system to which he had belonged for so long.

Also, in the minds of some, having a patriotic spirit did not necessarily contradict a pro-German attitude and a good dose of anti-Semitism, as the following denunciation letter shows. The letter was sent from Le Thor, a small town near Avignon, by a retired captain, Julien Bonpuis, a World War I veteran.

Le Thor, March 20, 1943

Monsieur the prefect,

I have gone through a complicated process to send my son to work in Germany (Fernand BONPUIS), and I accompanied him to Avignon to be sure that he would leave. . . . I would like you to verify whether he really left. . . .

This letter is aimed at showing my determination to see him do his duty as I had done in the past on the battlefield, but there is a machination hatched by the foreigners against our renewal. Here are the facts.

We have in Le Thor a Jewish family: the father Stern (who fled after the arrival of the Germans) and two daughters who live here and are spreading anti-French propaganda. They have done all they could to prevent the departure of my son; the older one, Yvonne, even threw herself at my son,[3] the second one, Maidy, is in the process of destroying another honorable French family.

It is therefore my duty (local chief of the veterans' legion and father of a large family) to report all this to you and ask for immediate expulsion of these Jewesses.[4]

After an investigation, Autrand's police services found out that Fernand Bonpuis had not left for Germany but had likely remained close to his fiancée in the area. A little note handwritten by a subordinate informs Autrand of this finding. The file against Stern did not result in much more than a commitment of the police to keep an eye on his family.

Unlike Captain Bonpuis, the political association l'Amicale de France was intensely anti-German.[5] Until this association was officially dismantled in August 1941 by the Vichy government, and its files seized by the services of Aimé Autrand, its members (under the leadership of Jacques Petit, a Parisian lawyer who had moved to a village near Avignon) advocated severing the ties with Germany. They deemed the Vichy government too soft against both the Jews and the Germans, and they felt betrayed by Maréchal Pétain when he started advocating a compromising attitude toward Germany. In their anti-Semitic hysteria, they found an enthusiastic ally in Xavier Vallat, the commissioner general for Jewish affairs in Vichy. To avoid being outflanked by the zealots of the Amicale and to induce its supporters to toe the line, the Vichy administration decided to dissolve the association. When the police seized its files, they found virulent anti-Semitic and pro-Fascist material, as well as a letter from Jean Girbeau, the bishop of Nimes and a notorious anti-Semite,[6] asking for "material about the Jews to enable [him] to educate [his] parishioners about that race." In the files of the association, I also found membership lists and a list of contributors, among them Berton and Sicard, the owners of the famous Avignon hardware store, who donated 10,000 francs to the Amicale. Little did I know, when my mother and I went to buy our hand-operated vegetable blender at Berton and Sicard's, that the store owners—and, indirectly, we—were contributing to the Amicale war chest. The Vaucluse archive director's comment echoes in my head: "You will see names of people you knew."

The Vichy government's unspoken official position fell midway between total alignment with Germany and total independence. Disposing of the Jews was one subject about which all factions could agree, but there was some disagreement about how brutally to eliminate them. Implementing an agreed-upon anti-Jewish policy would be an easy way to attempt to regain French sovereignty. For better or for worse, by working for the Vichy government Aimé Autrand found himself implementing its "moderate" position. Interestingly, this attitude is reflected in the Jewish individual police files, consisting of dozens of investigations conducted against Jews.[7] Although triggered by hostile denunciation letters and vicious SEC reports, most of the investigations did not result in any severe administrative actions, illustrating the reluctance of the administration—and of Autrand—to go beyond the collective measures against the Jews and harass individuals. Was this reluctance the result of personal moderation or political caution? Whatever the answer to this question, Autrand needed to be sufficiently tolerant of Vichy's state anti-Semitism to continue serving.

Informed by a letter, dated January 31, 1942, from the commissioner for Jewish affairs, Xavier Vallat, that two Jews, Levy and Naquet, were still serving as elected commissioners in the Avignon Association of Reserve Officers, Autrand has a friendly chat with each one of them. As a result, Levy agrees to resign, but Naquet holds firm. On March 13, 1942, Vallat suggests considering Naquet "automatically outgoing by virtue of the Law of June 2, 1941, article 2, paragraph 1, which forbids Jews to belong to any assembly resulting from election." On March 19, 1942, Autrand writes:

> **I am honored to inform you that the Administrative Council of the association mentioned above no longer includes any Jewish member.**
>
> **You will find included the new board composition that I have just received from the President. . . .[8]**

In another case, H. Femy, Nov'Hotel owner in Avignon, sends a complaint about a young Jewish hotel guest, Pierre Spira, accusing him of courting his daughter, "thus risking to compromise her by his advances, and causing great trouble for us." Femy adds, "For us to recover our lost tranquillity troubled by the misdeeds of Spira is the reason why I took the liberty of asking you to assign Pierre Spira, and his mother, to another residence, as far as possible from our town, since he is Jewish."

Six days later, Autrand directs the chief of the Avignon police to conduct an investigation:

Prefectorate
of Vaucluse
1st Division
2nd Bureau
No. D1 B2

Avignon, April 10, 1942

Confidential and Urgent

The Prefect of Vaucluse
to the Chief of Police
Avignon

I am honored to request that you provide as early as possible precise and confidential information about:

1. the religion
2. the morality
3. the behavior
4. the state of finances
5. the attitude toward the government

of Mr. Pierre Spira, domiciled 3 Rue Félicien David, in Avignon.

For the prefect
The delegated chief of division
Aimé Autrand

Autrand was faithfully implementing the anti-Jewish Vichy policies that culminated in the deportation and murder of the "foreign Jews" in August 1942, and made all the Jews in the area vulnerable to Nazi terror, both French and German, until the end of the war.

During the few days I spent at the archives, I became familiar with Autrand's handwriting and the twist of his signature. Interestingly, he had a weakness for turquoise ink at a time when purple ink was the trademark of good thrifty bureaucrats. At times, especially early in the war, he even used a red stamp for his function. His colorful signatures and handwritten annotations joyously contrast with the matter-of-fact black print or purple text of his subordinates, and with the grim consequences of the measures he was ordering. Did Autrand's hand ever tremble when he drafted the damning instructions against the Jews?

"Difficult times! What a confusion!" he probably thought to himself, while dipping his pen in the pot of green-blue ink. Everything had indeed become so complicated. For instance, he had received the conclusions of the subprefect of Carpentras, who had conducted an investigation against the Jew Alfred Nahon, following a request of the Police for Jewish Affairs in Marseille.

Sub-Prefectorate of Carpentras
Division D1 B2

Carpentras, December 22, 1942

The Sub-Prefect of Carpentras
to the Prefect of Vaucluse, . . .

By communicating to me the report of the SEC of Marseille related to the so-called Alfred NAHON, Israelite domiciled in Carpentras, . . . you have asked my opinion about the appropriateness of a measure of internment against the party of interest.

I am honored to advise you that since August 1941, date of the arrival of Monsieur NAHON in Carpentras, I have thought necessary to bring to your attention this individual who, under the alias of Henri HOURBON, was the representative, for the départements of the Bouches-du-Rhône, the Var, the Alpes-Maritimes, the Basses-Alpes, the Hautes-Alpes, the Gard, and the Vaucluse, of the group "Collaboration." Besides, this function has been taken away from him.

Indeed, through my reports of September 4 and 26, 1941, November 21 and 26, 1941, and January 4, 1942, I have kept you informed of the dealings of this character whose judiciary antecedents, Jewish origin, and questionable attitude made particularly suspect the nationalist and anti-Semitic opinions which he displays publicly. I did not change my mind about this individual.

However, we must notice that since his arrival at Carpentras, NAHON did not give rise to any unfavorable remark. He seldom goes out, does not seem to have any acquaintances, and does not attract any attention.

NAHON speaks very little. However, at the time of the Anglo-Saxon landing in North Africa, he expressed a condemnation of this aggression. On the other hand, he showed his satisfaction about the occupation of the Mediterranean coasts by the troops of the Axis. He stated that only the Germans were capable of saving us and that he approved of the measures taken against the Jews.

Such propositions coming from the mouth of an Israelite are very surprising; but, even if it is difficult to test their sincerity, they must nevertheless be recorded.

Under these conditions and in the absence of any proof of hostility manifested by NAHON against the Government, a measure of internment seems inappropriate to me.

Before going after Israelites who claim to be favorable to the Government's actions—whatever the reservation and the skepticism which are appropriate toward such declarations— it is a sane method to strike against those whose action is aimed against the Government. . . .

Consequently, it is my judgment that NAHON must be the target of a very attentive surveillance by the Police for Jewish Affairs. I have communicated this need to an inspector specialized in this kind of investigation who visited my office. I would be grateful to you to request those services to follow closely the activity of this individual.

Obviously, the author of the letter covered himself skillfully by referring to his past reports about Nahon. Only too happy to turn the problem back to the Police for Jewish Affairs, which had initiated the inquiry against Nahon a few weeks earlier, Autrand had written a resounding *oui* on the side of the last paragraph. It was so important not to be carried away by the zealots of Jewish Affairs.

In his "moderation," Autrand consistently took a middle-of-the-road position. He did not exhibit a clear behavior of his own, but would alternately borrow from either side. When he was directed to arrest the Jews, he arrested them, thus satisfying the desires of the anti-Semites. But he also probably showed some compassion by helping a few fugitives—or at least by closing his eyes. For instance, Autrand and the police knew that there were Jews who had eluded arrest in August 1942, since many of them were listed in the census of August 27, 1943. As the war progressed, anti-German sentiment became stronger, and French public opinion increasingly tilted away from Germany,[9] carrying the Vichy administration with it. Autrand shifted accordingly, recognizing the weakness of an excessive alignment with the Nazis. In 1943, his Gaullist side became more vocal, and he more readily expressed his patriotic positions. When faced with German demands, the man who, until the end of 1942, had methodically executed Vichy's anti-Jewish policies was now becoming sluggish and ready to use delaying tactics, like the rest of the Vichy administration. Yet even though there was a clear shift in his position, he still kept to the middle of the road. He did not go as far as to join the Resistance, but he did become more openly Gaullist, thereby risking arrest. In his "moderation," Autrand embodied all of France in one man: cruel and compassionate, submissive and independent, patriotic and racist, bold and cowardly, all in shades of gray.

Speaking of himself in the third person, Autrand masterfully captures his shift of conscience (and that of his peers) in a few painful lines:

> This is why, starting in July 1943, he was expecting every day to be arrested. When, indeed, starting at that date, a few members of the PPF and Militiamen understood that the police services of the prefectorate did not act with enough vigor against the terrorists and the Israelites, they publicly complained and did not hide their firm intention to initiate, without delay, the necessary complementary measures![10]

Indeed, Aimé Autrand was arrested on September 16, 1943,[11] in a punitive raid aimed at hundreds of French people from the *département* of Vaucluse, and sent to a German detention camp. By that time, he was considered a "Gaullist." By the fall of 1943, Autrand had seemingly become innocent again, a little Mitterand of sorts.[12]

27 | *The Cherry Farm*

A season is set for everything,
A time for every experience under heaven:
A time for being born and a time for dying.
A time for planting and a time for uprooting the planted;
A time for slaying and a time for healing,
A time for tearing down and a time for building up;
A time for weeping and a time for laughing,
A time for wailing and a time for dancing . . .
A time for silence and a time for speaking;
A time for loving and a time for hating;
A time for war and a time for peace.

—Ecclesiastes 3:1–8

During my week in the archives, I was so absorbed by the documents passing in front of my eyes that I did not pay much attention to the other people in the reading room until the last day of my visit. At the table next to me, an older man, probably retired, is reading with a magnifying glass a bound package of very old handwritten documents. I can see the title on the filing box: "Land Rights, 16th Century." Further away, a woman is discussing with an attendant which file she needs next. The seats are filled with studious people poring over yellowing sheets, methodically taking notes. Nobody is looking up, each one absorbed in his own little world.

The attendant at the desk smiles at me. She is the clerk who records every file I take out. A few days ago, after she became aware of the topic of my research, she asked me to find information concerning a Jewish family who were her neighbors during the war and were deported. "Very nice people," she said. "I used to play with their daughter a lot. But I never saw them again. Somebody told me that they were deported and died. I wonder how I can find out what happened to them." But I was not able to do much for her, except find the traces of the census of her friends.

A warm ray of winter sun bursts into the reading room through the huge Gothic window. I return to my documents for one last look and retrieve the Individual Jewish Files,[1] which are filled with denunciation letters, some anonymous and others openly signed. In fact, every one of the files in this collection was opened because of a denunciation by a private citizen. One of these letters was particularly hostile and evoked familiar names and places. It was written by a woman living in the small town of Pernes, between Carpentras and Avignon, a few weeks after the raid against the foreign Jews on August 26, 1942.

Pernes, September 19, 1942

Monsieur the Prefect,

I am honored and obligated at an hour when the Jewish problem is becoming more acute and I understand all the damage this race has inflicted upon us, and is unfortunately still inflicting, to inform you of the following facts: . . .

. . . On November 1, 1933, I saw that the farm that I had rented to Abraham Estryn was now occupied by his brother and other suspect foreigners. . . . The behavior of this gang of Jews was questionable, and I advised the prefect to have them

expelled. But, I must believe that dark powers intervened because the brother of Abraham Estryn is still around.

Abraham is said to be dead, but his brother took his place on the farm of Madame and Monsieur Vève. These people have no children, and Abraham had told me that he was loved like a son since Madame Vève was polishing his shoes and that Monsieur Vève would one day give him his property. . . . I had well understood that greed alone was keeping them in this family.

This Jew, Estryn, whose first name I ignore, continues to entertain the same dream as his brother, and he has entered this country by using deception. Are we going to let him defraud these naive peasants and spread his insidious propaganda because this is his reason for being here? . . .

On the same occasion, I must warn you that the Jews, in order to find a shelter and escape the measures aimed at men between the ages of 18 and 50, are trying by <u>all possible means</u> to rent farms in the area; others who were clever enough to buy properties are trying to pass as "peasants." They are very skilled in camouflage and staging.

It is painful for me to face this Jew who has fraudulently entered this country by abusing my ignorance and naïveté, and I would become an accomplice if I did not inform you, at a time when this race is the cause of all our miseries.

Receive Monsieur the Prefect the assurance of my highest respect and total devotion.

Madame L. Galy

Pinchas Estryn, the unnamed brother of Abraham, was a friend of our family's who was arrested on August 26, 1942, and taken to Les Milles, near Marseille. He had been targeted by the police in the preliminary list of 111 Jews, but he was able to bribe his way out of the camp. His return to the Vève farm was apparently not appreciated by Madame Galy.

The police initiated an investigation, but they did not find much cooperation among the stiff-necked villagers of Venasques. They interrogated seven witnesses, who were unsparing in their praise of the Estryn brothers. The police report states that Abraham Estryn was a prisoner of war and not dead, as Madame Galy suggested. The report concludes: "The behavior, the morality, and the attitude from the national point of view of the Estryn brothers did not lead, to date, to any unfavorable observation. Anyway, Pinchas Estryn will be subjected to a discreet surveillance."[2] The report also provides the address of Monsieur and Madame Vève: "Belle-Croix neighborhood in VENASQUE."

Could Monsieur and Madame Vève be the French owners of the cherry farm where my mother and I spent the last few hours together before her fatal return to Le Pontet? Would I finally be able to set my foot on the exact spot where we separated forever? Was this letter another one of these fragments of information that seemed to come my way miraculously during the past two years?

Claire Steltzer volunteered to help locate the place. Indeed, she remembered the Vèves and Pinchas Estryn, and she accompanied me to "old Vève's farm" in Venasques. Once more, we took the familiar road between the mountain and the valley. Patches of vineyards and cherry trees accompany us all the way to the center of the minuscule village. Since Claire had forgotten how to get there, we asked the oldest person we could find in the village, and indeed he remembered Monsieur and Madame Vève. "The farm is down there on the road to Carpentras, next to the Sacred Cross, on your right. But," he warned us, "the farm now belongs to Germans." Clearly, he did not seem to appreciate this new facet of history. He was probably more comfortable in the past. Now it was no longer possible to differentiate clearly between friend and foe solely on the basis of which language people spoke and where they lived.

Soon I am standing in the middle of the gravel yard, in the middle of the past, trying to reconnect with it. The farm and the barn have been remodeled to fit the new owners' idea of a vacation home in the country. Ironically, they are German citizens who fell in love with the area. The old farmhouse I knew peeks here and there through the new, stylish facade. Windows and glass doors replace the bulky walls. The dark kitchen has become an open area. The decrepit plaster has yielded to a new rustic look.

Next to the old Vève farmstead, a new house has been built over what used to be the cherry orchard. There are now new neighbors a stone's throw away. The blue sky of 1944 is now gone, hidden by the thickness of pine and oak trees that have replaced the sparse rows of cherry trees.

A familiar sight appears at the end of the long yard, away from the farm. Could this be true? There stands the large portal where my mother faded away. It is now condemned and locked with a chain because the new owners have opened up an entrance next to the house. The old farmers always liked to see visitors from a distance; people today prefer easy access.

Then, in the middle of that yard, I feel myself come full circle. I am standing again next to the young boy who subdued the mule, and as I look toward the condemned portal at the end of the yard, I see my mother leave as she did forty-eight years ago. This time, when she moves away, I walk with her down the gravel road, accompanying her for her last voyage. For I know already where she is going, every step she will take, from the return trip to our store on the old bus to the crematorium at Auschwitz a month later. I know because I have finally walked the entire distance with her, until the bitter end.

Although I know now the brutality of her arrest and the despair of her surrender, I have so far not been able to locate her "steel-hearted" assailants. Their only "fingerprint" was their "accent of Marseille," according to the 1991 testimony of my neighbor, Gaston Vernet. How could such a fragile clue guide me to the truth?

28 | *The French Connection*

If aggressors are wrong up there, they are right down here.

—Napoleon Bonaparte, *Maxims*

December 1993–April 1994

It is by accident that Paul Jankowski, a professor at Brandeis University and author of a book on fascism in Marseille,[1] brought to my attention, in December 1993, the Palmièri gang, a band of gangsters who had worked for the Nazis in Marseille and the southeast of France. After having worked for the Parti Populaire Française (PPF), these prewar gangsters had chosen the Nazis, unlike the gang of Antoine Guerrini, who had gambled on the Resistance. Having spent a year in Marseille to research his book, Jankowski had noticed in the archives of the *département* of Bouches du Rhône that Palmièri and his gang paid several visits to Avignon in the spring of 1944. Although I had already spotted Palmièri's name in the investigation files against the SD of the Marseille region (which I had received from Serge Klarsfeld in

1992),[2] it was my conversation with Jankowski that led me to ask for file access. Jankowski gave me important new details about the anti-Jewish operations of this Marseille gangster. In contrast to the results of my first request to Marseille, which went unfulfilled, this time the permission arrived quickly, and in April 1994 I was authorized to examine the Palmièri files.[3] Would I be able to find the traces of the Census of the Jews which was sent to Marseille by the police of Vaucluse on October 27, 1943?[4] Did Palmièri operate alone, or did he have profound links to the Avignon prefectorate?

It is the anonymous denunciation of Palmièri, one of the first file documents, that triggered the legal proceedings against him and his acolytes. Its text is cited here in its simplicity, with most of its style and punctuation errors:

> **Mr. the security chief, it is a patriot who has suffered who writes to you, he writes you to designate to popular justice four gangsters of the Gestapo. These are the three Palmièri brothers living at La Madrague Ville I name them Charlot Palmièri No. 1 agent of the Gestapo this one used to conduct searches at the homes of Jewish people and bring them to Rue Paradis, he took possession and stole all their money it is he, himself, who boasted about it with the money of his victims he bought a villa to his mistress at the Corniche; his brother Alfred Palmièri took the French people to deliver to Rue Honorat so they can be sent to Germany as to the third having been rejected by the Gestapo because of his handicap being humpbacked he served as an informer to his two brothers this three individuals dangerous for the population are still free and strut about at La Madrague Ville Cap Janet. The fourth agent is nicknamed Nitou he too took patriots to Rue Paradis; he just bought at l'Estaque the Bar Moutier for 500 thousand francs. all this money is only money stolen to his victims. mr. the chief of security I do not want to give you my name; not because of cowardice because these four gangsters deserve the most exemplary punishment; . . . I believe it is my duty to**

**designate them so that popular justice hits them hard,
because they benefited during 5 years of the misery and suffering of the people.**

**PS in case they are not arrested I will write directly to the
CDL [Comité de Libération][5]**

After a preliminary investigation, arrest warrants were
issued against Charles Palmièri and his gang. On his capture, the
gang leader was questioned by Judge Larrat, who had no difficulty in obtaining a full and detailed confession. At the beginning,
Palmièri made his gang available to Paul Kompe of Marseille's SD
to track down *résistants* and collect intelligence against them.
Kompe provided Palmièri with an apartment at 8, rue Paradis in
Marseille, as well as a warehouse at the same address, a few
blocks away from the SD offices. He received the order to open
the "Merle" office, a trading enterprise, which was to serve him as
a front. Initially, he was asked to get hold of black-market stock-
piles in exchange for a 3 percent commission on the seized merchandise, in addition to a salary of 10,000 francs a month. He then
established a network of informers on the *résistants* and even
took action against the latter. This is how Palmièri describes the
role of a certain Frézet to the judge who had noticed the name
among the documents seized in his apartment:

> **Frézet Marius, this is the bookstore owner who lived below
> my office. Kompe from rue Paradis told me that it was agreed
> that if customers were to buy too many maps at Frézet's store,
> he would tap against our wall to warn us to arrest the cus-
> tomers; I had made my associates aware of this, and during
> one of my absences, Heiter[6] arrested one person who had
> bought such maps and was later released.[7]**

The jurisdiction of the Palmièri gang spanned most of the
départements of the southeast: Bouches du Rhône, Vaucluse, Var,
Alpes Maritimes, Basses Alpes, and even Drome. At the beginning of 1944, Palmièri's mission would change:

Toward March 1944, Kompe told me then that we will take our orders from Bauer, officer of the 4B Section of the Gestapo (anti-Jewish repression). However, we would have to continue to keep Kompe informed about our activity. From this time on, it is mostly my brother Alfred who served as a liaison with Bauer; I myself did not go often to see Bauer. My office had a double role:

1. To arrest the Jews (we were in this case accompanied by a German in plain clothes) who were named in lists provided by Bauer. These were mostly foreign Jews, mostly German, registered on lists provided to the Gestapo by the prefectorate, or rather by the prefectorates of the interested départements. I cannot specify the number of Jews arrested by the bureau "Merle," say 200.

2. To transfer the Jews already arrested in the neighboring départements to the Gestapo of Marseille; the bureau actually transferred 44 or 54 German Jews detained in a convent of Basses Alpes by the French authorities, we made 2 or 3 transfers from Avignon, one transfer of 11 Jews detained in the Gendarmerie of Manosque.[8]

Palmièri was to receive 1,000 francs per arrested Jew. When he declares having received the census lists of *foreign Jews* prepared by the prefectorates, his testimony raises a natural question: why was the focus on foreign Jews? We already know that the Vichy government did not particularly like the idea of delivering the French Jews to the Nazis, an attitude clearly reflected in the deportation statistics. If Palmièri had benefited from random leaks in the prefectorates, he would have received the names of both French and foreign Jews. This establishes without a doubt that in 1944 the Vichy government continued sacrificing the foreign Jews to provide a measure of protection to French Jews.

Driven by a stream of personal testimonies, the interrogation of Palmièri proceeds little by little to establish the scope of his activities and that of his men. The following testimony is representative of the methods of the gang:

On March 30, 1944, around 7:00 A.M., I was arrested by
agents of the Gestapo of Avignon in the bus to Orange, where
I intended to sell merchandise in the outdoor market.

My husband was with me, but he was not bothered
because he is a Catholic while I am Jewish. . . .

I must bring to your attention that at the time of my arrest
in the bus to Orange, the Gestapo also arrested Monsieur Elie
ANGEL, who was later deported.

I want to add that at the time of my arrest, while I was
putting up some resistance and my husband was trying to prevent me from leaving the bus, the man who arrested me vio-
lently kicked my husband, who fell to the ground. This
Gestapo man was accompanied by an accomplice, to whom he
said, "Go and bring the revolver! We will shoot him," while
pointing at my husband. . . .

On the photographs which you are showing me, I categor-
ically recognize the perpetrator of my arrest, named Charles
Palmièri. He is the one who beat my husband and threatened
to kill him with his revolver.[9]

One testimony after another describes the brutality and the
extortion perpetrated by the members of the Palmièri gang:

Among the photographs presented to her, Lucie Politi recognizes Charles Palmièri. She indicates that he is the one who
interrogated her at the Sainte-Anne prison in Avignon, where
she had been incarcerated. She mentions that Palmièri stole
from her 10,000 francs out of 20,000 she possessed.[10]

Enormous amounts of money—10,000, 100,000, or even
200,000 francs—were taken from the victims, sometimes to set
them free. This is confirmed by the signed confession of Palmièri
himself:

we were in charge of arresting Jews; . . . sometimes in a raid
some Jews would give us money (100,000 or 200,000 francs)
and we set them free; of course we kept the money. Once in a
while, we could find jewelry belonging to Jews.[11]

On April 5, 1945, Palmièri gives details on transportation: "As I was saying, we would leave by car with my Citroën or that of my brother, later with the truck which we got from Bauer and which was driven by Simon or one of the others."

One testimony, that of Estrea Asseo, indicates that she was arrested by Lucien Blanc, an accomplice of Palmièri in Avignon. Although Estrea was able to name Lucien Blanc when I met her in 1992 in Avignon, she thought he was a *milicien*, a fact refuted by Judge Fabre's statement to Palmièri:

> **The woman Estrea Asseo, merchant rue du Chaperon Rouge in Avignon, witnessed your operation at the store of Denise Mitrani. She [Estrea Asseo] herself was arrested on June 6, 1944, by Lucien Blanc and Bergeron while you were arresting other people in that store. Bergeron brought Estrea Asseo to you, and you took her to the Avignon police to verify her identity, then you took her to the barracks of the 7th Engineering Regiment in Avignon, then to the Sainte-Anne prison, where you forced her to surrender part of her money. She was later deported to a camp in Germany.[12]**

The testimonies of numerous people establish a clear image of Palmièri: greedy, unscrupulous, and cold. He had sensed the vulnerability of the Jews, who had been transformed into pariahs by the Nazis and their collaborators. He exploited their weakness without caring about the consequences. In his case, anti-Semitism played a minor role; he had chosen to act this way because it served his financial objectives. Besides, he had had a brush with the law early in his life. Born in 1911, he was sentenced twice in 1929 for theft; in 1933 for smuggling; in 1935 for carrying illegal weapons, bankruptcy and theft, and car theft; in 1937 for theft and possession of stolen goods; in 1941 for assault and bodily harm; and in 1942 for theft. In 1936 he had joined Simon Sabiani's PPF to support the candidacy of his brother Alfred, an alcoholic, who ran for office and lost in the 1937 elections in the first district of Marseille.[13] He then moved to Paris, where he married Jacqueline

Payeur in 1940. There, he also tightened his ties to the PPF through Jacques Doriot, its leader, who was a regular customer at his wife's bar, Le Mirliton. This connection would prove useful, since Doriot was able to reduce a prison sentence Palmièri had received for black-market activities between the "free" zone and Paris. Well worthy of her husband, who returned to Marseille in 1942, Jacqueline remained in Paris, where she bought a bar jointly with her husband and conducted shady activities, which would earn her four citations, four closures, and 130,000 francs in fines. Later, she would become the lover of François Heiter, an interpreter at the service of the Germans. She arranged a job for Heiter with her husband in 1943. Toward the end of the war, she would dump Palmièri to live with Heiter, by whom she had become pregnant.

Faced with the enormity of the facts, the judge called upon a psychiatrist to check the sanity of the accused at the time of the crimes. The psychiatrist's report is remarkable in its banality:

I, undersigned, G. A. Rousselier, expert from the Institute of Legal Medicine and Psychiatry at the University of Paris, expert attached to the courts, requested on April 22, 1945, by ordinance of Monsieur Judge Fabre, examining magistrate in Marseille, to examine Charles Palmièri, with the mandate:

"To state whether he was insane at the time of his action in the spirit of Article 64 of the Penal Code.

"Whether psychiatric or biological examination detects, in this individual, any mental or psychological abnormality susceptible of diminishing his responsibility."

. . . Therefore, from a medical viewpoint, the study of the Palmièri case, done in a psychiatric sense, yielded only negative results, as far as personal and hereditary factors, his personal history, his present state, and the period corresponding to the charges against him.

Medically speaking, this man does not dissimulate any

hidden trouble; he does not attempt to simulate nonexistent problems.

He is perfectly able to act in his own defense.

He is fully responsible, and he does not exhibit anything which could serve to lower his penal responsibility based on any medical grounds.

Besides, this charged man, very direct in his statements, asserts that he never had any antinational intentions; he pretends he can explain his acts solely based upon his political convictions, and that he had, by conviction, wanted to fight against the "internationals"[14] and the Jews. He maintained his statements clearly, the evaluation of which does not fall in the range of a strictly medical document.[15]

The psychiatrist added an ironic note by mentioning that Palmièri indicates "his wife has always been faithful to him."

During his interrogation by Judge Larrat, Palmièri provided more specific details about the Vaucluse:

The other lists of Jews in the following towns and villages: Avignon, Ville-Laure, La Palud, Cadenet, Saint Romain Viennois, Saint Didier, Carpentras, Vedène, Orange, Perthuis, La Tour d'Aygues, Lauris, Gordes, Beaumont de Perthuis, Vaison la Romaine, Bollène, Puymèras, Mérindol, Beaume de Venise, Mallemort du Comtat, Cavaillon, Malaucènes, Montfavet, Le Thor, Goult, Le Pontet, Le Crestet, Chateauneuf du Pape, Sorgues, Entraygues, are lists which were established by the French authorities during the Census of the Jews. They were communicated to Bauer and were sent to us much later.

I had sent these lists to my Avignon agents, specifically to Mouillade, so that he could find out whether these Jews of the census still lived at their declared addresses.[16]

On May 29, 1945, Judge Jean Fabre of the Court of Justice of Marseille asked the examining magistrate of Avignon to "verify in the archives of the service which had been in charge of the census (Prefecture of Police) whether the attached lists [of

Avignon Jews, which were found in Palmièri's office] matched the lists of Jews in the census."[17] Four weeks later, the response arrived from Avignon, confirming once again the singling out of the foreign Jews a few weeks before the Allied landing in Normandy:

> From our investigations, it results that the attached list including 109 names of Israelites from Avignon is the integral copy of a complementary list of Jews residing in Vaucluse as of May 14, 1944. This list was sent upon request by the Service of Foreigners of the Prefectorate of Avignon to the Regional Prefectorate of Marseille around May 15, 1944.[18]

In his interrogation, Palmièri alluded to his Avignon associates, more specifically to the role of Gaston Mouillade of Montfavet, a small village two kilometers away from Le Pontet. Mouillade, who had participated in most of the raids in Vaucluse, admits that he had arranged for the arrest of Blaise Bounias and two women whom he suspected of working for the Resistance. In addition, he had stated to Reau, an employee of the prefectorate: "We are performing the cleanup because it is necessary to force the Gaullists to lower their tone. As far as I am concerned, I have decided to act energetically, because if the Americans were to land, my skin would not sell for much." In addition, according to the interrogation of Mouillade by Commissaire Chazalon, Reau was providing him with intelligence:

> A short time thereafter, Reau tried to meet Mouillade to provide him with the following tip: "Charles Vallabrègue and his sister are said to be hidden in the département, thanks to Mr. Clapier, former Cabinet Director of Mr. Daladier, who is said to have made one of his properties available to them."
> In July 1943, Mouillade participated in the arrest of the Stern family in Le Thor. . . .
> In April 1943, Mouillade had sought information about Mrs. Lamorlette, General Secretary of the Prefecture, Autrand and Plaindoux, Division Chiefs.[19]

It is strange to find among the documents concerning Palmièri and his gang a reference to Autrand, which corroborates Autrand's statements that his Gaullist opinions had caused him trouble with the collaborators.[20] It is probably after Reau provided information about Autrand's Gaullist opinions that the latter was placed on medical leave on May 1, 1943.[21] Plaindoux was also placed on medical leave the same day. In contrast to his blind collaboration until 1942, when he deported foreign Jews who had sought refuge under what they thought would be the protection of France, Autrand now distances himself from Vichy. Has he become sensitive about the fact that the Germans are robbing the French of their autonomy, or has he started hearing about the German military losses in the Soviet Union and North Africa?

In his deposition, Mouillade also mentions his own role as an informer against the Jews of Avignon area:

> On March 30, 1944, I met in Avignon around 5 P.M. Mr. Poutet of l'Isle sur Sorgue.
>
> The boss had ordered me to contact this man about the list of Jews in l'Isle sur Sorgue.
>
> Invited by Mr. Poutet to accompany him to his home and have dinner with him, I accepted. We left for l'Isle by car in company of Mr. De Cazal.[22]

Because of his connection with the informants of the prefectorate, with Palmièri the gang leader, and with the Nazis, Mouillade, our Montfavet neighbor, had become, unbeknownst to us, our most fearsome enemy.

But let us return to Palmièri's file. An essential document can be found in the midst of hundreds of testimonies against this thug and his gang. This poorly written document records a confrontation that took place in Marseille on July 20, 1945, between Moïse Benyacar from Le Pontet, a survivor of Auschwitz, and Charles Palmièri:

Moïse Benyacar:

I was arrested in Le Pontet on June 6, 1944, at half past noon, by 5 men, among whom Charles Palmièri being now present. I was arrested together with my wife and a baby, three and a half months old, we were brought to the village hall of Le Pontet, there were brought first my sister-in-law Mrs. Kremer, presently deported and without any news, Mrs. Levander [sic] from Le Pontet, presently deported and without any news, as well as Mrs. Bitran who was freed and is now in Avignon. . . . We were taken by the same people to the barracks of the Engineering Regiment, and then the Sainte-Anne prison then to Drancy, Auswich [sic], Bukenwal [sic], and Dachau, where I was liberated from. My wife and my child were deported at the same time as I, and I have no news from them.

Charles Palmièri:

I do not contest having made the arrest in company of Billartz who was the boss, he belonged to the Gestapo of Marseille under the orders of Bauer, also were present Bergeron and Blanc, Bride was with us that day, I do not know whether he stayed at the village hall or went to the house of Benyacar. I want to make it known that one member of our team told to the wife of Benyacar not to come, this happened after the departure of the German Billartz, but the woman said that she did not want to separate from her husband and she came with her child.

Moïse Benyacar:

I want to specify that at the village hall of Le Pontet
1. Mrs. Levander [sic]
2. Mrs. Bitran
3. Mrs. KREMER and her child, 6 years old

myself, my wife and my child. In total, 5 adults and two children . . .

Palmièri:

I do not contest that it is my team who arrested these 5 people.[23]

By providing me with the identity of the men who came to arrest my mother in the middle of the day on June 6, 1944, this document, buried for decades in the archives, becomes the final piece in my puzzle. Although it is impossible to know which of the five were the two "steel-hearted" men who dragged her out of our neighbor Gaston Vernet's kitchen, Gaston's testimony still resonates in my memory. "They spoke French with the accent of Marseille," he said. "A short moment later, they came back with a truck to load the merchandise." It is this detail from Gaston's testimony, together with my conversation with Paul Jankowski, that put me back on the track of Palmièri.

At the time of his testimony, Moïse Benyacar did not yet know the truth about the fate of his wife and his child. According to Serge Klarsfeld, the Benyacar family was deported from Drancy to Auschwitz on June 30, 1944, together with sixty-six other deportees from Vaucluse. Lisette and Sylvain Benyacar perished in deportation. When I spoke with him on November 1, 1995, Moïse Benyacar still remembered his brief detention at the Le Pontet village hall, in the company of the other prisoners. "It was half past noon, and there was no German present," he states, "just *miliciens*.[24] I remember your mother as if it were yesterday. I knew both of you well. In front of our captors, we were all in a profound distress."

None of the Avignon members of the Palmièri gang escaped a well-deserved fate. Pierre Josselme from Montafavet was killed by the police during a street fight in Avignon in February 1944. The others were delivered to justice, rapidly judged, and executed by firing squad: Louis Bergeron, nicknamed "Toto," in Orléans in 1944; Gaston Mouillade in Avignon in 1944; and Lucien Blanc in Nimes in 1945. However, Charles Palmièri himself almost escaped the judgment of man. Having fled with the SD ahead of the Allies, he was parachuted into France by the Germans, together with his brother Alfred and a few acolytes, to organize sabotage operations. Captured upon landing by the Gendarmerie, Alfred committed suicide by poisoning himself, while Charles volunteered to serve the Paris Police for the Surveillance of the Territory, which utilized him for intelligence with the intention of transferring him later to Orléans with similar goals. Fortunately, and unfortunately for him, Palmièri's results in Paris were dismal, as indicated by the following report of August 25, 1945:

> **Paris, August 25, 1945**
> **Préfecture de Police**
> **Direction de la**
> **Police Judicière**
> **REPORT**
>
> The investigation done according to the prescriptions of the investigation request attached provides the following information:
>
> Mr. Briel, Commissaire of Police at the Direction of Surveillance of the Territory [DST] in Orléans, could not be interviewed.
>
> Mr. Bernard, Commissaire Divisionnaire at the Direction of the Surveillance of the Territory, declared after being consulted:
>
> "Charles Palmièri was supposed to be transferred to Mr. Briel, Commissaire of Police at the DST of Orléans, who intended to use him for police operations, but because of the lack of results obtained in Paris between Mr. Orabona and Palmièri, this project was abandoned and Palmièri was delivered to the Court of Justice of Marseille."[25]

Had Palmièri been more effective, the DST would probably have kept using him, sparing him the inconvenience of justice. Of course, Palmièri used his short employment by the DST in his defense. He even brought up his help to *résistants*, members of the AJAX network in the police:

> by the intermediary of Commissaire Regnier, I made contact with Mr. Mercury, whose personal security was then threatened. . . . I also gave him indications and warned him that a

wide investigation was about to begin about the resisting activity of parts of the police (AJAX network). . . . I have therefore forewarned the AJAX network against the activities of the German counterintelligence.[26]

Palmièri was careful to remember that someday he might need the police. Nevertheless, the numerous testimonies and the serious charges against him resulted in a death sentence; he was executed in 1946. He left behind his brother Victor, whose death sentence was commuted to life imprisonment, and his wife, Jacqueline.

A report of the Mouillade trial testifies to the prevalent state of mind at that time, so similar in some aspects to today's attitudes:

> While returning to you the request for investigation attached, I am honored to send you the present report, established at your request after consultation at the Archives of the Court of Justice of Avignon, about the files of Gaston Frederic Mouillade, sentenced to death on October 7, 1944 . . .
>
> He had been sentenced three times before for breach of trust and swindle . . .
>
> ### COPY OF THE QUESTIONS TO THE JURY AND THE RESPONSES:
>
> 1. Is the accused Frederic Gaston Mouillade guilty of having belonged to the PPF, an organization aimed at helping enterprises of all kinds by Germany against France, while these two nations were at war?
>
> <u>Yes, by majority.</u>
>
> 2. Is the accused guilty, being French, of belonging to the Gestapo?
>
> <u>Yes, by majority.</u>
>
> 3. Is the accused guilty of having delivered or denounced <u>French people</u> [my emphasis] to an enemy organization and of having arrested them or caused this organization to arrest them?

<u>Yes, by majority.</u>

4. Are there any extenuating circumstances in favor of the accused?

<u>No, by majority.</u>[27]

In the questions posed to the jury, the judge makes no mention that most of the victims of Mouillade and his gang were Jewish. Although a large number had been both Jews and foreigners, only their supposed French nationality is mentioned, as if Mouillade had been guilty only of treason against France. This early omission of the Jewish side of French collaboration was to mark the beginning of fifty years of unease.[28]

Robert Bailly, another historian of wartime Avignon, never specifically mentions the Jewish refugees in the "free" zone in his 1986 study. The closest reference he makes describes them as follows: "The invasion of the forces of the Reich pushed down a crowd of refugees who, *in the image of their ancestors of bygone times,* were taking to the road ahead of the invader, without knowing where they were going and in ignorance of everything about the place where they would someday land!"[29] According to Bailly, the only arrests of Jews were made by the Gestapo, whose agents "were not only Germans, but . . . also included French members."[30]

29 | *The Anatomy of National Amnesia*

The Jew does not belong to any place except that place in which he makes money: would he not just as easily betray the king on behalf of the emperor as he would the emperor for the king?

—François Marie Arouet de Voltaire

1944–1993

In the spontaneous postwar trials as well as in the more orderly purge, popular justice did very little to dissipate the dark cloud of shame that had engulfed French national pride. When I examined the minutes of the 1945 trials in the Purge Files,[1] there were no traces of proceedings against people like Aimé Autrand or Gros, our neighbor the restaurant owner. No trace of Berton and Sicard. There was no trace either of the tens of "Aryan" administrators of Jewish assets. Instead, I found a few insignificant cases.

The shoemaker from Le Pontet, André Mazoyer, was accused by two angry villagers of overpricing the repair of a pair of shoes. However, the case against him was deemed futile and dismissed. The Mouret brothers, textile manufacturers from Avignon, were accused of collaboration because they had supplied uniforms to the German air base in the village of Pujaut near Avignon. They were exonerated after proving that they had used their trips to the German base to gather military information for British intelligence and that they had repeatedly volunteered their pickup truck to the Resistance for weapons traffic.

I could have testified on behalf of both of the parties because I knew them well. The shoemaker was living with Madame Gaffet, the mother of my friend René. They remained friendly with us in the worst of times, although the villagers did not like their lifestyle. During the war, the Mouret brothers had been kind enough to provide merchandise to my mother at a time when it was not politically correct to sell to Jews. I still have the postcard they sent to my mother after she came to their factory and they were absent. "Madame Levandel," they wrote on November 26, 1943, "we regret we were unable to meet you at your last visit to our Factory, and we would be grateful for you to tell us which of our products you are interested in, so that we can prepare a shipment."

The purge file of Jacques Petit, the leader of l'Amicale, the Fascist organization dissolved by Vichy in 1941, confirms the relatively moderate position of Aimé Autrand. Petit is charged with having denounced Autrand in 1941 for having "renewed the dwelling authorization of the Spaniard Aguilas."

The relative emptiness of the collaboration files leaves me puzzled. The files do not reflect the intense emotions that overwhelmed the immediate postwar months , nor do they mention the number of trials that took place in the *département* of Vaucluse. The police, reflecting many segments of the society of Vaucluse, were more or less inclined to forget. This attitude, in turn, may have encouraged some individuals to purge the purge files. Since the summary tribunals did not readily accept the authority of the government, it is possible that the information flow to the police was limited. With the recent resurfacing of private purge material,[2] it has become evident that important material was prevented from reaching the police files by individuals who either feared the evidence or did not trust the police.

Aimé Autrand's late "conversion to Gaullism" in the fall of 1943 and his arrest on September 16, 1943, provided him with a powerful shield when he came back to Avignon in March 1944. Joseph Cucumel, a courageous *résistant* who had joined the opposition as early as July 1940 and was named secretary of the prefectorate after the Liberation, granted me an interview on December 26, 1994. He confirmed that, during the war, he was aware of the activities of numerous collaborators, among them Autrand. In 1940, he even strongly objected to Autrand's remaining in the Vichy administration. After the Liberation, he could have confirmed his suspicions, since he had access to all the secret files. But he had preferred to keep silent, not wanting to be perceived as vindictive. After the Liberation, he reinstated Autrand as division chief (division D3); today he chooses to remain publicly silent out of "respect for the families."

Cucumel responds to my puzzlement by pointing me to the purge committee under the direction of Max Fischer, a famous *résistant* named vice-prefect of Avignon on August 26, 1944: "Since he was in charge of examining the files of all the civil servants in place during the war, he ought to know!" During my visit to his Paris residence in September 1995, Fischer shared with me his view of the past. After joining the Vaucluse Resistance as a refugee from Paris, he became the closest aide of Colonel Beynes, the chief of the Vaucluse sector. Since he had no prewar connections to the area and since he had not been informed of Autrand's wartime role, he had not instructed his committee to charge him with any wrongdoing. "It was impractical to blindly examine all the wartime administration files," states Fischer.

In a common postscript of Vichy history, Autrand was later

given a job at the Avignon archives, "thereby putting the wolf in charge of the sheep." To add insult to injury, Autrand was appointed by "nomination of his peers" to the Committee of World War II History (Comité d'Histoire de la Second Guerre Mondiale) led by Henri Michel, who was later given the title of chief inspector of national education and asked by the French government to establish the true historical significance of the war. Autrand's arrest on September 16, 1943, had easily provided him a clean bill of health, since no one was much concerned about the "lost Jews of 1942." No one paid much attention either to Autrand's role in creating and maintaining the census lists that made the Jews vulnerable to the Nazis.

Interestingly, Autrand's past is eloquently captured in an unclassified document that reports the visit of a Vichy official to Avignon. Unlike the classified W series, this document has remained publicly available since the end of the war, for Henri Michel and everyone else to see:

VISIT TO THE PREFECTORATE OF VAUCLUSE
on October 21, 1941

1 - Discussion with General VALLIN, prefect of Vaucluse.

Cordial discussion that did not reveal a clear position on the question.

The prefect brought to my attention that the wife of his general-secretary, Mr. LAMORLETT, is Jewish, and is keeping too high a profile.

2 - Met Mr. AUTRAN [sic], 1st Division, who is focusing on the Jewish question.

1,500 Jews in Vaucluse, 346 of whom are refugees from the occupied zone

500 Jews approximately in Avignon

50 Jews approximately in Carpentras, mainly rich refugees (Hotel of the Princes, . . .)

No suspected failure to register.

> The census files are currently ready and are about to be
> shipped to Vichy; a verification is being conducted on a central
> record and will probably be established on one of the lists.
>   One can expect a good collaboration from Mr. AUTRAN
> [sic].[3]

This document contradicts Autrand's version of events, according to which his boss, Louis Vallin, was required, in November 1940, to move him away because he was suspected of having "too loyally served the Republican regime,"[4] and therefore of harboring anti-Vichy sentiments. In fact, this 1941 interview by a Vichy bureaucrat finds Autrand more engaged than his boss.

It has now become overwhelmingly clear that Autrand's participation in the Vichy administration was known when he was reinserted into respectability after the war. In a private communication (May 14, 1993), Robert Paxton, a scholar of the Vichy era, recalled that, in the early 1970s, he had brought the past position of Aimé Autrand to the attention of the head of the Committee of World War II History, Henri Michel, who reacted angrily to the messenger. A glimpse at another side of Autrand's personality was provided by the testimony of Claude Levy, a retired historian and past member of Michel's committee. Levy remembers that Autrand was not taken seriously by his fellows on the committee because "he was not a respected historian." He also added that the committee and its leader did not care much about the Jewish aspect of the war. These two testimonies raise important questions: why was Aimé Autrand selected for the committee, and did the other members of the committee close their eyes on his past?

To complete his metamorphosis, in 1949 Autrand applied to the Ministry of Veterans Affairs for the status of deportee, a status reserved for inmates of the infamous death camps. To his great chagrin, however, his request and those of thirty-eight other coapplicants from Avignon were denied. They had been sent to the labor camp at Linz, Austria, not to a death camp. In 1954, after years of sterile proceedings, Autrand approached Jean Nicolai, president of the Association of the Deportees of Vaucluse, in an attempt to break this barrier, and requested a recommendation, without mentioning the actual location of his detention. After a brief investigation, Nicolai realized the trap and sent to the Department of Veterans Affairs a letter of denial sealing forever the fate of Autrand's request.

I was fortunate to hear this story from Nicolai himself in June 1993. Nicolai brought to our meeting a copy of Autrand's book that had been personally inscribed by the author. Autrand's handwriting and signature bore an extraordinary resemblance to those on the letter and drafts I had found in the police archives of Vaucluse, dissipating any possible doubt I might have had that Autrand was indeed the chief of Section D1, the same man who implemented Vichy's measures against the Jews.

In his 1965 book, Autrand complains bitterly about "discrimination" against the thirty-nine Linz inmates of Avignon, who

> never pretended to compare their fate to that of their less fortunate comrades deported to the so-called "slow death" camps, such as Auschwitz, Dachau, or others, but this was not a reason sufficient to conclude that the deportees from Vaucluse to Linz had been privileged by fate, that they did not suffer, and that consequently they did not deserve the title of deportee, nor internee, solely under the pretext that the labor camps situated around the German factories of Linz were not included in the concentration camps endorsed by the investigators of the French government. . . .
>
> Under these conditions, isn't it appropriate to consider as unjust, cruel, and humiliating the attitude of the members of the national commission of deportees toward this category of war victims, and aren't we fearful, by such unjustly discriminating methods, of discouraging, in the future, the best of intentions?[5]

After the war, Autrand was one of the numerous beneficiaries of the "Vichy amnesia" that descended upon French society. The typical resistance of the current French administration to open up the archive files is a testimony to the continuing power of this amnesia. In fact, the current administration seems determined to put as much distance as possible between today's France and the crimes of its earlier Vichy administration. In addition to hiding the role of Vichy, the present government is attempting to eliminate from history the existence of the hunted Jews themselves. This conspiracy of silence creates an unexpected alliance of results—if not of intentions—between the silent French establishment and the historical revisionists. This attitude is pervasive in France today, even among those with the best of intentions, for example, the helpful employee who served as my mentor in the Avignon archives. During a relaxed chat, I mentioned my surprise when I realized that Aimé Autrand had "forgotten" to include in his book the list of Jews he himself had deported on August 26, 1942. Since she had studied the files before I was authorized to see them, she was not surprised at all. Instead, she responded, "I can understand his omission because he did not consider them *his own* Jews."

The result—and maybe the cause—of this government's state of mind is a strong desire to separate Vichy collaboration from its betrayal of the Jews. It is significant that no French war criminal has ever been sentenced in France for crimes against the Jews. In contrast, it has been very easy to mobilize the French justice system against German Nazis like Klaus Barbie. For fifty years, French collaboration has been portrayed as a victimless crime or, in the worst case, as a vague, infamous association with the Nazis. By the same token, the deportations of Jews by the Vichy government, if noticed at all, have remained a perpetratorless crime. Doesn't Jean Favier, the former chief of the French National Archives, reflect this state of mind when he qualifies, in an official letter, the Census of the Jews as "the files of self-denunciation of the Jews"?[6] Had he been motivated by an elementary concern for historical truth, Favier did not need an exemption to verify that the initial census of June 1941 in the "free" zone was "secretly done" by the prefectoral administration, thereby leaving little choice to the interested parties.[7] In addition, the public threats toward those who would dare evade these measures were not designed to promote any free choice among the hunted Jews.

Amid the reluctance of the French government to face the past, a debate has been raging about the authenticity of the recently discovered Census of Paris Jews. The question now being debated is whether the file consists of the original census cards or later (partial) copies. Although this debate may have academic value, it is misleading, because it focuses the attention on the wrong issue. The more important questions are whether Vichy performed the Census of the Jews and whether this census was used to deport the Jews. It is in the power of the current administration to move on to these issues and to settle this controversy by showing and authenticating the actual Jewish census lists, which lay under a thick layer of dusty silence in the regional police archives. Most of the prefectorates are harboring lists similar to the ones I saw in Avignon. By disclosing the census lists as well as releasing other collaboration files, the government could lead its people out of denial. By refusing to show the material or limiting access to it, French officials affirm their desire to preserve the doubt and thereby play into the hands of those who deny the Holocaust for ideological reasons. By doing so, they are also covering up their own fifty-year-long "Vichy amnesia." In trying to keep the role of Aimé Autrand hidden, the police hypocritically claim to be acting in the name of "privacy and family honor." This "privacy," though, just so happens to be my personal truth as well. As to "family honor," everyone knows that children of heroes are not necessarily heroes. The same goes for all other character traits.

More significant than the current administration's denial of the most elementary right to know by individual victims of war crimes is its role in the occultation of a fundamental historical truth. The wartime archives of the Vaucluse police undeniably demonstrate the continuity of the administrative institutions before, during, and after the war. Amid the prewar political turmoil and the frequent wartime replacement of the prefects, Aimé Autrand faithfully provided administrative continuity. Secretary of the prefectorate of Vaucluse before the war, he was also part of the inner circle of Edouard Daladier, the mayor of Avignon who would become prime minister.[8] After the war, his reintegration into the system as the key authority on the wartime history of Vaucluse, as the conduit through which the *département* of Vaucluse inherits its past, allowed for a seamless presentation of events, implicitly condoning Vichy actions by refusing to condemn them.

This continuity has traditionally been assured by the French provincial notables who have carried forward the indispensable threads of social and political responsibility of the bourgeois reigning class, a responsibility that often transcends the deepest differences between opposite ends of the political spectrum. The notables formed a tightly knit caste whose membership ranges from liberal socialists ("true republicans," as they love to call themselves) to right-wing nationalists ("true French," in their own words). Situating Autrand in the body of local notables was an important gap I needed to bridge in my research.

Jean Garcin, member of a prominent Vaucluse family, eagerly agreed to share his views about the historical events he helped to shape fifty years earlier. Our encounter took place in Chateauneuf-de-Gadagne at l'Oustaladou du Moulin, the Garcin family property hidden behind a tall wall at the end of a private alley of plane trees. The redbrick complex lies beyond a heavy iron gate next to the River Sorgue, which crosses the property. The living quarters and the offices are adjacent to the paper mill that provided much of the family wealth for generations. Garcin's secretary, who was expecting me, welcomes me outside and shows me to a reception room through a side entrance. The wooden ceiling beams and the rustic furniture attest to the Provençal style of the room. A large antique kitchen oven with a huge hood fills one corner of the room. The secretary clears a large bowl of fresh flowers from the massive wooden table. "It will be easier for you to work," she says, and adds, "Do you want some coffee while waiting for Monsieur le Président?" She is referring to the forty-five-year-long reign of Jean Garcin as member and president-elect of the General Council of Vaucluse, the governing body of the *département*.

Jean Garcin, a lean, energetic seventy-six-year-old man, enters the room. He introduces himself and adds, "You know, my wife is Jewish. We first met when she was working as a liaison for Bourgès-Mounoury and Chaban-Delmas in Lyon,[9] and I was the Resistance commander of six southeastern *départements*, including Vaucluse, where, together with my father and my uncle, I started my fight against the Nazis."[10] As he describes his Resistance days, he explains his role in details. "I used experts to design for me the cheapest way to destroy enemy targets," he says, "and a mechanical engineer advised me to lay a small dose of dynamite on the piston articulation of a locomotive instead of using a massive amount to blow up the entire machine. This way, we could hope to reuse the equipment after the war. A chemical engineer had a similar role for chemical plants. I was a *man of action!*" Garcin projects the image of a singleminded, methodical commander whose sole concern was to slow down the German military effort. He tells about his rescues of *résistants* who had fallen into the hands of the Nazis. However, Garcin does not mention freeing any Jewish victims of Vichy and the Nazis. He concentrated all his effort on military targets.

"Did you know Aimé Autrand?" I ask. "Of course, I knew him well," replies Garcin. "He was the friend of my uncle who had served as president of the General Council of Vaucluse before the war. Autrand used to visit our house regularly and discuss political matters with my uncle. My family has had a long liberal political tradition in spite of the wealth you can see around here." I bring back the name of Autrand to avoid a drift in our conversation. "In the name of the General Council of Vaucluse, I myself commissioned his book about the war," stresses Garcin, "and I urged the past members of the Resistance to cooperate with him." Since Garcin does not mention the Jews, I sharpen my questions.

"Did you know that Autrand was a collaborator? Did you know that he constructed lists of Jews as a member of the Vichy administration before German occupation?" I read to Garcin the October 21, 1941, visit report by a high-ranking Vichy official, promising that Autrand would be a good collaborator. Either shocked by my revelation or politically cautious, Garcin waits for my next question.

I decide to explore further Autrand's postwar role. "In retrospect, it may have been a mistake to ask Autrand to write his book," I venture. Garcin energetically interrupts me. "Not at all!" he states with authority. "He was the best-qualified person, because being part of the administration during the war, he knew how the system worked from within." Although he clearly knew that Autrand held a high position in the Vichy police, Garcin did not seem to make the connection between Autrand's job and the deportation of Jews, as if the Jews had been spontaneously deported. I can barely resist my mounting sense of anger, but I pursue my interview, looking Garcin straight in the eye to better capture his reaction to my next question. "Monsieur Garcin," I ask slowly, "if you had known he had deported one *résistant*, what would you have done?" Garcin the commander, who harbors no sympathy for traitors, even hypothetical ones, menacingly proclaims, "I would have liquidated him on the spot."[11] Hoping to create a parallel, I ask my next question, "And if you had known that he had deported many Jews?" Garcin, who does not like to be cornered—physically or intellectually—predictably reacts, "This is a hypothetical question." "So was my previous question!" I state, refusing to give up. "Since I have the proof that he indeed deported Jews in August 1942, doesn't that make the question less hypothetical?" Garcin, the man of action, reacts with a typical fatalism often reserved for the Holocaust and the Jews, "If he had refused to do the job, others would certainly have done it in his place." I can't help but say, "The bottom line is that he did not refuse. Did he?" Definitely irritated by my persistence, Garcin ignores my question and takes control of the interview. He now looks me straight in the eye and picks up the age-old stereotype about the

Jews, "You want to separate the Jews from the rest of us." Unable to contain my emotion any longer and forgetting that I am the guest, I shoot back, "Did *the rest of you* not separate the Jews by abandoning them?" Conscious that we are on a collision course but unwilling to give up his position, Garcin looks away from me and up to the ceiling, clearly signaling his wish to disengage. "I wonder," he says as if speaking to himself, "whether the Jews would have joined the Resistance if they had not been hunted."

It is now my turn to remain silent. About to ask whether his traditional suspicion of Jewish patriotism held true for his wife too, I realized the futility of our dialogue. His tunnel vision did not include the Jews. He was focused on a single goal, to the exclusion of all others. Military collaboration with the Nazis was the sole collaboration that interested him. Racial collaboration did not matter, particularly since he never saw the trains of Jews being deported across his military jurisdiction. There may even have been a strategic advantage to letting these trains carry their load; they were diverting equipment and personnel from the German war effort. The Jews had become hostages to the weakening of their enemies.

One can easily understand why Autrand would have wanted to "forget" his own role, but I find it sad and tragic that Garcin, a man who otherwise acted according to the highest moral imperative, entirely missed the Jewish dimension of the war. Had he not, he would have risen above the rest of us and become righteous among the nations. In fact, even with the benefit of history, he does not seem to recognize his blindness of those days.[12]

Garcin interrupts my wandering thoughts as he disapprovingly points to my notes. "Why are you doing *this?*" he asks. In his mind, the Jews must now have a good reason to stand between France and a glorious past, and as far as he is concerned, he is ready to give up their memory fifty years later. I answer his question with another question, "Monsieur Garcin, were you frightened during the war?" "Never," comes the response, "I was a man of action." By describing himself for a second time as a man of action, Garcin reminds me of my powerlessness as a child, and I react, "I was terrorized because I was a child of inaction." With a nod of the head, Garcin acknowledges that he understands, but he definitely feels uncomfortable with inaction, even that of a child. "What have you done with your fears since then?" he asks me. "After I grew up," I responded, "I put my life at the service of my people wherever they lived in fear. Now, I have become a man of reflection, since I am no longer afraid. That is the reason why I am doing *this*," I conclude, pointing to my notes on the table. Clearly, Garcin remains unconvinced. The only acceptable way would have been for the Jews to settle their accounts swiftly during the war and forget everything thereafter. A true man of action does not look back, lest he turn into a pillar of salt.

To release the tension of our abrasive dialogue, I shift away from the Jews for a while, noting that Autrand's service was probably responsible for the arrest and deportation of tens of "red Spaniards" to Dachau, Maidanek, Mauthausen, and Buchenwald between 1939 and 1942.[13] With a sharp flash of interest in his eyes, Garcin mentions that, as a teenager, he had almost volunteered for the Spanish war on the side of the Republicans, for whom he felt sympathy. He decided to stay put, though, after he learned from his uncle that doing so might jeopardize his future in France. Seemingly preferring my interest in the "red Spaniards" to my work about the Jews of Vaucluse, he asks me to keep him informed on the progress of my investigation about the Spaniards.

In an attempt to come back to Autrand's role, I mention my desire to talk about other collaborators, like Bonpuis from the neighboring village of Le Thor. "Bonpuis," he interrupts, "I knew well this *collabo*. He had a large number of children, ten or eleven, if I remember well." "Obviously, nothing happened to him after he supported the Germans," I interject. "But Monsieur," he objects, "we could not have locked up all the collaborators. There was no room for all of them. Although I came too late for our village guard, who had just been shot, I contributed to calming down the spirits after the Liberation. Soon, I became chief of security for the seventh region commander, who asked me to resolve the problem of prison overcrowding. So I went from town to town and released every prisoner without a file opened yet. I am sure that, in the process, I released a good number of criminals." I ask him, "Was this a reconciliation of sorts between people who had made choices on opposite sides of the fence?" Garcin shoots back, "I made no choice. I did what I was programmed to do by my family. I hope you realize that my uncle's first name was Voltaire." Clearly, for Garcin as for any other Frenchman, being given the first name Voltaire at birth is as good as a lifetime endorsement for one's liberalism by the father of French anticlericalism. "When I speak," he continues, "it is my family who speaks. I sucked my attitude with the milk of my mother in this kitchen of my grandmother." Garcin makes a broad gesture around the room, and his eyes linger on the large kitchen stove. He explains that his mother, a suffragette in 1920, instilled in him the enlightened, anticlerical liberalism that had long been the trademark of his family. By the same token, Garcin also explains why the difference between himself and Autrand was not as significant as I had implied, since one's attitude is predetermined by one's family. Once again, the bonds of notability override political differences.

Ignoring the next visitor waiting outside and the repeated signals of his secretary, Garcin continues the dialogue well over one hour beyond the allotted time with the passion of a real man of action. As I get up to leave, I am subjected to a well-tuned parting ritual. The attentive secretary loads me with patriotic pamphlets, artistically printed on the best paper from the mills of Jean Garcin. A passage on one of them, the Déclaration des Droits de l'Homme et du Citoyen,[14] provides an ironic signature to our meeting: "ARTICLE XV. Society is entitled to require from every civil servant an accounting of his administration." This article could have been written for Autrand personally.

On my way to the door, I mend the fences with a compliment on Garcin's vitality. "You know," he says, "I was beaten in the 1992 elections. In spite of winning my district by a landslide, I found myself in a tie, and *he* [Régis Deroudhile, the eighty-three-year-old mayor of Le Pontet] won because *they* broke the tie by seniority. It is ironic to be sent home at the age of seventy-six for being too young!" His secretary appears again. "Monsieur le Président," she says, "your next guest has been waiting for a long time." For her, Jean Garcin will always remain Monsieur le Président.

At the end of my visit, I realized that, in his smooth reinsertion into provincial notability, Autrand had benefited from the complicity of people like Berton and Sicard, who had a personal interest in remaining silent, and others who, determined like Garcin not to stir the mud, had preferred to look the other way and concentrate instead on the glories of the past. The fate of the Jews was never a point of contention between Autrand and his peers.

Incidentally, the Vaucluse seemingly wants to remain silent not only about the crimes against the Jews, but about the few descendants of criminals who still benefit from these crimes. I have recently followed a rumor, which had persisted for decades, stating that an "Aryan" administrator had kept the assets of Jews who died in the death camps. This notorious anti-Semite, sentenced to death in 1944, got his sentence commuted to life imprisonment and was finally pardoned after the intervention of the clergy. After his death of old age, his family continued to benefit from the product of his crimes. The confession of a family member recently confirmed these facts. How many additional fortunes were acquired in the same way? If you ask country people, they will readily tell you.

In the meantime, a new request for an exemption—initiated on December 12, 1993—to help solidify my research[15] became the object of endless haggling. I was first authorized on March 29, 1994, to see two or three pages selected by a bureaucrat in the file F7 14900, but three other files were denied me (F7 14887, 14895, and 14897). After a letter of protest in early May 1994, and with the support of well-known historian Pierre Vidal-Naquet regarding the quality of my work, the "study" of my request was "restarted" by the National Archives on May 19, 1994. Vidal-Naquet was asked to *"be the warrant of* [my] *discretion"* in case of a satisfactory outcome. Finally, in September 1994, two of my three remaining requests were granted with substantial limitations (F7 14895 and 14897); the third was denied *"by the Ministry of Internal Affairs . . . according to the decree No. 79-1038 of December 3, 1979"* (my emphasis). As in the previous case, I am authorized to see only extracts, but this time I am shown only insignificant official government publications, documents not controlled by the decree of 1979 anyway! Such severely restricted authorizations undoubtedly allowed Jean Favier to improve his statistics and to brag publicly that he refused only four requests in fourteen years.[16]

Having myself benefited, like a handful of other researchers,[17] from help of influential people, I was submitted to a paralyzing procedure that renders any serious work impractical unless one is stubborn as a mule and has the longevity of a redwood tree. These administrative obstacles, whether deliberate or not, obstruct well-intended historical work, often stopping it altogether.

Ironically, as the Vaucluse correspondent of the National Committee of World War II History, Aimé Autrand was granted unlimited access to the police archives documenting his own crimes. Since he knew the ins and outs of the collaboration machine, he naturally received the support of Jean Garcin, while I, a victim, would have been prevented from learning these ins and outs had I not benefited from considerable influence. Autrand returned Garcin's favor by dedicating four pages of his book to Garcin's Resistance role. As he writes with gratitude in the preface to his book:

> The so-called "Committee of World War II History" . . .
> is permanently helped . . . by qualified *département* correspondents, who were exceptionally granted all access needed for research and investigation, particularly for the consultation of archive documents before the expiration of the normally expected delays [until full declassification].[18]

After this long detour through the past, the time has finally come to examine the present and draw up a balance sheet. But how far have we really come? On July 16, 1995, during the fifty-third anniversary commemoration of the Vel d'Hiv arrests, President Jacques Chirac accepted French responsibility for the persecution of the Jews, a significant move that seems to have created a real opening. In particular, he ordered the trial of Maurice Papon,[19] which had been blocked for fifteen years largely by his predecessor, François Mitterrand, himself a man with an ambivalent connection to the Vichy regime.[20] After six months of proceedings and considerable national debate, Papon was finally sentenced to a ten-year prison term on April 2, 1998.

France recently granted to the Holocaust Memorial Museum in Washington, D.C., the privilege of microfilming the Vichy archives concerning the persecution of Jews, Gypsies, Freemasons, and other undesirables.[21] Of course, the agreement is subjected to the "usual restrictions determined by the law,"[22] a statement that must be interpreted in the light of the recent report by Guy Braibant about the French Archives.[23] The report, largely inspired by Sonia Combe's controversial book *Les Archives interdites*,[24] brings to light various grave shortcomings in the administration of the archives. For example, several public entities have violated the law of 1979 by not delivering "sensitive" material to the national archives. The report also recognizes arbitrary exercise of administrative authority in granting or denying selective limited access to permitted material. In addition, it brings to light the illegality of successive government decrees aimed at tightening archive control.[25] Finally, it suggests forty measures aimed at increasing the contents of the archives, opening them up, and managing them more effectively. Braibant's report, however, never mentions the Gendarmerie archives, which "benefit" from the exception granted to the military in the law of 1979. Indeed, the Gendarmerie, a branch of the military, does not have to deliver its archives to the public, although its role is strictly that of a civilian police force. This exception allows it to cover up its wartime implementation of the Vichy government's anti-Semitic policies. Another significant hole in the report is the totality of the economic archives holding the secret of all the confiscated Jewish assets—real and others—that ended in the French national coffers or in private hands.

Although Prime Minister Lionel Jospin has recently clarified the intentions of his government to open up the Vichy archives,[26] this opening, scheduled for 1998, has since been postponed. In her answer to the first of two "written questions to the Minister of Culture and Communication" presented on my behalf by Senator Guy Penne, Mme. Catherine Trautman has expressed the intention to grant access to every interested party—not just historians.[27] However, the second "written question," which deals with the opening of the Gendarmerie and finance archives, has remained unanswered for almost a year. On the bright side, the Mattéoli Commission, chartered by Prime Minister Jospin to examine the economic spoliation of the Jews of France, recently published an interim report that provides a broad overview of the sources of information on this subject.[28] As experience may have taught us many times over, a large number of studies are not necessarily aimed at resolving the issues once and for all.

Judging by France's reluctance to address the darkest side of its past, we may have to wait another one hundred years, which is how long it took for the French army to accept the conclusions of the Dreyfus affair. In 1895, Alfred Dreyfus was falsely accused of high treason as a result of an anti-Semitic conspiracy. Sentenced to exile by a martial court, the decision was reversed and he was cleared, due to the discovery of evidence fabricated by members of the high military command. However, it was only on September 7, 1995, after a hundred-year-long silence, that Brigadier General Jean-Louis Mourrut issued, on behalf of the army, a statement recognizing the innocence of Captain Dreyfus.[29] Will the true role of the Gendarmerie be exposed before 2045? Will the French government produce a full list of Jewish assets robbed by the Vichy administration and by individuals in time to make restitution to the victims possible?

In Lieu of an Epilogue

At the end of my voyage, I cannot repress a feeling that overwhelms me as I contemplate the three years that have just passed. Indeed, I have the impression of having been accompanied by an invisible force: sometimes, by my side, it helped me to overcome a profound nausea in the face of horror; sometimes, slightly ahead of me, it unearthed my next discovery and put it within my hand's reach.

Little by little, I became aware of a clear connection between all the people who had a role in the deportation of my mother and so many others. The Autrands, bureaucrats without much conscience who registered and arrested the Jews under their protection; the Bérards, conscientious small village employees who prepared the raw material village by village; the Palmièris, who arrested them to resell them like merchandise; the Bauers, who bought them to better destroy them—all these people had more or less lost their aptitude for humanity, the capacity for putting oneself in someone else's skin, which is the source of compassion. To my great surprise, I realized that none of them had guns to their heads forcing them to do the job. That was reserved for the victims and their helpers.

In contrast, all those, who, like the Brès, retained their humanity in spite of their precarious conditions, rose above their peers. If they were able to respond to the needs of others, it is because they could still look at the world through the eyes of the victims.

Along the way, I also met the Gravediggers of Memory, who are doing their best to keep the truth buried. Of course, most do not subscribe to a Nazi ideology. A number of them, war heroes who had not paid attention to the Jewish tragedy, are now irritated by a truth capable of tarnishing their glory of yesteryear. A few who did not make the right choice have a strong motivation to hide an embarrassing past they know too well. Some members of today's administration feel a deep solidarity with the servants of Vichy, "whose sole fault was to have done their duty." Others, finally, distinguished members of the historical establishment, are afraid of losing their privilege as historians at the king's court, a position for which they had toiled so hard. Each for a different reason willingly set out on a road that led them to play into the hands of the Assassins of Memory.[1]

Another intriguing silence deserves particular attention. Admiral William D. Leahy, the U.S. ambassador at Vichy from January 1941 to May 1942, must have had firsthand knowledge of the measures against the Jews and of the first deportation from Drancy in March 1942. Yet. in his 1950 autobiography,[2] he remains remarkably discreet about the real dimensions of the Jewish tragedy, mentioning only that "there had been some discrimination against the Jews at Vichy, aimed principally at getting hold of their money." This post facto revision of history raises significant questions about Leahy's role during the war and that of his government.

Fortunately, a new generation of historians, no longer willing to worship the golden calf of silence, is making its way from the margins to the center stage. One by one, these individuals are exploring the roads of collaboration that were opened up twenty-seven years ago by the early work of Robert Paxton.

During my voyage, my sympathizers made a lot of remarks for my own good and asked a lot of questions. I was advised not to be so Jewish. I was told that I should not set myself apart, that I should look at the world more evenly. That, better to embrace differences, I would have to renounce mine. That the Jew in me looked too possessive of the war. They recommended that I not be so judgmental. Autrand, after all, needed to provide for his family. He was simply executing orders, he was not alone, and, had he refused, someone else would have done the job in his place. In addition, staying at the service of Vichy had its positive side too, if only to help a few poor souls. As to Bérard, he could not have suspected the consequences of his Census of the Jews. Everyone was scared. Everyone was hungry.

I was reminded that there were only eighty active members of the Resistance in Vaucluse. That they were courageous but not well-organized amateurs. That they did not know, and that, had they known, they would have been no match. That it was July 1944 before they received machine guns, their only heavy weapons, because the Allies and De Gaulle saw them as gangsters and Communists. I was also told that I had allowed myself to be fooled by the large number of "delayed-action resistants" who took a stand only after everything was over.

It was unfair for me to require, people said, that at the Liberation justice be rendered against all the Vichy functionaries. Besides, the "guilty" ones had already redeemed themselves by turning Gaullist. Anyway, no one knew—neither during nor after the war. And even if people did know, there was, in the justice of the Liberation, room only for those criminals too hardened to turn their coats on time.

I was told, in so many words, that my story—our story—had been inevitable. That I would have been better off not to try too hard to understand. That I should have left the disturbing past in its archive boxes. That I should have kept quiet about some facts, because, by speaking, I will hurt innocent people. That families will be implicated.

IN LIEU OF AN EPILOGUE

I was even asked what I would have done in the place of the actors of this drama—a painful question I wished I could escape, since I had been a victim too young to play a role.

Had I been in Autrand's place, would I have stayed in the administration in 1940? Would I have performed the Census of the Jews as early as 1941? On August 26, 1942, would I have executed Vichy's orders to arrest them? Would I, instead, have joined the Resistance?

Had I been an ordinary villager, would I have seen the hunted Jews? Would I have welcomed them to my home, or would I have denounced them? And if I had been Bérard, the mayor of Le Pontet's aide, would I have provided to Vichy the list of my neighbors?

Had I been Garcin, would I have spared some of my explosives to stop the trains of infamy and sent a few of my men to free the deported Jews from their sealed cars?

At the end of the war, if I had been charged with the restoration of order, would I have rendered justice to all the victims by sentencing everyone who had betrayed them? Or would I have done my utmost to forget as quickly as possible?

Had I been Favier, the director of the Archives of France, would I have helped to establish the truth? Or would I have presided over ambiguity?

And you, the reader, what would you have done? What would we do, you and I, if, unfortunately, things were to start all over again?

Notes

Foreword

1. See Nechama Tec, *When Light Pierced the Darkness* (New York: Oxford University Press, 1986), a study of non-Jewish rescuers of Jews in Poland.
2. Pierre Laborit, *L'Opinion Française sous Vichy* (Paris: Le Seuil, 1990).
3. Asher Cohen, *Persécutions et sauvetages: Juifs et Français sous l'Occupation et sous Vichy* (Paris: Cerf, 1993), 238–39.

The Cherry Season

1. Norman B. Spector, *The Complete Fables of Jean de La Fontaine* (Evanston, Ill.: Northwestern University Press, 1988), 5.

The Waltz of Names

1. Isaac originates from the Hebrew word for laughter.
2. *Pinkas Hakehilot*, The Notebook of the Communities, Spertus College, Chicago.
3. Naturalization file 27453X46, Ministry of Social Affairs, Health, and Urbanism.

Inside My Little Circle

1. "Flavored with little glazed onions" means "first-class" for the French, who find much inspiration in their cooking.
2. *Le Statut des Juifs de Vichy* (Paris: Association des Fils et Filles de Déportés Juifs de France, 1990), 30.
3. November 30, 1995.
4. *Les Tsiganes en France, 1939–1946* (Paris: CNRS Editions, 1994).
5. Law No. 2333 of June 2, 1941. See *Les Juifs sous l'Occupation: Recueil des Textes Officiels Français et Allemands 1940/1944* (Paris: Association des Fils et Filles de Déportés Juifs de France, 1982).
6. Law No. 3086 of July 22, 1941. See ibid.
7. Document from the Centre de Documentation Juive Contemporaine, Paris. Many administrators are listed, among others Henri de Camaret, Lucien and Yvon de Cazalet, Paul and Marcel Morreau, Jean Lagrance, Henri Lemaire, Charles Bonnard, Paul Ely, Jean Bley, Henri de Courtois, Georges Bonjean, and Jean Sacresta.
8. Document LXI-40, Centre de Documentation Juive Contemporaine, Paris.
9. Document 7w15, Archives of the Prefecture of Vaucluse, Avignon.
10. Aimé Autrand, *Le Département du Vaucluse: De la Défaite à la Libération* (Avignon: Editions Aubanel, 1965).
11. *Pinkas Hakehilot*, The Notebook of the Communities, Spertus College, Chicago.

Maréchal, Here We Are

1. Georges Brun, *Les Juifs du Pape à Carpentras* (Carpentras: Le Nombre d'Or, 1975), 206.
2. *Les Juifs sous l'Occupation: Recueil des Textes Officiels Français et Allemands 1940/1944* (Paris: Association des Fils et Filles de Déportés Juifs de France, 1982).
3. M. R. Marrus and R. O. Paxton, *Vichy et les Juifs* (Paris: Calman-Lévy, 1981); English translation: *Vichy France and the Jews* (New York: Schocken Books, 1983).
4. *Les Juifs sous l'Occupation*, 155.
5. Ibid., 22.
6. Ibid., 163.
7. *Liste des Israélites étrangers entrés en France depuis le 1ᵉʳ Janvier 1936 qui doivent faire l'objet des mesures prévues par les instructions de M. le Ministre Secrétaire d'Etat à l'Interieur en date des 5 et 15 Aout 1942,*

Document 7w16, Archives of the Prefecture of Vaucluse, Avignon.

8. *Les Juifs sous l'Occupation,* 164.

9. Serge Klarsfeld, *Vichy—Auschwitz,* vol. 1 (Paris: Editions Fayard, 1983), 339–40.

10. Ibid., 342–55.

11. Ibid., 321.

12. Ibid., 355.

13. Stephane Courtois and Adam Rayski, *Qui savait quoi?* (Paris: Editions de la Découverte, 1987).

14. *Memorial to the Jews Deported from France,* ed. Serge Klarsfeld (New York: Beate Klarsfeld Foundation, 1975).

15. Klarsfeld, *Vichy–Auschwitz.*

16. Robert O. Paxton, special supplement to the French newspaper *Libération,* no. 3776, July 13, 1993.

17. Department for Investigation and Control, the successor to the Police for Jewish Affairs.

18. Klarsfeld, *Vichy—Auschwitz,* 458.

19. Ibid., 466.

20. Susan Zuccotti, *The Holocaust, the French, and the Jews* (New York: Basic Books, 1993), 155.

21. Joseph Weill, *Contribution à l'Histoire des Camps d'Internement dans l'Anti-France* (Paris: Centre de Documentation Juive Contemporaine, 1946).

22. Marrus and Paxton, *Vichy et les Juifs.*

23. Aimé Autrand, *Le Département du Vaucluse: De la Défaite à la Libération* (Avignon: Editions Aubanel, 1965), 29, 153–66.

24. Memo from Donald A. Lowrie, dated August 10, 1942, cited in Klarsfeld, *Vichy—Auschwitz,* 324–27.

The "Foreign" Jews of 1942

1. Telegram No. 2765-Pol.9.

2. Serge Klarsfeld, *Vichy—Auschwitz,* vol. 1 (Paris: Editions Fayard, 1983), 457.

3. André Laserre, *Frontières et camps: Le refuge en Suisse de 1933 à 1945* (Lausanne: Editions Payot, 1995).

4. Sabine Zeitoun, *L'Oeuvre de Secours aux Enfants (OSE) sous l'Occupation en France* (Paris: Editions L'Harmattan, 1990).

5. The shipment of the 1814 Jewish males was Nazi retaliation for the assassination of Lieutenant Colonel Winkler and Major Nussbaum in

Paris on February 13, 1943 (*Memorial to the Jews Deported from France*, ed. Serge Klarsfeld [New York: Beate Klarsfeld Foundation, 1975]).

6. The list of dormant Swiss accounts can be found on the Web at http://www.dormantaccounts.ch.

7. Document XCII-121, p. 51, UGIF Archives, YIVO (Yiddishe Vissenshaft Organizatie), New York.

8. Document XCII-120, p. 55, UGIF Archives, YIVO, New York.

Les Français parlent aux Français

1. Bernard Wasserstein, *Britain and the Jews of Europe, 1939–1944* (Oxford: Clarendon Press, 1979), 297.

2. *Un appareil* means "an appliance"; TSF stands for *téléphonie sans fil* (wireless telephony).

3. *Les Juifs sous l'Occupation: Recueil des Textes Officiels Français et Allemands 1940/1944* (Paris: Association des Fils et Filles de Déportés Juifs de France, 1982).

4. Document LXI-102, Centre de Documentation Juive Contemporaine, Paris.

David and Goliath

1. Raphaël Alibert to Charles Pomaret, July 1, 1940, in *Le Statut des Juifs de Vichy* (Paris: Association des Files et Filles de Déportés Juifs de France, 1990), 30.

2. Serge Klarsfeld, *Le Calendrier de la Persécution des Juifs en France, 1940–1944* (Paris: Association des Fils et Filles de Déportés Juifs de France and the Beate Klarsfeld Foundation, 1993), 18.

3. Ibid., 203.

4. George Olekhnovitch, "La jurisprudence actuelle du Conseil d'Etat en matière d'acquisition, de retrait et de perte de la nationalité Française," *Revue Critique de Droit International Privé* 2 (April–June 1992): 363–93.

5. Bernard Laguerre, "Les Dénaturalisés de Vichy," *Vingtième Siècle Revue d'Histoire* 20 (October–December 1988): 3–15.

6. File No. 191113-DX-47, Ministère des Affaires Sociales et de l'Intégration, March 11, 1993.

7. Klarsfeld, *Le Calendrier de la Persécution des Juifs en France,* 817–18.

He Is Not Like the Rest of Us

1. Document 4w2774, Archives of the Prefecture of Vaucluse, Avignon.
2. Ibid.
3. We were registered on August 27, 1943. Document 7w15, Archives of the Prefecture of Vaucluse, Avignon.
4. Augustine, *The City of God*, chapter 18.
5. The Oeuvre de Secours aux Enfants (Institution for Relief to Children) was sponsored by the American Jewish Joint Distribution Committee (Joint, for short).
6. OSE report of September 6, 1943.
7. In *Le Département du Vaucluse: De la Défaite à la Libération* (Avignon: Editions Aubanel, 1965), Aimé Autrand documents that Beccarud was sent to Buchenwald on September 26, 1943, and did not come back.
8. Serge Klarsfeld, Vaucluse Collaboration Cleanup Files.
9. The Palombo family was deported from Drancy to Auschwitz by convoy 71 on April 13, 1944. *Memorial to the Jews Deported from France*, ed. Serge Klarsfeld (New York: Beate Klarsfeld Foundation, 1975).
10. Aluminum strips of the appropriate length were able to confuse the long-wave radar of the German antiaircraft batteries.

The Steltzers

1. *Garrigue* is the local name for the bush area that is covered in wild lavender, thyme, rosemary, and briar.

He Who Saves One Single Life . . .

1. SD = Sicherheitsdienst (Security Service of the SS), also a branch of the German Reich security.
2. The FFI (Forces Françaises de l'Intérieur) was a secret Gaullist army that fought a guerilla war against the Nazis.
3. Report of the Délégué Régional du Service des Recherches des Crimes de Guerre Ennemis (Regional Delegate of the Service of Research about Enemy War Crimes), July 12, 1946. The report was used for the indictment of members of the SD in Avignon.

The Liberation

1. Herbert Lottman, *The People's Anger: Justice and Revenge in Post-Liberation France* (London: Hutchinson, 1986), 30.
2. *Collabo* was a common short version of the word "collaborator."

Back to the Steltzers

1. Claire related this anecdote to me in a letter. The incident made such an impression on her that she even remembers the name of the soldier.

Back to Normal

1. Private communication by Bernard Rochwerger, Avignon.
2. *Brit milah*, Hebrew for "circumcision," literally means "convenant of the circumcision."

The Family Souret

1. The Armenian people were victimized by their neighbors, the Turks, who conducted countless mass murders at the beginning of this century. Like the Jews, many Armenians were forced into a precarious exile. For more information, see Henri Verneuil, *Mayrig* (Paris: Editions Laffond, 1991). There is also a movie version of this book.
2. Fiery water.
3. Hunter's style.

In My Mother's Shoes

1. Dispatch 2765, August 5, 1942.

A Souret or a Lewendel?

1. Cross-referenced lists of Seized Jewish Assets and Aryan Administrators, Centre de Documentation Juive Contemporaine, Paris.

Do Not Turn Around

1. Nechama Tec, *When Light Pierced the Darkness* (Oxford: Oxford University Press, 1986), xi.

2. Annette Wieviorka, "1992, Reflexions sur une commémoration," *Annales, 48ᵉ année* 3 (May–June 1993): 703–14.

"Political" Deportee Number 23925

1. Pierre Vidal-Naquet, "L'année 1942 et les Juifs en France," colloquium at the Ecole des Hautes Etudes en Sciences Sociales, Paris, June 15–16, 1992.

2. *Memorial to the Jews Deported from France,* ed. Serge Klarsfeld (New York: Beate Klarsfeld Foundation, 1975), 574.

3. Georges Wellers, *L'Etoile jaune à l'heure de Vichy: De Drancy à Auschwitz* (Paris: Editions Fayard, 1973).

4. The revisionists, a small group of neo-Fascists with international political connections, argue that the Holocaust never took place and that Jews are trying to manipulate the Gentile world through guilt about the Holocaust. Unfortunately, denying that the Holocaust occurred, or at least minimizing its scope and significance, is not a position reserved for revisionists alone. See Pierre Vidal-Naquet, *Les Assassins de la Mémoire* (Paris: Editions de la Découverte, 1987).

5. Apparently, this "act of disappearance" (read "death certificate") was necessary for my father to be recognized as a widower.

6. The granting of the title of "political deportee" was a collective measure decided by the French Parliament in an attempt to acknowledge limited responsibility.

7. Zeev Sternhell, *Ni Droite, Ni Gauche* (Paris: Editions du Seuil, 1983).

8. Bernard-Henri Levy, *L'Idéologie Française* (Paris: Editions Grasset, 1981).

9. Estrea Zaharia Asseo, *Les Souvenirs d'une rescapée* (Paris: La Pensée Universelle, 1974).

10. Drancy arrival list of June 13, 1944; personal communication from Serge Klarsfeld. As far as the size of the group of deportees is concerned, this list is probably a more reliable document than the account of Estrea Asseo.

11. Sara Lewendel personal file, Veterans Affairs Archives, Paris.

12. Annette Kahn, *Le Fichier* (Paris: Editions Robert Laffont, 1993).

13. *Le Fichier Juif: Rapport de Commission présidée par René Rémond au premier ministre* (Paris: Editions Plon, 1996).

14. Wellers, *L'Etoile jaune à l'heure de Vichy.*

15. *Le Monde,* February 4, 1997, pp. 9 and 16.

NOTES

16. Tom Bower, *Nazi Gold* (New York: HarperCollins, 1997).

17. Drancy receipt book No. 146, Centre de Documentation Juive Contemporaine, Paris.

18. Sara Lewendel personal file, Veterans Affairs Archives, Paris.

19. See Adelaïde Hautval, *Médecine et crimes contre l'humanité* (Arles: Editions Actes Sud, 1991). Hautval, a Protestant woman, was sent to Auschwitz in 1942 because she defended a Jewish family being brutalized in the street by the Gestapo. The German justification was: "Since you defend them, you will share their fate." She served as a doctor in Bloc 10 but refused to collaborate in medical experiments. She came back to tell her story.

20. Document C-1, p. 80, UGIF Archives, YIVO, New York.

21. Document CXI-104, p. 16, UGIF Archives, YIVO, New York.

22. Law No. 5047 of November 29, 1941, signed by Maréchal Pétain.

23. Decree No. 1477 of June 5, 1944. See *Les Juifs sous l'Occupation: Recueil des Textes Officiels Français et Allemands 1940/1944* (Paris: Association des Fils et Filles de Déportés Juifs de France, 1982).

Close Calls

1. Gilbert Michlin, private communication, June 1993.

2. Sara Lewendel personal file, Veterans Affairs Archives, Paris.

3. Sabine Zeitoun, *L'Oeuvre de Secours aux Enfants (OSE) sous l'Occupation en France* (Paris: Editions L'Harmattan, 1990).

4. Richard I. Cohen, *The Burden of Conscience: French Jewish Leadership during the Holocaust* (Bloomington: Indiana University Press, 1987).

5. Echoing the title of the book by Stéphane Courtois and Adam Rayski, *Qui savait quoi?* (*Who Knew What?*) (Paris: Editions de la Découverte, 1987).

6. Jean-François Steiner, *Treblinka* (Paris: Editions Fayard, 1966); English translation by Helen Weaver, *Treblinka* (New York: Simon and Schuster, 1967).

The Train of Memory

1. Until May 1944, the trains were unloaded in the old train station of Oświęcim, between Auschwitz I and Auschwitz II. To expedite the extermination of the Jews, the tracks were extended right up to the crematoria of Birkenau. After May 1944, the convoys were unloaded onto the Birkenau ramp.

2. A survivor of convoy 76 who participated in the Train of Memory, Henri Stermann, described the descent from the train in graphic detail. "You can write that down," he said to me. His voice was even and his words precise. From the unloading ramp, he was taken to work, while my mother was led immediately to the gas chamber. Henri Stermann and his older brother survived; his younger brother, sister, and parents did not.

3. The crematoria were destroyed when the Germans retreated ahead of the Red Army.

4. The corpses were scooped into the crematoria by members of the Sonderkommando. To conceal information about the mass murders, the Nazis periodically exterminated members of the Sonderkommando and replaced them with new workers.

"The Germans Did It"

1. M. R. Marrus and R. O. Paxton, *Vichy France and the Jews* (New York: Schocken Books, 1983), 302.

2. The postwar trials focused on "collaboration with the enemy in time of war," according to Article 75 of the French penal code.

3. In the Avignon archives of the *département* of Vaucluse, the directory lists the following resources: individual purge files (sections 22w15, 22w16, and 22w17); seized documents on the collaboration organization L'Amicale de France (sections 4w1814 and 4w1815); collaboration groups (section 8w4); Parti Franciste (section 4w9479); various reports concerning *résistants* and *miliciens* (section 36w4).

4. "London File" No. 2383. The SD indictment files can be found in the archives of the Centre de Documentation Juive Contemporaine in Paris and are currently unsorted. All of the quotations in this chapter were extracted from these indictment files. The Gestapo of Avignon is covered in the indictment files.

5. Commissaire Léon Castellan to Judge Cruciani, Document No. 5598 SRPJ, June 29, 1948, and appendix (File 2107145; July 28, 1947).

6. Judgment of December 18, 1948.

7. Gendarmerie report No. 2, March 1, 1950.

8. Report of Commissaire Léon Castellan in response to Judge Cruciani, Document No. 9525 SRPJ, October 7, 1946.

9. Didier Epelbaum, *Aloïs Brunner* (Paris: Calman-Lévy, 1990).

10. Response to Judge Cruciani's request by Lieutenant Colonel Pétré, delegate of the Ministry of Justice for the 15th Region, File No. 364.

11. As a point of reference, in those days a newspaper cost 0.30 francs.

12. Gendarmerie report No. 492, April 29, 1946.

13. Gendarmerie report No. 626, June 7, 1946.

14. Epelbaum, *Aloïs Brunner.*

15. *Chicago Sun Times,* November 1, 1987.

16. Epelbaum, *Aloïs Brunner.*

17. Document 7w15, Archives of the Prefecture of Vaucluse, Avignon.

18. Asher Cohen, *Persécutions et sauvetages: Juifs et Français sous l'Occupation et sous Vichy* (Paris: Cerf, 1993).

19. Dispatch No. 2765 P, August 5, 1942 (modified August 18, 1942), in *Les Juifs sous l'Occupation: Recueil des Textes Officiels Français et Allemands 1940/1944* (Paris: Association des Fils et Filles de Déportés Juifs de France, 1982).

The "Papon" of Avignon

1. Maurice Papon faithfully served Vichy as secretary of the regional prefectorate of Bordeaux, where he methodically hunted the Jews, until 1943, when he supposedly joined the Resistance. After the war he was appointed to various police positions. In 1958 he became a trusted associate of de Gaulle, who named him head of the Paris police. From that position, unchallenged, he went on to a remarkable career. See Michel Slitinski, *L'Affaire Papon* (Paris: Editions A. Moreau, 1983).

2. Bernard Lambert, *Dossiers d'accusation: Bousquet, Papon, Touvier* (Paris: Editions de la Fédération Nationale des Déportés et Internés Résistants et Patriotes, 1990), 178–79.

3. Aimé Autrand, *Le Département du Vaucluse: De la Défaite à la Libération* (Avignon: Editions Aubanel, 1965).

4. Mesures contre les Juifs, 27w16.

5. Victor Basch was the president of the League of Human Rights until 1939. He was assassinated by the French Militia in Lyon.

6. André Halimi, *La Délation sous l'Occupation* (Paris: Editions Alain Moreau, 1983), 40–41.

7. Serge Klarsfeld, *Le Calendrier de la Persécution des Juifs en France, 1940–1944* (Paris: Association des Fils et Filles de Déportés Juifs de France and the Beate Klarsfeld Foundation, 1993), 567 and 580.

8. Serge Klarsfeld, *Vichy—Auschwitz,* vol. 1 (Paris: Editions Fayard, 1983), 374.

9. According to the file on seized Jewish assets at the Centre de Documentation Juive Contemporaine in Paris, P.M.F. was taken over by Henry Le Maire (administrator No. 4091), residing at 4b, rue de Grivolas, Avignon.

10. The full text of the final report can be found in file 27w16 (Mesures contre les Juifs).

11. The OSE was officially set up to care for needy children. The Jews (and apparently the French police) were aware of its rescue activities. Thousands of Jewish children owe their lives to the OSE.

12. Files of the Bobryker children, provided by Vivette Samuel, OSE Archives, Paris.

13. Michelle Cone, *Artists under Vichy: A Case of Prejudice and Persecution* (Princeton, N.J.: Princeton University Press, 1992).

14. Renée Poznanski, *Etre Juif en France pendant la Seconde Guerre Mondiale* (Paris: Hachette, 1994).

15. Recensement des Juifs, 27w15.

16. Literally, the "official newspaper"—a repository of all French government decisions as they occur.

17. Régis Déroudilhe, *Le Pontet* (Avignon: Editions Aubanel, 1982).

18. Document dated July 28, 1943, in the Vaucluse police file 235w6.

19. Lebon had replaced Henri de Camaret in his function as the SEC representative in Avignon. Camaret, in the meantime, continued to administer dozens of properties confiscated from Jews.

The Victim and the Hangman All in One

1. Aimé Autrand, *Le Département du Vaucluse: De la Défaite à la Libération* (Avignon: Editions Aubanel, 1965), 231–32.

2. Ibid., 29.

3. In French, the phrase "threw herself" expresses the contempt of the author of the letter.

4. Dossiers Individuels des Juifs (Individual Jewish Files), 7w17.

5. Seized file: l'Amicale de France (The Friends of France), 4w1814 and 4w1815.

6. Robert Zaretsky, *Nîmes at War: Religion, Politics, and Public Opinion in the Gard, 1938–1944* (Philadelphia: University of Pennsylvania Press, 1995), 113–17.

7. Dossiers Individuels des Juifs, 7w17.

8. Ibid.

9. Although Pierre Laborit rightfully provides a more nuanced view

in his book *L'Opinion Française sous Vichy* (Paris: Editions le Seuil, 1990), one cannot deny the significant effect of German military losses.

10. Autrand, *Le Département du Vaucluse*, 232.

11. Listes d'Arrestations (Lists of Arrests), 6w37.

12. While he was serving in the Vichy administration, François Mitterand, the former French president, was nominated to receive the Francisque, the highest decoration handed out by Maréchal Pétain to reward allegiance. Much later, Mitterand, like Autrand, joined the Gaullists. Ironically, the Francisque was granted to Mitterand in 1943, when he was already in London. See Pierre Péan, *Une Jeunesse Bien Française: François Mitterand, 1934–1947* (Paris: Editions Fayard, 1994).

The Cherry Farm

1. Dossiers Individuels des Juifs, 7w17.

2. Mesures contre les Juifs, 27w16.

The French Connection

1. Paul Jankowski, *Communism and Collaboration: Simon Sabiani and Politics in Marseille, 1919–1944* (New Haven, Conn.: Yale University Press, 1989).

2. Report of Commissaire Léon Castellan in response to Judge Cruciani, No. 9525 SRPJ, October 7, 1946.

3. Dossier Palmièri, Archives Départmentales des Bouches du Rhône, 55w148.

4. Census of the Jews, Prefecture of Avignon, 27w15.

5. Anonymous letter, which triggered the investigation of Palmièri and his gang; Document No. 2.

6. Heiter, a gang member, served as an interpreter.

7. Interrogation of Charles Palmièri by Judge Larrat, March 10 to April 6, 1945, No. 28, p. 27.

8. Ibid., p. 19.

9. Deposition of Madame Perugi, née Leon, Juliette, Avignon, June 20, 1945.

10. Commisaire of Mobile Police Victor Roton, May 25, 1945.

11. Interrogation of Charles Palmièri by Judge Larrat, March 10 to April 6, 1945, No. 28, p. 19.

12. Interrogation of Charles Palmièri by Judge Jean Fabre, March 14, 1946, No. 873, p. 15.

13. Jankowski, *Communism and Collaboration*, 113.

14. "Internationals" is an epithet signifying Communists and their sympathizers.

15. Document 38.

16. Interrogation of Charles Palmièri by Judge Larrat, March 10 to April 6, 1945, No. 28, p. 38.

17. Palmièri files, Archives Départementales des Bouches du Rhône, 55w148, No. 449.

18. Ibid., No. 468.

19. Deposition of Mouillade in front of Commissaire Chazalon, September 1944, No. 53.

20. Aimé Autrand, *Le Département du Vaucluse: De la Défaite à la Libération* (Avignon: Editions Aubanel, 1965).

21. Personal communication of Mrs. Hollard, Archives Départementales de Vaucluse, April 11, 1994.

22. Report of Agent Mouillade about the case of Bounias from Cavaillon (Vaucluse); copy of documents from the Mouillade file No. C. J. 1791/44.

23. Report from the confrontation led by Judge Jean Fabre, Marseille, July 20, 1945, No. 255.

24. Like many others, Moïse Benyacar wrongly uses the term "miliciens" to designate the members of the Palmièri gang.

25. Document 860.

26. Interrogation of Charles Palmièri by Judge Larrat, March 10 to April 6, 1945, No. 28, p. 50.

27. Report of Commissaire Victor Rotton about the Mouillade case, May 2, 1945.

28. Annette Wieviorka, *Déportation et génocide: Entre la mémoire et l'oubli* (Paris: Plon, 1992).

29. Robert Bailly, *Histoire d'Avignon et des Avignonnais pendant la dernière guerre* (Avignon: Editions A. Barthélemy, 1986), 39.

30. Ibid., 114.

The Anatomy of National Amnesia

1. Dossiers d'Epuration (Purge Files), 22w15, 22w16, and 22w17.

2. Private purge files, discovered by Serge Klarsfeld.

3. Document LXXIII-7 & 8, Centre de Documentation Juive Contemporaine, Paris.

4. Aimé Autrand, *Le Département du Vaucluse: De la Défaite à la Libération* (Avignon: Editions Aubanel, 1965), 231–32.

5. Ibid., 233.

6. Jean Favier, in a letter to a book editor.

7. Census of the Jews, Archives du Département de Vaucluse, Avignon, file 7w15.

8. Elisabeth du Réau, *Edouard Daladier, 1884–1970* (Paris: Editions Fayard, 1993).

9. Bourgès-Mounoury and Chaban-Delmas were two notable national leaders of the French Resistance.

10. Garcin's nom-de-guerre was Colonel Bayard.

11. Interestingly, some critics of Garcin still maintain that he was excessively trigger-happy.

12. In his preface to *Le Train fantôme* (Paris: Les Etudes Sorguaises, 1991), Garcin ignores the Jewish deportees of the convoy that crossed the Vaucluse in August 1944. Answering his own rhetorical question "Who were they?" simply, he says, "French *résistants*, Spanish republicans, Italian anti-Fascists." His conclusions is sadly ironic: "Oblivion is death, death of civilization, death of man" (pp. 5, 6).

13. According to a private communication from Mr. Hayez, director of the archives of Vaucluse (November 30, 1995), division D1 took care of the files of the Spaniards ("Reds" and others) before and during the war. These files, which Autrand followed until 1943, mention several "regroupings" aimed at concentrating hundreds of Spaniards from the Vaucluse in camps in the Vaucluse (GTE 148), Ariège (Le Vernet), and Gard (Jonquières Saint Vincent). The deportation of some of these Spaniards—which Autrand recorded after the war in the name of the Committee of World War II History—is not mentioned anywhere in the archives of Vaucluse.

14. The 1789 French Bill of Rights of Men and Citizens.

15. F7 14887: Arrest and internment of Jews; F7 14895: Measures against the Jews; F7 14897: Expulsion of foreigners (Belgians, Spaniards, and Swiss); F7 14900: Prefects and regional prefects, police intendants, and police prefectorate.

16. Peter Hellmann, private communication following his interview of Jean Favier in 1993.

17. Sonia Combe, *Les Archives interdites: Les Peurs Françaises face au passé proche* (Paris: Albin Michel, 1994).

18. Autrand, *Le Département du Vaucluse*, 11.

19. Bernard Lambert, *Dossiers d'accusation: Bousquet, Papon, Touvier* (Paris: Editions de la Fédération Nationale des Déportés et Internés Résistants et Patriotes, 1990).

20. Pierre Péan, *Une Jeunesse Bien Française: François Mitterand, 1934–1947* (Paris: Editions Fayard, 1994).

21. Personal communication from Marilyn August of the Associated Press, February 12, 1996.

22. Law No. 79-18 of January 3, 1979.

23. Les Archives en France, *Rapport au premier ministre*, La Documentation Française, Paris, May 1996.

24. Combe, *Les Archives interdites.*

25. Decrees 79-1038, 79-1040, etc.

26. *Circulaire du 2 octobre relative à l'accès aux archives publiques, Journal Officiel,* October 3, 1997.

27. *Réponses des ministres aux questions écrites, Journal Officiel,* November 27, 1997.

28. Prime Minister's Commission for the Study of Spoliations of the Jews of France, April to December 1997, La Documentation Française, Paris, December 1997.

29. *Libération,* No. 4453, September 12, 1995.

In Lieu of an Epilogue

1. Pierre Vidal-Naquet, *Les Assassins de la Mémoire* (Paris: Editions de la Découverte, 1987).

2. William D. Leahy, *I Was There* (New York: Wittlesey House, 1950).